# Tennyson and Madness

*Ann C. Colley*

# TENNYSON
# And Madness

The University of Georgia Press

Athens

Printed in the United States of America
Designed by Francisca Vassy
Set in 10 on 12 point Bembo type

The paper in this book meets the guidelines for permanence
and durability of the Committee on Production Guidelines for
Book Longevity of the Council on Library Resources.

Library of Congress Cataloging in Publication Data

Colley, Ann C.
  Tennyson and madness.

  Includes bibliographical references and index.
    1. Tennyson, Alfred Tennyson, Baron, 1809–1892—Knowl-
edge—Psychology. 2. Tennyson, Alfred Tennyson, Baron, 1809–
1892—Criticism and interpretation. 3. Mental illness in literature.
4. Literature and mental illness. I. Title.
PR5592.P74C64 1983      821'.8      82–13689
ISBN 0–8203–0648–7

To my father, Henry Harris Cheetham, who believed, lived, and taught Mrs. Wiggs's philosophy:

> In the mud and scum of things
> Something always, always sings.

From Alice Caldwell Hegan's *Mrs. Wiggs of the Cabbage Patch* (1901)

# Contents

# Acknowledgments

 should like to thank Judith K. Moore, J. Scott Colley, and, most especially, Thomas F. Dillingham for their reading of my manuscript and for their valuable suggestions. I am indebted to the staff of the Cambridge University Library and that of the Tennyson Research Centre, Lincoln, for their gracious assistance.

In the summers of 1976 and 1979 I attended seminars for college teachers sponsored by the National Endowment for the Humanities at the University of California, Berkeley, and at Princeton University. During those seminars Professor U. C. Knoepflmacher and Professor Ralph Freedman gave me encouragement and my work direction.

I should also like to thank Joyce Garnier for spending many hours discussing Tennyson with me; Robert Buffington for believing in my work; my colleagues Professor Arlene I. Clift and Professor Betty J. Overton for their generous support. Finally my thanks go to my friend and daughter, Gwen.

# Tennyson and Madness

# Introduction

ithout any doubt, Tennyson was acutely sensitive to inquisitive biographical studies. So vehement was he in his dislike that even today critics are sensitive to his objections and vulnerable to Shakespeare's epitaph that Tennyson threw at biographers: "Cursed be he that moves my bones." The twentieth-century critic Ralph Wilson Rader is an example. In his study of *Maud*, he introduces his "exposé" of the poet's intimate friendship with Rosa Baring by reminding the reader that Tennyson would not have been pleased with such a study.[1] He apologetically quotes "To———, After Reading a Life and Letters"—a poem written by Tennyson in 1849 to damn Lord Houghton and Thomas Medwin for tearing Keats's and Byron's hearts to shreds "before the crowd" like carrion vultures:

> For now the Poet cannot die,
> Nor leave his music as old,
>   But round him ere he scarce be cold
>   Begins the scandal and the cry.[2]

Just over thirty years later, Carlyle was scarcely cold before a friend of Tennyson and Carlyle's, J. A. Froude, published *Thomas Carlyle: A History of His Life in London, 1836–1881*. The publication of Froude's book revived the bitter sentiment of Tennyson's 1849 poem; moreover, the book brought the poem's verses closer to home: Froude had exposed Carlyle's mental instability to the "crowd." He had told his readers, for example, of Carlyle's experiences at Dr. James M. Gully's establishment in Malvern.[3] Understandably Tennyson, who had also been a patient of Dr. Gully's and had suffered periods of severe instability, felt angry and threatened. Tennyson reacted with brutal imagery. In response to a question about the biography, he told a visitor to Farringford: "I don't want to be ripped up like a hog when I'm dead."[4] As Tennyson grew older, his almost pathological mistrust of biography increased—a mistrust that, at one point, resulted in his instructing his son Hallam to burn the existing letters exchanged between him and Emily before their marriage, a time of particularly severe mental anguish for them. It was inevitable that such a strong dislike for biographical studies would catch his contemporaries' attention. As a result, several felt obligated to speak of Tennyson's profound dislike of inquisitive biography, his yearning for privacy; others felt obligated to include his opinion that it is folly to fancy that "all that a poet says in his verse must have some local meaning, or a personal reference."[5] Other biographers were to skim the surface of Tennyson's life and to defend their position by stating their belief that the poet's life resides in his work. For example, in his preface to the *Memoir*, Hallam wrote: "For my own part, I feel strongly that no biographer could so truly give him as he gives himself in his own work."[6] Following Hallam's path Thomas R. Lounsbury records what Tennyson told Francis Turner Palgrave several times: "The poet's work is his life, and no one has a right to ask for more."[7]

Although Hallam, Palgrave, and Lounsbury chose their words to defend their subject, they were not being inaccurate in insisting that Tennyson's work is his life, for Tennyson does truly "give himself" in his poetry. From the time he began composing poetry, he attempted to evolve a poetic form from the raw and often painful materials of his life. He rarely averted his attention from that on which he feared the carrion critics or brutal butcher might feed. As Sir Charles Tennyson points out, "many of his poems are clearly products of specific situations."[8] Tennyson was by no means a person who hid from himself and his anxieties. His dislike of biographical studies does not mean he was, as some critics would have it, an evasive poet. The point needs to be emphasized that Tennyson objected to these studies because he did not want the Houghtons, the Medwins, or the Froudes to do the telling; and, furthermore, he did not want the public to become so involved in the minutiae that they lost sight of his artistry. Tennyson as much disliked those who might pry into his private life, as he objected to those who might be blind to his creative independence from those intimacies. He once said as much to his coachman, William Knight: "There are some curious creatures who go about fishing for the people, and searching for the places, which they fancy must have given rise to our poems. They don't understand, or believe, that we have any imagination of our own, to *create* the people or the place."[9]

Although he grew impatient with those "curious creatures" who forgot that he was a creator, his strong dislike for any biographical study of a writer's work was closely linked to his desire to keep within the circle of intimate friends experiences like those which sent him to Dr. Gully's establishment. By no means did he want such painful times to be exposed before the public. But the problem for Tennyson was that his life was full of such experiences. As Robert Martin emphasizes in his recent biography of Tennyson, they were all too frequent.[10] Madness and morbidity were always present. His sense of the relative importance of his poetry and of his life was potentially most vulnerable to inquisitive biographers who would sooner remember his instability than recall his poetry. From the time Tennyson was a child in the early 1800s until his death in 1892, the specter of madness was always to hover over him and often to come dangerously near. True to form, however, he never turned his attention away from that specter. He chose to face it, and in the process he learned as much as he could about madness and watched his family, his friends, and himself for any signs of its terrible presence. At times he institutionalized himself in attempts to rid himself of it.

Because Tennyson faced the threat of madness, it was inevitable that he would transpose his experiences and his knowledge of insanity into his poetry.[11] The result is that much of the poetry is "private" in the sense that it is brimming with multiple brushes with madness. His imagery, subject matter, preoccupations, and style are all affected by his understanding and fear of insanity. A majority of the poetry takes its shape from a creative force that is fighting to remain sane and is therefore constantly moderating its own "wilder" impulses. Madness ends up being more than material for biography; it also emerges as a means by which readers can appreciate more fully Tennyson's artistry. The point of this book, then, is not merely to uncover "inquisitively" all of Tennyson's experiences with madness. On the contrary, its major thrust is to reveal how carefully Tennyson studied these experiences and how he used that knowledge and combined it with his understanding of madness as a literary metaphor to create poems that not only address madness but also take their shape from the poet's engagement with it. These poems are larger in number than many may expect. In fact, few poems written by Tennyson escape the influence of his anxiety. Hence, madness becomes not only a way of approaching a few obvious pieces like *The Princess* or *Maud*, but also a means of discussing a major portion of his life's work.

To begin to understand how Tennyson's experiences with madness shaped his poetic posture it is necessary to think of Tennyson as an observer of that madness and not, as some might claim, its victim. Although there are episodes in Tennyson's life to suggest that he could easily consider himself a victim of the morbidity that surrounded him, there are many more to demonstrate that he fought against this temptation and chose instead to stand outside of himself and adopt the role of an observer of the instability he found threatening yet fascinating. This role helped him survive and helped him simultaneously engage and distance himself from that instability. One way in which he regarded madness from an observer's perspective was to consider it within the context of the literary metaphor that neutralized the threat of insanity by treating it either as a cliché or as a symbol of the wrongs affecting the cultural and social milieux. The other and more courageous way, however, was to study the instability firsthand. One example of his adopting that role occurs in the late 1830s when in order better to understand the insane and, as he said, to "study the ravings of the demented at firsthand," he visited Dr. Matthew Allen and his private asylum.[12] What is noteworthy about Tennyson's visits to this asylum is not just the sense they give of his compulsion to look at and study the instability hovering about him, but also the opportunity they offer to explore the coincidence that at the same time Tennyson was visiting Dr. Allen's institution the severely despondent poet John Clare was also present, but as Dr. Allen's patient.[13] The proximity of these two poets is perhaps not especially significant in itself—for instance, there is no evidence that the two met—but the fact that Clare was the inmate while Tennyson was the observer is. Their antithetical posture at the asylum illustrates the differences in their poetic posture and demonstrates, quite vividly, Tennyson's decision to adopt the observer's role and therefore to write poetry not only from the perspective of a poet sensitive to madness as a literary metaphor but also from the perspective of one who is scientific, almost clinical, in his approach to madness. The poems show how Tennyson fought to separate himself from those like Clare who chose not to be observers and consequently lost control over their morbidity and became lost in the dark passages of their minds.[14] To study madness was to prevent enclosure. Because of the importance of this role to Tennyson's poetry, it is worthwhile to examine the implications of these poets' antithetical position at the asylum.

Both Clare and Tennyson were unusually sensitive to their moods. Letters written more than ten years before he became Dr. Allen's patient show that Clare was a person excessively aware of his physical and emotional ups and downs. Like Tennyson, he constantly watched himself for symptoms, and so from 1822 on his letters are rather full of accounts of his mental health. In 1825, feeling desperate and suicidal, he traveled to London to seek help from Dr. George Darling. By March 1831, sleeplessness and apprehension over the return of the "blue devils" affected Clare so badly that he was telling his publisher, John Taylor, that his future held nothing but "a stupid & stunning apathy or lingering madness & death." It was Taylor who arranged with Allen that Clare should enter the asylum in 1837.

Because of their heightened sensitivity to their moods and their anxiety concerning the motions of their minds, Clare and Tennyson, true to their shared Romantic tradition, often explored their dreams and visions. As Keats had in his letters, Clare wrote accounts of his dreams in journals; Tennyson recorded his in journals and through conversations with family and friends.[15] As might be expected, many of these experiences appeared in their poetry. Clare's nightly visions created "The Dream" and "The Nightmare"; Tennyson's dreams helped form many of his poems. That they shared this interest in dreams, however, is not as important as the manner in which Clare and Tennyson translated these dreams into their poetry. In translating his dreams, Clare demonstrates how much of an inmate he really is, how locked in he is by his moods and by his willingness to indulge in their darkness; Tennyson demonstrates how carefully he guards against that possibility by adopting the pose of an observer, a pose that mirrors his contemporaries' anxieties as much as it does his own.

Following the example of the Romantic poets who took the dream and attempted to reproduce it with sensuous language and poetic form, Clare tends to concentrate wholly on the dream's activity and to become lost in its horror, its pleasure, and its imagery. Rarely is there an introduction, rarely is there any reflection on the dream's nature, and almost never is there an attempt to understand the reason for the dream.

On the other hand, Tennyson takes pains to explore and interpret his dreams, even to moralize them. He is not as comfortable as Keats with sensuous dream imagery. Although Keats equates the dreamer and the madman in "The Fall of Hyperion," that equation is not a threatening one. Keats passes it off as if it were more a convention than a reality. Tennyson, obviously, cannot. He is not as willing as Keats to give in to the dream's power and indulge in an activity in which neither the will nor the voluntary powers play a role. Unlike Keats, he does not wish to "dream it every night." Fearing the dream's power to unbalance him, he is compelled to frame the dream within an almost clinical context, and in this way control the sensuous excesses. For him, to dissect and be clinical was not to murder but to temper and to survive. It is no wonder then that throughout his poetry narrators either comment analytically on the action or stand above it, looking down on the depths or gazing beyond, surveying as well as anticipating. And it is no wonder that the poetry is crowded with personae who are, like himself, at once in the depths of despair yet detached enough to question, explore, and analyze their actions. Moreover, it is not surprising to find Tennyson searching through history, mythology, and folklore to discover means of observing how others, like himself, deal with similar difficulties and feelings. His poetic preoccupation with Greek mythology after Arthur Henry Hallam's death is typical of this tendency. The dilemmas facing Ulysses, Tithon, Tiresias, Semele, and Proserpina helped him gain a perspective on his own suffering, on his fears about moving forward without Hallam, and on his suicidal longings.

Clare less frequently distances himself from, questions, or resists his dreams in his poetic recreations of them. Even with his personal fears regarding his growing insanity, he is far less timid than Tennyson, more willing to embrace the Romantic impulse, and thus to accept intuitive perception as truth rather than to feel the need to temper that moment or intuition by engaging in a clinical analysis. He is less willing to dissect, more willing to agree with someone, like Keats, who could compare the "Imagination" to "Truth" or to "Adam's dream," and periodically long "for a Life of Sensations rather than of Thoughts!" [16]

This tendency not to analyze experience affects the way in which Clare approaches and represents himself. Just as he had let his dreams remain as experiences to be felt rather than analyzed, so does he allow himself to embrace his distressing moments rather than to stand back and take account. Of course, there are moments when he tries to adopt the observer's posture, as when he wrote, "My life hath been one love—no, blot it out,— / My life hath been one chain of contradictions" ("Child Harold"). But most of his poems do not demonstrate this posture. Most demonstrate his choice not to resist himself and in Tennyson's sense his failure to keep a distance. "The Fate of Genius" illustrates this inclination when it shows Clare conforming to the pose of the neglected genius and speaking of himself as frail. He identifies with other "natural geniuses," Stephen Duck and Robert Bloomfield, anticipating the time when he too will meet their fate by dying forgotten, sick, and mad. He is their "kindred heart." He is not receptive to the wisdom of his acquaintance and hero, Charles Lamb, who argued that geniuses or poets are not, contrary to public opinion, necessarily insane. [17]

In his poems Clare repeatedly makes himself the subject or the victim. There are exceptions—as when he writes about the villagers, the wild life, and people he admires—but often these become mirrors or extensions of himself. Moreover, they do not lead the poet out of himself. Rather, they turn him in on himself and let him remain there. The resulting obsessive concern resembles the self-indulgence that Tennyson and his anxious contemporaries recognized and fought so hard to overcome.

One effect of Clare's poetic posture is his tendency to keep a majority of his poems locked into the past. Influenced by a Romantic nostalgia for times gone by, for childhood, Clare mourns the loss of his boyhood, the vanished pleasures of youth, and the goodness of the past. Unlike Tennyson, he can only see an Eden in the idyllic past. For him, the present is the funeral of the past. Clare resists the future and hence resists change. In his poem "On Youth," for instance, Clare can only speak of youth's sweet joys that have "gone astray." He is only aware of the pains of the present. On the other hand, almost in conscious opposition to this enclosed posture, Tennyson's poem "Youth" illustrates just how aware Tennyson was of the danger of the futile temptation to remain in the past or to hide in the floundering present. Caught between the voices of the past, "come back," and those of the future, "come along," his speaker feels confused but knows he must not stand still. He must heed the future's call:

> Yet well I know that nothing stays,
>     And I must traverse yonder plain:
> Sooner or later from the haze
>     The second voice will peal again.
>                                    [ll. 53–56]

The sentiment is repeated in "Ulysses," "The Lotos-Eaters," and "Morte d'Arthur" and reinforces Tennyson's anxious contempt for those like Clare who resisted the future and chose to yield to the past or remain idle and barren in the present—an anxiety that was all the stronger since Tennyson recognized the impulse within himself to remain still and to fall into the suspect pleasures of idleness and self-pity. He recognized that he could have quite easily given in to the impulses to linger in the sensuous, to stay among the lotos-eaters. He was just as aware as Keats of the temptations to "build a sort of mental Cottage of feelings quiet and pleasant," to disregard the world around him. However, like Keats, he also realized "Alas! this never can be."[18] But, unlike Keats, the temptation to remain with that mental cottage is far less for Tennyson, who, along with his contemporaries, is much more alert to the dangers of confining oneself and feeding off one's feelings.

Clare, however, had difficulty leaving the cottage behind and moving ahead. He was always looking backward, to home, a perspective that trapped him in the memory of his first love, Mary Joyce. Her image possessed his mind. Even after her death in 1838, Clare seems to have insisted that she was still alive, and he continued to write letters to her. When he escaped from the asylum, his one driving thought was to see her again. The poems written while he was at the asylum vividly illustrate this obsession, for Clare addressed one poem after another to Mary, all varying the theme "I sleep with Thee, and Wake with Thee." He begins to resemble those lovers declining into madness encountered in Tennyson's poetry. Like many of them, Clare slipped into a delusive state in which he was not sure what was real and what was a dream. He became an example of what Tennyson feared and what Allen warned against: that those who improperly "indulge" in their "thoughts and feelings" become incapable of resisting any other train of thought and lose control.[19] In the end it is not difficult to realize why at Allen's asylum it was Clare and not Tennyson who was the inmate. Clare and his poems are very much trapped in what Keats identified as the "dark passages" belonging to his contemporaries' "Chamber of Maiden-Thought." Like many of the Romantics Keats had in mind, Clare could not find his way out of that chamber. He and his poetry are lost among the dark passages of that chamber's conviction "that the World is full of Misery and Heartbreak, Pain, Sickness and oppression."[20] This conviction and its accompanying uncertainties, its "Mist," unbalance and trap Clare as they were to restrict so many of his mentors. He is rarely able, and perhaps even unwilling, to understand or to shed light on that darkness. As Keats pointed out, only rarely can a person, a "Genius" like Wordsworth, discover how to light up that darkness. If Keats had not died he might also have identified Tennyson as such a genius. Compared to Clare's enclosed and dark thoughts, Tennyson's openness and understanding are all the more noticeable. He and his poetry fight against Romantic enclosure by adopting the pose of the observer who constantly attempts and occasionally succeeds in shedding light on the chamber's vision of misery and pain. The impetus, though, for this struggle did not come from Tennyson alone. It also belonged to the mood of his age, which feared the excesses of the Romantics and, therefore, anxiously explored the darkness, using analytical and clinical tools. The Victorians did not want to become victims of that darkness and believed that one way to overcome such a fate was to attempt to understand, to shed light on the misery and pain. The Victorians, in fact, adopted most earnestly Keats's sense that "extensive knowledge is needful to thinking people—it takes away the heat and fever; and helps, by widening speculation, to ease the Burden of the Mystery."[21] Tennyson as the observer and the Victorian is shaped by this need.

Because Tennyson was an observer, he was keenly aware of his contemporaries' various views of madness. He was sensitive to the fact that madness was a word that stood for a diverse and complex range of unstable behavior and morality, ranging from sinful thoughts to hypochondria, to obsessive thinking and mania. And he was sensitive to the Victorians' comprehension of madness as a composite of older theories and newer clinical studies. In composing his poetry Tennyson combined his understanding of these various views with his knowledge of madness as a literary metaphor and, of course, with the knowledge that emanated from his numerous and sometimes excruciatingly painful personal encounters with instability. This study of Tennyson's poetry, therefore, opens with a discussion of the phenomenon of "mad humanity" in the nineteenth century and of the conventional and shifting treatments of madness in literature, and then moves on to describe his personal experiences. These opening discussions prepare the way for the major part of this study that explores the ways in which the phenomena of the "mad humanity," literary madness, and his personal experiences complement (and sometimes contradict) each other in Tennyson's poetry and influence not only the character and structure of his poems but also his preoccupation with the necessity of "sublime repression" and his belief in the supremacy of the will.

## Chapter One

# Mad Humanity

Hysterics, raving lunatics, locked attics, mismanaged asylums, insane delusions, threats of inherited or impending madness, and societies tyrannized by undisciplined passions are all too familiar in nineteenth-century English literature. Examples occur in the novels, for instance, of George Meredith, Charles Dickens, Charlotte Brontë, and William Makepeace Thackeray, and in the poetry of Robert Browning and Tennyson.[1]

If all this madness were confined to fiction or poetry it might easily be understood, even dismissed, as being merely a device to quicken the action or intensify the work's sympathetic or moralistic tone. Such is not the case, however, for madness does not abide solely in those imaginative and metaphoric enclosures. Rather, it is part of those enclosures because the nation's consciousness pushed it there. Hence, Brontë's Mrs. Rochester, locked within the tower of Thornfield Hall, and Browning's madhouse cells exist not just because they are formed by a literary convention, but because they are nurtured by an age almost overwhelmed by its sense of instability.[2] They are extensions of the nineteenth-century sensitivity to madness—a madness that was a pressing and threatening reality.

This sensitivity not only emerges in the century's poetry and fiction but also often surfaces elsewhere. The essays of Thomas Babington Macaulay, Thomas Carlyle, John Henry Newman, and John Stuart Mill, for instance, rarely escape allusions to the tormented mind. It was most natural for Macaulay to understand Suraja Dowlah's dissolute behavior as a form of madness; for Carlyle to castigate the chaos whirling around him as madness; and for Newman, in his lectures on *The Idea of the University* (1852), to allude to the "deranged" person and, moreover, to demonstrate a lively concern for the "overstimulated" mind that runs the risk of becoming "as impotent" as that of "the madman."[3] Of course Mill was no madman, but his references to his breakdown and his subsequent studies in abnormal psychology are to be expected. However, Mill is not alone. Few Victorian autobiographies, lives, or, for that matter, collections of letters overlook their subjects' "mental crises."

Just why the English would be so absorbed by their mental health is an intriguing question. One answer rests with the physicians and their newly found preoccupation with "nerves" and "madness." Toward the end of the eighteenth century and following the investigations into King George III's madness (1798), it became acceptable and indeed fashionable for physicians to show a professional interest in madness.[4] Such was the impact of their interest that by the middle of the nineteenth century the most prominent as well as the most fashionable among them were involved in fathoming the mysteries of madness, nervous diseases, and the nervous system. Brimming with definitions, clinical studies, statistics, and engraved illustrations, their books are monuments to this surge of interest in the subject. If the therapies of our own time were not themselves so various and so inclusive, one might be amused by the bewildering variety of approaches and solutions to mental problems found in nineteenth-century England.

Exploring the mysteries of madness, however, had its difficulties, for the physicians were well aware that their comprehension of psychology was inadequate, that their understanding had come from moral philosophers and books and not from firsthand observation. They were in full agreement with the great French psychiatrist Philippe Pinel, who in 1801 declared that the field was one replete with "so many errors to rectify, and so many prejudices to remove."[5] To begin correcting these errors and prejudices the English physicians followed the lessons found in texts written by several prominent French doctors who had undertaken a much more scientific approach to their patients. Like their mentors, these Englishmen started to collect clinical evidence. And they did it with gusto. For instance, following the example of Pinel, Thomas Percival in 1803 suggested that "a regular journal should be kept of every species of malady"; in 1804 Joseph Mason Cox published careful descriptions of twenty case histories in his book *Practical Observations of the Insane*; in 1810 John Haslam began to perform autopsies on the brains of dead asylum inmates; and eventually, in 1830, John Conolly strongly advised every medical student to take part of his training in a lunatic asylum, so that he could have firsthand experience and therefore be "as familiar with disorders of the mind as with other disorders."[6] Conolly was not alone in promoting such clinical studies. Sir Benjamin Brodie, one of Tennyson's doctors, also urged this training. When lecturing to medical students in the 1830s, Brodie encouraged the students to recognize the importance of "nervous diseases," for "in one shape or another you will meet them at every turn of your future practice."[7]

As might be expected, given the public's sensitivity to madness, this newly acquired interest in clinical psychology did not stay within the

limits of the medical profession. Rather it broke out of those limits into
a network, like the nerves under study, touching and reaching the body
of people. Indeed, one idiosyncracy of nineteenth-century England is the
extent to which these specialized studies ran over into the more popular
journals and magazines reviewing the arts and the political scene.[8] This
proclivity to publish studies of madness began as early as 1809 when the
*Quarterly Review* consigned considerable space to a discussion of Haslam's *Observations on Madness and Melancholy*, Pinel's *Treatise on Insanity*,
and Thomas Arnold's *On the Management of the Insane*. Throughout the
ensuing decades, the journal was to continue its interest by reviewing
more books on the subject. Sometimes journals reprinted articles that
had appeared in *The Lancet*, and frequently *Fraser's Magazine*, *The Nineteenth Century*, *Belgravia*, *Macmillan's Magazine*, *St. James' Magazine*, *The
Athenaeum*, *Household Words*, and *The Cornhill Magazine* included articles
written especially for them by those involved in the treatment of the
insane.[9]

One reason these reviews and articles traveled beyond the professional
journals into the laymen's magazines was the age's sense of its mad humanity—a sense stimulated by the physicians' avid interest in the phenomenon. It would be safe to say that a majority feared that madness
was spreading in epidemic proportions from man to man, from generation to generation, and from region to region. Many saw madness as a
monster lying beneath the surface, waiting to be given an opportunity
to rise and consume their England. As one contemporary put it, there is
"an immense amount of latent brain disease in the community, only
awaiting for a sufficient exciting cause to make itself patent to the world."[10]
Most found that "exciting cause" in the quickened pace of modern life.
They feared that the "crowding and jostling" age was straining people's
minds to the breaking point. From their point of view, increased wealth,
poverty, idleness, recklessness, and of course alcoholism caused insanity.
To make matters worse, doctors compounded people's fears by subscribing to the thought that insanity was "The English Malady" and by considering seriously whether insanity prevailed more in England than
in other countries.[11] That concern lingered persistently throughout the
century.

However, the doctors were not entirely to blame for the alarm. New
legislation and special parliamentary committees also added to the public's sense of a mad humanity.[12] Parliamentary reports and acts eventually
benefited the inmates, but in the meantime fed the public's anxieties by
constantly drawing attention to columns of statistics showing an increase
in the number of mental patients. Rather than consider the possibility
that there were greater numbers of people suffering from insanity be-

cause better records were being kept, many jumped all too quickly to the conclusion that insanity was infecting the nation.

Such fears brought with them the compulsion to define insanity. However, as most readily acknowledged, the task was difficult. In fact, so numerous were references to the difficulty that a cliché, not unlike an epic's apologetic beginning, was born: few could open a discussion of insanity without explaining their own inadequacies in the face of such an enormous and amorphous beast as madness. The cliché also inevitably found its way into the parliamentary committee hearings. On one occasion, a committee member asked the physician Samuel Fort Simmons, "Have you been in the habit of classifying the different descriptions of mental disorder?" Simmons's reply is predictable: "—That is a matter of so much difficulty, that I have not attempted it any more than the common distinction of mania and melancholia."[13]

When Simmons was answering the committee member's question in 1812, people were still more or less content to cling to the traditional way of classifying madness according to the ancient divisions of mania and melancholia. By the middle of the century, however, most were not so content. They searched for more accurate divisions of insanity into species and subspecies—a search that uncovered so many subspecies that these well-meaning attempts often bordered on the ludicrous and seemed a parody of the scientific method they were emulating.[14] But all this zealous activity was not in vain, for the physicians soon came to the emphatic and helpful conclusion that mania and melancholia were not mutually exclusive states. Rather, they were states that fluctuate and combine in a variety of ways.[15] The results of this new consciousness were at first chaotic, but eventually an order pressed through the seemingly endless lists of species, bringing with it an understanding that madness could now be divided into four basic, yet fluctuating, types: (1) melancholia or monomania, (2) mania or delirium, (3) partial insanity, and (4) moral insanity.

Although still bearing its traditional trappings, melancholia was linked specifically to severe depression and monomania, the exclusive preoccupation with a single idea or object—the *idée fixe*. People recognized its dangers and were willing to attribute much suffering to its grip. By subscribing to the *idée fixe*, the English were once more following the French lead, for it had been Jean Étienne Dominique Esquirol (1820) who had insisted on substituting the word *monomania* for *melancholy*. As he said, the word "Melancholy . . . should be left exclusively to moralists and poets, who, in their expressions, are not obliged to employ so much precision as physicians."[16]

Violence, tempestuous passion, and fury—all the traditional ways of describing mania—still clung to the Victorians' comprehension of this form of madness. Because wild behavior continued to dominate the popular image of madness, even as late as 1815 the public could pay a penny in hopes of seeing the maniacs rage in Bethlehem.[17]

Partial insanity was a catchall phrase for the multiple subspecies of insanity. The phrase allowed physicians to describe those many cases in which a person retained part of his or her reason, who lost control over one or two subjects, or who suffered from periodic aberrations. Of all the forms of partial insanity, hypochondria and hysteria were the most common and the most controversial. Some physicians insisted on considering them as distinctly different forms of insanity, but others, the more enlightened, insisted that these were two words naming the same disease. Those who distinguished between the two did so because, of course, from the beginning hysteria had been a disease associated solely with women, not men, since hysteria had been supposed to originate in an infected uterus. They had difficulty applying the term to their male patients. On the other hand, those who did not distinguish between the two experienced few qualms, for they acted under the conviction that hypochondria and hysteria were nervous diseases originating in the patient's imagination. More typically, however, nineteenth-century physicians got caught in the middle of the controversy. For example, several eminent physicians readily admitted that males and females displayed and suffered from similar hysterical symptoms, but they also admitted that they did not feel at ease calling the disease by its "feminine" name, "hysteria." Tennyson's Dr. Benjamin Brodie is one example. In 1836 he was honest enough to admit that he had described cases "as if the symptoms were peculiar to the female sex; but it is not so in reality; and I have known several (though by comparison certainly rare) instances of males being affected in the same manner. I employ the term hysteria because it is in common use, and because it would be inconvenient to change it for another."[18]

Another of Tennyson's physicians, Sir James Paget, also recognized that men can be affected "in the same manner," but like Brodie he could not change his habits. He chose to dwell almost exclusively on cases of women suffering from hysteric tumors or hysteric diseases of the spine or pelvis. Undoubtedly the century's predisposition to think of women as being more nervous than men encouraged the prejudice and led to the practice of calling women hysterics and men hypochondriacs, even though many physicians knew better.

These "imaginary diseases" and their elusive nature both intrigued and bothered physicians. Frequently they would examine the hypochondriacal or hysterical patient after his or her death to demonstrate to themselves and their public that even after "the most minute dissections," as Brodie wrote, there is "nothing . . . different from what there would have been" if the disease had "never existed."[19] Doctors were never totally content, however, to pronounce these diseases as entirely imaginary. The hypochondriac's or hysteric's complaints seemed to them to exist within a strange and irritating borderland between a real physical complaint and an imaginary one.

Moral insanity, the other major species of insanity, is almost too "Victorian" to be true. Perhaps only in the Victorian era would people associate a lack of morality or "a perversion of moral sense" with madness. In the nineteenth-century mind, the patient suffering from this form of insanity might have full possession of his intellectual faculties but not full possession of his feelings and personal habits. In the 1830s Dr. James Cowles Prichard defined moral insanity by using the phrase "self-government"—a phrase that was to become the rallying cry of those who feared any form of excess and who believed that lack of control over feelings or habits automatically put people into the vicious grip of insanity.[20]

At the foundation of all these forms of madness was a common demon—faulty reasoning. Continuing the preceding century's practice, people in the nineteenth century often spoke of insanity as being the opposite of reason and good sense, "as light is to darkness, straight to crooked."[21] False reasoning linked ideas in mad ways. So acceptable was this concept that in the 1843 trial of Daniel McNaughton the judge acquitted the would-be assassin of Sir Robert Peel on the grounds that he lacked reason and therefore was mad.[22] False reason, however, was not the only demon. False sensory impressions were also to blame. As the century progressed, these false impressions were to become the more menacing demon. With the growing knowledge of the body's physiological processes, physicians were intrigued with how people perceive the outside world, how the sense impressions reach the brain, and how those impressions form an understanding of the outer reality. They spent considerable time tracing the initial sensory impression as it ran along the intricate network of nerves into the brain. Their interest in following these impressions led them away from the tradition of allowing associationism and "unreason" to explain abnormal behavior. Madness could now also be thought of in physiological terms. Madness could be nothing more than an erroneous perception or a "false report" from the senses. The idea that mad men and women suffered from a faulty sensory network that misrepresented the world by modifying and disfiguring their surroundings intrigued the physicians. Delusions, hallucinations, and illusions were not necessarily the children of false reasoning, chaotic associations, but the offspring of "the false report" of a person's senses.[23]

Because madness could be synonymous with faulty perception, anything that contributed to self-deception or to a mistaken impression was thought responsible for causing confusion. The self-conscious, moralistic public had no difficulty in identifying the guilty ogres. Depending on their prejudices and persuasions, laymen and physicians churned out lists, even longer than those identifying subspecies, of insanity's physical and moral causes. The physical causes were variations on those recognized hundreds of years before: accidents, shocks, sunstroke, starvation, old age, changing seasons, the moon, lack of sleep, alcoholism, hereditary traits, and determination of blood to the brain. Of these, the last three absorbed most of the period's energy.[24] Alcoholism reared its threatening head time and time again. Haslam listed it first among the physical causes. Many other physicians, believing in its destructive power, attempted to study alcoholism in a scientific manner. In 1804, for example, Thomas Trotter presented the first clinical evidence that alcoholism produced more mental afflictions than corporeal diseases. Throughout the century people picked up Trotter's conclusion and painted horrific pictures of madness prompted by intemperance. They went so far as to warn the public that drink's mad consequences reached beyond those who indulged—that children would inherit the malady "drink" from their fathers.[25]

The concept of inherited madness visible in the temperance movement's warnings was very much alive in other discussions of insanity. The specter of inherited madness had in fact hung over discussions of insanity for as long as people had recognized the disease, but in the nineteenth century hereditary influences showed themselves more clearly and more menacingly than before. By 1814 the specter was visible enough for physicians like Joseph Adams to devote a book to the subject. His *The Hereditary Properties of Disease*, along with numerous other texts, prompted debates and provoked people to question the theory's finer points. For example, several wondered whether a child born before the parent's attack of madness would be more or less likely to inherit the tendency.[26] In these debates the fact that the child would inherit madness was of course a given. As the period moved on, clinical evidence, statistics, collections of family histories, and interviews with patients all combined to leave little doubt in the public's or the physicians' minds that insanity, or, at least the propensity to it, passed from generation to generation.[27]

The state of a patient's blood has always been associated with madness, and nineteenth-century physicians shared that assumption. Like their predecessors they talked about the impurities in the blood, but unlike their predecessors they chose to center much of their discussion on the blood's circulation. As Ilza Veith, the historian, has pointed out, nineteenth-century physicians recognized a connection between the emotions and the rapidity or slowness with which the blood moved through the body and circulated in the brain's blood vessels.[28] Putting it quite simply, too much blood gushing into the brain caused mental chaos; too little created depression.

The physicians' sensitivity to a physiological cause, like the blood's circulation, is indicative of the period's energetic belief in insanity's physiological roots. Many physicians vehemently stressed the body's influence over the mind. In 1827, for example, the surgeon of Lancaster County Lunatic Asylum, Paul Slade Knight, insisted that "an over zeal for religion, or a violent excitement of some one of the passions, is frequently the inevitable result of the corporeal affections, by which . . . the mind is constantly influenced." He continued by writing, "I have no hesitation to declare . . . that in every case of deranged intellect the disease proceeds immediately from corporeal disorder."[29] In 1847 *The Zoist*, subtitled *A Journal of Cerebral Physiology*, also came out strongly with the opinion that "madness is a derangement of the function of the brain." Supporting this school of thought, many physicians dissected brains, searching for inflamed membranes and examining blood vessels, in the hope of connecting "specific symptoms of mental disorder with specific morbid conditions of the encephalon."[30] The nineteenth century's enthusiasm for phrenology belongs to this conviction, for phrenology was originally one means of establishing a physiological basis of madness.

The nineteenth century would have not lived up to its reputation as a century preoccupied with its morals had it not also identified causes of madness resulting from the conduct of the emotions. Most of these causes are predictable, for they mirror the Victorians' anxiety concerning the threat posed by the new commercial age, the loosening of sexual mores, the changes in the political and social order, the redefinition, for example, of women's education, and the zeal with which religious evangelicalism was spreading throughout the country. The subsequent list of what the Victorians called moral causes is self-righteously long: excessive fears, griefs, domestic misfortune, fanaticism, disappointments in love, religious devotion, terror, anger, pride, ambition, indulgence in any passion, anxiety, overwork, nervous shock, unexpected accession of wealth, unexpected loss of wealth—anything excessive was on everyone's list.[31] Any of these excesses could lead a susceptible person, like those with hereditary predispositions, into the locked room or the asylum. Such was the Victorians' preoccupation with these excesses that

poulticed on consequence of injuries produced by the use of handcuffs."[41] Terribly disturbed by what he found, Hill began introducing reforms. By degrees the asylum left behind forced feedings, plunge baths, tranquilizing chairs, chained legs, locked and darkened rooms, and whippings. So effective were Hill's reforms that by 1837 the asylum's board was able to report: "The present House Surgeon has expressed his own belief, founded on experience in this house, that it may be possible to conduct an Institution for the Insane without having recourse to the employment of any Instruments of Restraint whatsoever."[42]

Using his work at Lincoln as an example, Hill became a pioneer in trying to convince people that asylums need not depend on the older coercive methods, that personal attention was more effective than physical coercion in controlling and healing madness. Change did not come easily. *The Further Report of the Commission on Lunacy* issued in 1847 showed, for example, that even in those asylums advocating more gentle treatment there were struggles between those who believed and those who did not believe in the reforms. Binding, cupping, leeching, cold bathing, and blistering continued. Stubborn asylum directors exclaimed, "*What! Let loose a Madman! Why, he will tear us to pieces!*"[43] Hill, however, was not without his supporters. Tennyson's friend Dr. Matthew Allen, the director of an asylum at High Beech near Epping Forest, shared Hill's enthusiasm for nonrestrictive methods. Allen abhorred "a direct system of coercion" and firmly believed that "harsh measures" always increase the evils that they should pretend to cure. His mild system gave his patients more freedom to move about the asylum's grounds and, in some cases, to discharge themselves. He felt it better to risk a few "accidents"—suicides and escapes—and to treat his patients as if they were still "reasonable human beings" than subject them to physical coercion. Even so, Allen was not beyond making an exception for "ferocious and furious maniacs."[44]

The increasingly strong reaction to older restrictive methods meant that new ones had to replace them. In an age willing to recognize moral insanity, it is not surprising that moral management would be the answer for the majority. "Mildness and firmness" were the key to this treatment. Together these qualities helped the patient recover or develop powers of self-government which he had lost or never been allowed to have. Through moral management, the will would regain its "supremacy" and control the body and its animal spirits. Advocates stubbornly clung to the belief that when "man has power over himself" he can control and prevent insanity. Madness was understood, in John Abercrombie's words, as the loss of that power to master the mind.[45] The will and its controlling power were essential to a healthy mind. A loss of will meant disaster.

That loss explained numerous cases of partial insanity. For instance Paget relied on the principle to explain hypochondria. He maintains that a "strong will is, I think, less common among these patients than is a want of will. Sometimes there is a general feebleness of will: the patients can do nothing for themselves; can trust themselves in nothing; but commit themselves to someone with a stronger will, and an appearance, if not a reality, of more knowledge. Hence, among these patients are the most numerous subjects of mesmerism, spiritualism, and other supposed forces of which the chief evidence is the power of a strong will over a weak one."[46]

The pressures to govern oneself must have been enormous and, rather than have cured, must have exacerbated many people's nervousness. Perhaps no more vivid illustration of this pressure exists than in the machinery created to encourage a young boy to govern himself and break the habit of masturbation. Masturbation, of course, was thought to be a major cause of insanity. Alexander Comfort, in his study of sexuality *The Anxiety Makers*, reproduces illustrations of two machines sold to parents in the 1880s, the "Electric Alarum" and the spiked or toothed "Penile Ring." Both were designed to awaken the sleeping boy if he had a nightly erection or if he involuntarily abused himself. Another method was to tie the sleeping boy's hands to the sides of his bed.[47] The alternative was the asylum. Young women were not exempt from the pressure for self-government. To aid a woman in battling against her "fatal" habits, physicians by the mid-nineteenth century had developed a sinister technique by which they either removed her clitoris or severed the connecting nerves—all in the hope of producing better self-government and reducing instances of insanity.[48]

Because of the importance given to self-government, parents and teachers also suffered their share of anxieties. In the popular mind these adults were held almost entirely responsible for nurturing the child's will.[49] Physicians and reformers preached in hyperboles to mothers and fathers, especially to mothers, that one slip, one false example, might ruin their children forever. In fact, one of the most convincing arguments in the nineteenth century in favor of women's education was that if women were responsible for the children's moral well-being they had better be educated so that their weak wills might not corrupt their children's.[50] By all means, it was necessary to remove a person from an environment that did not encourage self-government. This necessity took many people away from home. For those who could afford it, a foreign tour was the answer. It was one way of separating the sufferer from the malignant influence of home. For others, a private asylum or an hydropathic establishment offered a respite from evil influences. The principle was to divert the diseased mind away from itself.

In the long run, the methods used in purging a patient or increasing his will's power or in diverting his mind away from itself were never as disturbing to people as the widespread technique of treating all forms of madness with drugs and "physic." The toxic properties of these medicines and the doctors' habit of relying too heavily on drugs, particularly opium, alarmed many, and either sent physicians searching for safer medication or sent them completely away from any type of physic. For those who were most alarmed, the water cure offered a way of treating nervous disorders without having to prescribe drugs. Much of the popularity of this cure and the sudden surge of hydropathic establishments in England in the 1830s and 1840s can be attributed to the reaction against medicinal cures. Dr. James M. Gully, the hydropathic physician who was to become Tennyson's doctor and friend, was among "the very earliest practitioners to realize that the startling, immediate benefits of drugs were often attended by very serious long-term disadvantages."[51] Like other physicians of hydropathy, Gully outlawed drugs and, for that matter, any stimulant such as tea, coffee, and of course alcoholic drinks which would exacerbate the patient's nervous condition.

By the time people were going into the water cures, not only were they aware of the hazards of drugs, but, thanks to the proliferation of articles and discussions on insanity, much of the public and a majority of physicians were extraordinarily sophisticated on the subject of madness. But the fact that they took insanity more seriously, trying to understand and control it by amassing definitions, statistics, and clinical evidence, should not suggest that they were existing in a vacuum, protected against the infection of historical prejudices they were trying so hard to overcome. On the contrary, very few rid their understanding completely of their preconceptions or rid madness of its historical trappings. Not all their theories and conclusions were strictly "clinical." The columns of statistics barely shielded the reader's eyes from these ancient prejudices and conceptions. As the methods of physical coercion and restriction suggest, for example, few could forget the classical association of passionate bestiality with madness. Despite campaigns to humanize insanity, the passionate and destructive "animal spirits" still haunted Tennyson's contemporaries.

Moreover, their understanding of madness as a moral disease might be "Victorian," but it was also an heir to, or at least a variation on, the medieval idea that madness was a disease visited on those who had sinned. Madness was a punishment to cleanse the wicked of their excesses. Nineteenth-century fiction as well as pieces written by physicians indicate that this medieval sentiment was still very much alive in literary conventions and in more specialized writing. The number of villains in

Victorian fiction who are punished by going mad is quite remarkable, and the tendency of the doctors to consider madness as a "purge" is equally noteworthy.[52] This association of madness with evil or sin also helps explain why the nineteenth-century physicians and laymen persisted in wanting to punish the insane and put "the fear of God" into them. Perhaps even the Victorians' anxiety over the acquisition of wealth and new technology also parallels the medieval period's sense of madness as being the price of acquiring or knowing too much.

The century's indebtedness to historical theories on madness is also illustrated by the fact that Robert Burton's *Anatomy of Melancholy* came back into vogue, not only in Victorian drawing rooms, but also in the physicians' libraries.[53] It was a best-seller. The parallels between what Burton has to say about madness and what the nineteenth century had to say about insanity must be partially responsible for the book's popularity. These parallels are extensive: melancholy is a hereditary disease of the body and mind; idleness, ambition, drink, lust, lack of sleep, love, jealousy, immoderate exercise, impure blood, inflamed brains cause insanity; a "change of air" and bleeding cure it. Fear of a seething mass of mad humanity also finds its parallel in Burton's recognition that madness "is an inbred malady in every one of us . . . which if it be stirred up, or get ahead, will run *in infinitum*, and infinitely varies as we ourselves are severally addicted."[54]

Another historical conception of madness which carried over into nineteenth-century thought was the fear of "fantasy" or "imagination" unchecked by the will.[55] There was still the prejudice that "those in whom the imaginative faculty is inordinately developed," poets in particular, "are particularly liable to morbid affections of the mind." For this reason John Dryden's couplet on the subject introduced many a discussion on insanity and genius: "Great wits are sure to madness near allied, / And thin partitions do their bounds divide" (*Absalom and Achitophel*, 1: 162–63). The older sense of a madman as a raving maniac tormented by uncontrollable passions lingered too. Dissecting brains, collecting statistics, dividing madness into infinite subspecies did not succeed in burying the image of King Nebuchadnezzar, King Lear, and Don Quixote. The myths lived on, so that in the nineteenth century the understanding of madness was simultaneously naïve and sophisticated. Madness was historical as well as clinical. It mingled images of a raving lunatic with images of pitiable victims of modern society and conjured up images of morbidly affected brains preserved in laboratory jars.

But most of all, whether it had a historical or clinical basis, madness was ubiquitous. It was all-encompassing, including not only the maniacs and their extravagantly wild behavior, but also admitting those suffering

from any slight mental abnormality—from a hypochondriac complaining of imaginary pains in his side to someone momentarily weighted
down by a single idea or overcome by anxiety or depression. Anything
slightly excessive, irrational, or distorted might receive the label. No
wonder, then, that those living in nineteenth-century England were so
familiar with it and sensitive to it.

Those who were keenly aware of the madness around and in them could
not help but also be influenced by the multiple images of insanity available to them in literature. The familiar mad figures in the ancient Greek
drama, Renaissance literature, poetry and prose of the seventeenth- and
eighteenth-centuries, Gothic novels and melodramas, and Romantic texts
helped keep the phenomenon of madness in the forefront of their consciousness and gave them additional ways of shaping their understanding
of what it is to be "mad."[56] Like those portraits of madness in medical
texts, many literary portraits were at once traditional and inventive; others were extensions of scientific thought. All helped to create a more
complex vision of madness than the scientific models, however diverse.

To begin thinking about these literary images, it is necessary to acknowledge that madness in literature rarely exists for its own sake. Rather,
it lives as metaphor, as a means of addressing other issues. In his study
of Augustan madness and literature Max Byrd makes just that point. He
notices, for example, how frequently madness is a metaphor of tragedy.[57]
Examples are not hard to find. Madness obviously helps to objectify the
disorderly world of *King Lear*; it emphasizes Hamlet's tragic confusion;
and it brings the horror facing the Duchess of Malfi to a vivid pitch.
Where would the audience's sense of *The Duchess of Malfi*'s tragedy and
moral disorder be without Ferdinand's insanely perverted behavior? The
same question also has to be asked of the Gothic romances and the
nineteenth-century closet drama. Where would their terror, evil, and tragic
pathos be without the specter of insanity? Frequently madness looms
from under the main plot, reinforcing the prevailing sense of chaos or
despair. The Renaissance drama that Tennyson and a significant number
of nineteenth-century readers studied so assiduously offers striking examples. For instance, in the subplot of Thomas Middleton and William
Rowley's *The Changeling*, Antonio's mad disguise and "romantic" ex-
cursions into the madhouse to woo the keeper's wife mirror Beatrice's
crazy scheming and disguising and parallel the play's exposure of "the
bestial element in man."[58] Another example of such "mad" paralleling
comes in John Ford's *The Lover's Melancholy*. Here the mad masque not
only reveals how carefully Ford read Burton's *Anatomy*, but also, like

other Jacobean masques, exposes the tragic disorders plaguing the play's main characters.[59]

Madness as metaphor also belongs to satire. With all its traditional associations with violence, filth, and stupidity, madness offers the writer a splendid opportunity to exercise hyperbole and to speak graphically of fools and chaos. Perhaps one of the most vivid examples of this metaphor is in a poem Tennyson committed to memory—Alexander Pope's *The Dunciad*.[60] As Byrd points out, no one lives in that poem's chaotic world who is not mad.[61] Madness is crucial to Pope's savagely satirical thrust at a morally inferior and unreasonable state of affairs.

Jonathan Swift's satirical pieces equally burst with mad men and women.[62] For instance, in another poem Tennyson committed to memory, "The Legion Club," Swift uses the popular image of the raving maniac locked within a filthy cell to help him attack the folly of the Irish parliament. So enraged was Swift with the parliament that he condemns each member to his "proper cell."

> Let them, when they once get in
> Sell the Nation for a Pin;
> While they sit a picking Straws
> Let them rave of making Laws;
> While they never hold their Tongue,
> Let them dabble in their Dung;
> Let them form a grand Committee,
> How to plague and starve the City;
> Let them stare and storm and frown,
> When they see a Clergy-Gown.
> Let them, 'ere they crack a Louse,
> Call for th' Orders of the House;
> Let them with their gosling Quills,
> Scribble senseless Heads of Bills;
> We may, while they strain their Throats,
> Wipe our A——s with their V———.[63]

The Augustan world is not alone in locking its foolish leaders behind bars. Throughout the history of literature mad lawyers, priests, doctors, brokers, and educators have often paraded across the stage or have populated pages exposing hypocrisy and reinforcing the writer's sense of a lewd, egocentric, and doomed world. Recall the mad masque in *The Duchess of Malfi* with its procession of insane lawyers, priests, doctors, and brokers, and consider the lawyers and priests who, almost three hundred years later, inhabit the cells in Charles Robert Maturin's *Melmoth the Wanderer*.

As part of its illustration of such rottenness, madness also exposes any behavior that threatens to undo the existing order, a function that was to become important to Tennyson and the uses he made of madness in his poetry. In any number of literary works, madness characterizes the destructive mob and its challenge to the dominant social and political order; it also characterizes those who shake the religious order and the zealots whose schemes run wild. Consider the mad mobs that populate Augustan literature and that become standard in any piece about revolution or war. Consider also those "mad monks" and imprudent schemers who unsettle not only themselves, but also those they so easily contaminate. Madness, however, is a metaphor most often used to characterize the terrors associated with sexual pleasure, a pleasure that tyrannizes reason and eventually upsets the moral and social order. Such a metaphor occurs in Ford's *'Tis Pity She's a Whore* and centuries later enables writers of Victorian fiction to represent their heroes and heroines who lead sinful lives.[64] For Ford and these Victorian writers, madness is similar to what it was for the medieval world—a punishment visited on sinners who succumb to their lust. Tennyson's "Lucretius" belongs to this tradition.

Another aspect of madness as it functions metaphorically in literature is its accompanying freedom and its "cunning" or its devious nature. Within the tradition that mad men and women can say anything and get away with it, writers are freer to speak their minds through their mad characters. Because the mad have license to be strange and cunning, writers and their characters are also freer to play with time, to hatch plots, and to dissemble so that "the truth" may be discovered. Examples of such license belong to revenge tragedy. Fredson Bowers speaks of the importance of madness as a dramatic device in the revenge tradition and notes that in the later revenge tragedies, particularly, madness is consciously used by the protagonist to delay and to prepare plots.[65] The feigning of madness is essential to the plot of Shakespeare's *Titus Andronicus* and, of course, *Hamlet* when madness allows Hamlet to sneer at Polonius (and get away with it), to upbraid Claudius and Gertrude, and to plan his revenge.

Characters outside the revenge tradition also use madness to help them play with time and unveil the truth. Adam Overdo in Ben Jonson's *Bartholomew Fair* disguises himself as a madman-fool, a disguise that does not work as intended, for Overdo gets lost in his disguise. Being a fool himself, he misinterprets much of what he hears and sees. The disguise, instead, unveils Overdo. Thomas Percy's beggar Tom O'Bedlam is another example. He puts on the mad disguise not just to win sympathy but also, as in the case of one of the Tom O'Bedlam ballads, to show how "mad" Puritan enthusiasts are for their beliefs.

Sometimes these mad figures uncover such marvelous and necessary truths that, although wild in appearance, they possess a certain nobility. Many are the examples of frenzied yet noble poets; many are the examples of dreamers whose mad visions reveal a truth hidden from a saner eye. William Blake's stubborn contention that only the madman is free and fulfilled is very much in that tradition. Accompanying this tradition comes the paradox that madness heals; that it is sometimes necessary to be mad in order to be cured of moral obliquity, and that, at times, it is also necessary either to feign or suffer from the disorder to discover the order. Penelope B. R. Doob, in her study of medieval literature and madness, offers examples of this phenomenon, and so does John R. Reed, who remarks that in Victorian fiction temporary madness is often a positive state, for it permits the cleansing and renovating of a mind—a concept that complements the mad doctors' belief in purging as a part of their cure for insanity. Reed believes that the hero of Tennyson's *Maud* is purged—experiences a moral recovery—through temporary insanity.[66]

As might be expected, however, madness rarely is a positive state. More frequently it serves, as it does in scientific texts, as a warning. It reminds people how they and their institutions can so easily become lost in the "mists of error" and become divorced from the truth. Consequently, more abundant are the Don Quixotes who are lost in their dreams and hallucinations. Like Friedrich Schiller's Ghost-Seer ("The Ghost-Seer; or, Apparitionist"), they constantly misapprehend the world around them; they lose touch with reality and go insane. Such are the deceptive qualities of madness that often its victims cannot even recognize those closest to them. Manfred in Horace Walpole's *The Castle of Otranto*, for example, suffers so acutely from his mad passions that he does not know his daughter Matilda, a blindness that surely echoes the maddening Lear's failure to recognize Cordelia and her sincerity. Because these characters live blinded by error, like Balin and Balan in Tennyson's *Idylls of the King*, they wander into the wilderness as exiles, strangers to themselves, their friends, and their country. Their obsessions eventually trap them in cells or attics. Madness then becomes a metaphor of their confinement.

Madness is not in all cases a device to move the plot, enhance the tragedy, or mirror the chaos. It can also be a personal metaphor, thus coming closer to existing for its own sake. It may reflect the writer's perception that madness is a human, often most personal, affliction. For example, madness for Samuel Johnson was not, as Byrd notes, "the indispensable metaphor of folly, error, or malice that it was for Pope and his contemporaries."[67] It was a dreadful possibility. Johnson lived in fear of its threatening presence, a fear that also influenced the writings of anxious individuals like William Cowper, Christopher Smart, William

Collins, Samuel Taylor Coleridge, John Clare, Arthur Symons, and Tennyson, who could not help but represent madness as something at once metaphoric and real. They are, however, in the minority, for most writers think of madness in conventional terms only. Convention, not experience, shapes their images. Almost exclusively they rely on those images that have altered little since the ancient Greeks spoke either of the frenzied, god-possessed poets whose madness touches truth or of those whose strong passions make it impossible to bridle their horses. Of these two ancient images, that of the rider and horse dashing wildly into chaos has clung more stubbornly than the first (the *Idylls of the King*, for example, is one of many pieces to rely heavily on that image). The image remains because in people's minds madness has never quite separated itself from "unbridled passion." Consequently, both literary and scientific texts are brimming with lovers driven mad by excessive jealousy, with men and women driven insane by a lust for power or a religious fervor. Many are the unrequited, "crazed" lovers who crowd the medical texts as well as the traditional and modern love sonnets, who populate Burton's *Anatomy*, and who occasionally become the butt of comedy. Such lovers and mad tyrants inhabit the mad world of Jacobean drama;[68] they live on into the writing of Pope, Swift, and Johnson; they reappear in the gloomy recesses of late eighteenth- and early nineteenth-century poetry and roam the dark, delusive passages of Gothic fiction. Ann Radcliffe's *The Mysteries of Udolpho*, for example, revolves around the warning of Emily's dying father: to avoid horror and madness it is necessary to counterbalance the passions with reason. The father who himself is highly emotional fears his daughter will become "distempered," live in the distorted world of her imagination, and fall into "all the misery of superstition," all of which are "like one of those frightful fictions in which the wild genius of the poets sometimes delighted."[69] Throughout the novel, Emily in her constant battle to bridle her passions not only becomes the heir of the Jacobean drama's tragic and comic victims but also the child of the eighteenth century's overwhelming fear of the fancy or the imagination.

Such ruling passions later help consume and, paradoxically, enliven Byron's Childe Harold, who burns with feverish fires and wild ambitions, and they help tyrannize and madden many who roam through the novels of Scott, Trollope, Dickens, and Meredith. These passions help Scott advance his plots; allow Trollope to depict those who "cannot resolve the various demands of their passionate natures"; offer Dickens a means of illustrating the lunacy of society; and permit Meredith to explore the dangerous consequences of excessive passion.[70] Little wonder that the youthful Tennyson prefaced his poem on the passions with lines from *The Mysteries of Udolpho*! Emily's father's warning was still very much alive.

Not all conventional literary images of madness rely on mad lovers, ambitious tyrants, and foolish enthusiasts. They also draw on stock figures like Tom O'Bedlam, Crazy Kate, mad mothers, and wild hags.[71] Then there are the fools and knaves who suffer from the *idée fixe*, and there are the Romantic "untamed rebels" whose madness makes them simultaneously appealing and threatening. All these stock figures come bearing images mirroring their disorder: ripped and bizarre clothing, disheveled hair, poverty, bestiality, impotency, filth, and, of course, blindness. Like other mad figures, they too are consumed by feverish fires; they too are pursued by reminders of their living death. Such is the state of the mad and the foolish in *King Lear* and of the mad in *The Changeling* who "imitate the beasts and birds, / Singing or howling, braying, barking—all / As their wild fancies prompt 'em."[72] Similar are the madmen in *Melmoth the Wanderer* who shriek and live in impotent agony. They too are squalid, listless, and disgusting. Theirs is the condition that later causes Jane Eyre to wonder whether the growling Bertha Mason is "beast or human being."

All these conventional images are a vivid reminder of how persistent certain attitudes toward madness are, particularly those proclaiming its bestiality. Most of these attitudes cling so vigorously that a reader can hardly turn to a literary description of madness, irrespective of when it was composed, without discovering similar phrases. For instance, the above examples of the growling Bertha Mason and the barking mad in *The Changeling* are barely distinguishable from one another. Both mirror tenacious patterns of imagery which nearly defy history. Madness always seems to be clothed in clichés or to be locked into conventional patterns. However, despite this tendency, literary madness is not without its variety. There have been shifts in people's attitudes which have influenced the image patterns, have altered the emphasis, and have, in fact, lent historical perspective. In the medieval period, for example, most of the literature emphasizes how insanity is a divine punishment, even a test of a person's faith in God.[73] In the literature of the Renaissance, madness, although still carrying memories of divine punishment, loses many of its religious overtones and becomes more closely associated with the secular Ship of Fools metaphor. Insanity is a means of condemning social, political, and moral ills and of exposing the flaws that necessarily accompany excessive passion. In a sense, the literature of the period is like the metaphoric ship, for within its bowels it carries one fool or madman after another. Not all images of madness are terrifying, however. People in the Renaissance possessed the extraordinary ability to laugh at madness, to let it entertain. One reason is the belief that madness often does not last forever. It is curable or it is a mere disguise worn temporarily until a problem is resolved. M. C. Bradbrook is among several critics who notice this phenomenon and remark on how frequently madness becomes a jest. The drama often features the "comic madman" for whom sanity is always in sight.[74]

A hundred years later, though, such jests and comic madmen are missing, for the sense of an available sane world disappears. Madness in the Augustan Age is neither temporary nor entertaining; rather, it is a phenomenon to be feared. No divine inspiration attends madness. There are few fools to entertain; they are present to warn readers that the fancy lurks waiting to tyrannize anyone who gives in to its charms. Bedlam becomes a metaphor of the world. Toward the end of the eighteenth century, however, such a terrifying sense of madness begins to be qualified. A more charitable mood and, indeed, a growing willingness to experience the darker side of human experience emerge. Also, madness now begins to leave the public or social realm and enter the privacy of people's minds. Instead of satirizing the lawmakers as Swift does in "The Legion Club," writers pay more attention to the inner turmoil of those possessed by an obsessive love. This obsession neither touches nor threatens society. Instead of members of Parliament dabbling in their dung, there are the dreamlike figures, the recluses, in a poem like Thomas Warton's "The Pleasures of Melancholy," who surround themselves in provocative, gloomy landscapes to be "where thoughtful Melancholy loves to muse" and to be where their imagination or fancy may be released.

By the beginning of the Romantic period there is a significant shift in people's attitudes toward madness. Poets are more sympathetic toward those who suffer from madness. William Wordsworth in his "Mad Mother," for instance, does not dwell on the woman's bestiality but does dwell on her strong maternal affection for the child she carries in her arms. Wordsworth's sympathetic fascination with this mad mother, and of course with the idiot boy, the leech gatherer, and Peter Bell, is not an isolated incident. It is part of the growing fascination with the more extraordinary emotions and ways of life.[75] Although there is still an interest in and, indeed, a conscious effort to exercise the rational side of the mind, to think as Childe Harold says, "less wildly," there is simultaneously a magnificent effort to liberate and engage the less conscious levels of the mind, to face the irrational. The results of this effort vary. There are the Gothic novelists who, at the same time they warn their readers of the maddening consequences of excessive passion, ask them to wallow quite pleasurably in the melancholic setting and in the fancies of their fiction. Of all the Gothic writers perhaps Charles Maturin best portrays this fascination with violent emotion and this taste for perverse behavior. In *Melmoth the Wanderer* he uses madness as one means of journeying into the irrational. He takes his readers into, and traps his characters in, a madhouse to let them hear the cracks of the keeper's whip and the ravings of the inmates. This visit is not intended to expose the folly of the inmates as much as it is intended to let Maturin, the readers, and the characters wallow in the terrible, yet wonderfully exotic, agony of madness. Percy Bysshe Shelley's *The Cenci* makes similar demands. When the raped Beatrice "staggers wildly" across the stage, she becomes an instrument through which Shelley and the reader search for what Shelley spoke of as "the impenetrable mysteries of our being." This search, though, is not without its terrors. As Shelley admits, it also "terrifies its possessor at the darkness of the abyss to the brink of which it has conducted him."[76] As with Maturin, despite such terror, there is always a certain pleasure and growth; there is a sense of being on the verge of something new. Byron's Childe Harold and his Manfred are two more examples of those who glimpse the strange and unexplored regions of the suffering, irrational mind. They too are part of the growing willingness to meet the internal monsters that the Augustans were trying hard either to deny or to conquer. Samuel Taylor Coleridge and John Keats, with their interest in dreams, participate in this mood. For them too, meeting the internal monsters brought terror. Coleridge risked facing the "viper thoughts" that "coil around the mind," and Keats worried that his dreams might be considered those of a madman. However, for them there were rewards. It was worth taking the risk, for more is to be gained than to be lost in dreaming or in engaging the darker passages of the mind.

What is to be gained is similar to what the ancient Greeks suggested the frenzied poets gained: a personal relationship with the higher powers, a reaching out to a reality that lies beyond the restricting vision of everyday life. Many Romantics insisted on the ancient belief that poets, like geniuses, are "mad" and therefore privileged, for they possess powers that break through the enclosures of the "saner" mind. Madness and genius become close allies. Poets often celebrate their genius and their instability. Byron is one. In a letter to Thomas Moore (28 January 1817) he describes, with a touch of hyperbole, how he felt during the composition of *Childe Harold*: "I am glad you like it; it is a fine indistinct piece of poetical desolation, and my favorite. I was half mad during the time of its composition, between metaphysics, mountains, lakes, love unextinguishable, thoughts unutterable, and the nightmare of my own delinquencies."[77] Not only does Byron celebrate his madness, but so does his protagonist who admires Rousseau for making madness beautiful. Keats shares this sensibility. He also feels the desirability of experiencing "the wakeful anguish of the soul," of feeding "deep, deep upon" melancholy's "peerless eyes." Later in the century, Arthur Rimbaud shows his sympathy for this position when in a letter to Paul Demeny (15 May 1871) he claims that to be a visionary poet, he must work through a long, boundless, and systematized "dérèglement de tous les sens," through all forms of love, suffering, and madness.[78]

It is, however, Charles Baudelaire who intensifies Keats's recognition that melancholy "dwells with Beauty" and with "Joy." For him, "La mélancolie est toujours inséparable du sentiment du beau." In the spirit of this conviction, Baudelaire takes a perverse delight in madness and a lyrical pleasure in despair. Baudelaire's sensibility is anticipated by Goethe's *The Sorrows of Young Werther* and in the "Werther epidemic" that spread throughout Europe following the novel's publication. Many are the "beautiful suicides."[79]

Even though Tennyson admired *Les Fleurs du Mal* he was, as might be expected, horrified by it.[80] The Victorian laureate, like many of his contemporaries, could no longer feel comfortable with madness as an inspiriting power and could barely imagine a "beautiful suicide." (Matthew Arnold's *Empedocles on Etna* is perhaps an exception to this feeling. Empedocles' suicide is "beautiful" in that the act of throwing himself off the precipice is the one way in which he will become inspirited and whole. The suicide is, however, full of despair, for it is accompanied by an even stronger desire to find happiness and wholeness in life.) Arnold's and the other Victorians' attitudes toward madness almost retreat to the fearful one held by the Augustans. There are differences though. As is clear from the earlier discussion of scientific attitudes toward madness in the nineteenth century, the Victorians' sympathy for those who suffer from madness and the Victorians' understanding of the disease increases; like their mad doctors, they place more emphasis on the individual's responsibility to govern himself, to exert his will. Increasingly, literary madness becomes a metaphor for moral inadequacy—a view that complements the belief in "moral insanity." As was also true for the scientists, the Victorian writers simultaneously held society and inheritance responsible for any sort of aberrational behavior. No longer did mad men make a mad world. Now a mad world replete with mammonism, religious, scientific, and social upheaval unbalanced people.

The Victorians had their point of view, but they also held on to their literary inheritance. Hence, their literary images of madness share characteristics belonging to their predecessors. As before, madness is at once a dehumanizing and personal experience; it is a disguiser and a revealer, a source of tragedy and comedy, a phenomenon that paradoxically buries and releases the self, that hides and unveils the spiritual dimensions of life, and finally it is a representation of the limits and the freedom of existence. When Tennyson came to use madness in his poetry he was aware of this complex and historical imagery; consequently, it is impossible to read his poems without recalling his knowledge of scientific and literary images of madness. Both images offered him ways of transposing his private experiences with instability into a more public form.

## Chapter Two

# Brothers and Sisters
# in Misery

lfred Tennyson and his brothers and sisters were born into a
century keenly conscious of its mad humanity. They not only
inherited a world conscious of its "nerves" but also a family
excessively aware of its members' morbidity. "Black bloodedness" was a phrase none of the Tennysons took lightly.

The poet's unfortunate family history has only recently come to the
foreground. Before Sir Charles Tennyson's biography of his grandfather,
*Alfred Tennyson* (1949), most readers were not aware of the Tennysons'
black bloodedness. A few had caught glimpses of the instability hovering
about the Tennysons, but even those few had not realized the extent to
which this instability had touched so many members of the family and
had periodically absorbed their lives. Now, with the help of additional
biographical studies, notably Sir Charles Tennyson and Hope Dyson's
*The Tennysons: Background to Genius* (1974) and most recently Robert
Martin's *Tennyson: The Unquiet Heart* (1980), many more readers are informed. And, now that the facts so long hidden from the public's eye are
published, no biographical account can avoid the matter; few introduc-
tions to editions of Tennyson's work can close without alluding, at least
to some degree, to the family's entanglement with epilepsy, melancholia,
monomania, mania, hypochondria, hysteria, alcoholism, and drugs, and
to its members' trials in public and private asylums.

At the center of these accounts is the poet's nervous and moody father,
Dr. George Clayton Tennyson. Dr. Tennyson's troubles began at an early
age when his father, George Tennyson, disinherited him in favor of a
younger brother, Charles.[1] The specific reasons for his father's distrust
are not documented, but the unhappy effects are. The disinheritance forced
Dr. Tennyson to enter the church, a profession he would have rather
avoided. The subsequent financial instability preyed on his mind and
sharpened his anxiety, especially later when he was responsible for his
wife, Elizabeth, and their eleven children. Understandably, the disinher-

itance provoked an inveterate resentment. By the 1820s, when all eleven children were living at home in the Somersby Rectory, the effects of early misfortune combined with his increasingly nervous temperament to produce alarming results. Determined to give his children his best, Dr. Tennyson tutored them meticulously but at the expense of his mental health. Although he felt the "satisfaction in thinking that my boys will turn out to be clever men . . . in consequence of the exertions I have bestowed upon them,"[2] the satisfaction was not enough to counteract his emotional difficulties. These exertions proved to be too much, for they coupled with his already taut nerves to give birth to demons. His drinking became excessive. Immoderate doses of laudanum exaggerated his anxiety; "epileptic" seizures plagued and frightened him.[3] Anxiously, Dr. Tennyson watched his powers of control slipping away.[4] Hoping that a change of scene would restore his equilibrium, doctors prescribed various cures and sent him on European tours, but neither the cures nor the tours offered permanent relief.[5] Violent quarrels, one involving a knife and a loaded gun, paired with long, lethargic days of morbid introspection increased his depression and threw a shroud over the rectory, which, in former years, had enjoyed brighter moments.[6]

Dr. Tennyson's erratic, manic-depressive behavior deeply disturbed his wife. She threatened to leave Somersby, for, as Sir Charles Tennyson, Hope Dyson, and Robert Martin point out, Elizabeth "felt it unsafe either for herself or her children to remain any longer in the house."[7] Indeed the children also had emotional difficulties, especially Alfred. Throughout the 1820s, until the last month of his father's life, Alfred helped to look after his father and to guide the family. The poet never lost his respect and love for his father. His letters to relatives speak not only of his concern for his mother, and his brothers and sisters, but also of his overwhelming concern for "my poor father." After nursing Dr. Tennyson through a particularly dangerous series of seizures in 1825, he wrote, "No one but those who are continually with him can conceive what he suffers."[8] The pain of watching Dr. Tennyson's physical and mental health deteriorate took its toll. Alfred's sensitivity to his father's suffering was so acute, in fact, that he imagined himself going blind. According to those who remember, at times he threw himself on a grave in a nearby churchyard, "praying to be beneath the sod himself."[9] Poems written during these months mirror Tennyson's compassion for his father. For instance, the melancholic tone and image of the opening lines of an 1830s lyric seem to capture the son's despairing compassion for his sick father. In these lines, even though Alfred is writing about the sad spirit of autumn, the image of his own father's sad spirit is not far away.

A spirit haunts the year's last hours
Dwelling amid these yellowing bowers:
　　To himself he talks;
For at eventide, listening earnestly,
At his work you may hear him sob and sigh
　　In the walks.[10]

Other juvenilia capture his sensitivity toward his father's sense of injustice at being an exile. "The Exile's Harp," "Written by an Exile of Bassorah," and "The Outcast" are examples. At times these poems seem to rage for his father and to snarl at those who barred Dr. Tennyson from his inheritance of "the Hall."[11]

One of the most upsetting consequences of his father's sickness was the nagging fear that the unstable Dr. Tennyson was consciously drinking himself to death. A short piece, "The Grave of a Suicide," composed three years before Dr. Tennyson's death is not merely an abstract expression of melancholic verse. In the following two stanzas from the lyric, Alfred's anxiety concerning his father's growing despondency and "suicidal" tendencies contributes to the emotional force of the lines and accompanies the conventions learned from his reading of the pre-Romantic and Romantic poets.[12]

Poor soul! the dawning of thy life was dim;
　　Frowned the dark clouds upon thy natal day;
Soon rose thy cup of sorrow to the brim,
　　And hope itself but shed a doubtful ray.

That hope had fled, and all within was gloom;
　　That hope had fled—thy woe to phrenzy grew;
For thou, wed to misery from the womb—
　　Scarce one bright scene thy night or darkness knew!
　　　　　　　　　　　　　　　　[ll. 5–12]

The woe did indeed grow to frenzy, and Dr. Tennyson died on 16 March 1831. One week later, Alfred's older brother Charles wrote to a friend announcing the death. The letter describes the "phrenzy" of the father's last months: "He suffered little and after death his countenance which was strikingly lofty and peaceful, was I trust, an image of the condition of his soul, which on earth was daily racked by bitter fancies and tossed about by strong troubles."[13] Even though the death was natural, its suicidal implications hovered. As Christopher Ricks suggests, years afterward Alfred was still haunted by the thought. Over twenty years later, the specter of this "suicidal" threat helped him to create the fiction of *Maud*, his study of madness. Although by no means a literal representation of his father, the opening stanzas from part one are fraught with the potent memories and disturbing questions accompanying his father's final years.

### III

> Did he fling himself down? who knows? for a vast
>     speculation had failed,
> And ever he muttered and maddened, and ever
>     wanned with despair,
> And out he walked when the wind like a broken
>     wordling wailed,
> And the flying gold of the ruined woodlands drove
>     through the air.

### IV

> I remember the time, for the roots of my hair were
>     stirred
> By a shuffled step, by a dead weight trailed, by a
>     whispered fright,
> And my pulses closed their gates with a shock on my
>     heart as I heard
> The shrill-edged shriek of a mother divide
>     the shuddering night.                    [ll. 9–16]

Allusions to this ambiguous death continue to be heard in "The Voyage of Maeldune," a poem written when the poet was sixty years old.[14]

Alfred was, of course, not the only child to be touched by his father's difficulties.[15] By 1834, when he was twenty-five years old, the effects of the previous decade on his brothers and sisters were causing them all grave concern. His sister Emily, who was also upset by the death of her fiancé, Arthur Henry Hallam, suffered from headaches and hysterical pains in her side. She wrote, "My life is so wretched, that sooner than pass another year as the last, I would be content to follow my poor Father to the grave."[16] A younger brother Edward was irreversibly insane and had been sent to an asylum. A few years earlier, his mother had written, "He weeps bitterly sometimes, and says his mind is so unnotched he is scarcely able to endure his existence."[17] Septimus was suffering from nervousness and was growing disturbingly like his insane brother, so much so that the family was seeking assistance through private asylums. In January 1835 Alfred was feeling desperate about his brother's condition and wrote to their Uncle Charles that Septimus was "subject to fits of the most gloomy despondency accompanied with tears—or rather he spends whole days in that manner, complaining that he is neglected by all his relations, and blindly resigning himself to every morbid influence."[18] Arthur was rapidly becoming an alcoholic and was about to be sent away to the Crichton Institute for cures; Charles was "almost killing himself with laudanum," and the oldest brother, Frederick, was acting in a most eccentric manner. He had been sent down from Trinity College, Cambridge, after displaying a behavior described as being appropriate to an inhabitant of Swift's mad Laputa.[19] Another brother, Horatio, was less affected but was displaying signs of otherworldliness as was his sister Mary, who was wrapping herself up in a spiritual world. Cecilia was melancholic, and last, but hardly least, Matilda was acting in a peculiar way, a result, the family said, of her having been dropped on her head when she was a baby.[20] Years later, with few exceptions, their problems were to continue. Edward remained in an asylum until his death in 1890; Frederick, Charles, and Septimus continued to suffer from their nerves; Horatio remained in a mystical world; and three of the sisters, Mary, Cecilia, and Matilda, remained nervous and hypochondriacal—as Sir Charles Tennyson suggests, decidedly eccentric and manic-depressive.[21]

These brothers and sisters of Somersby were not only reacting to their father's problems. They were also reacting to the Tennyson family tradition that prompted one member to utter the sentiment, "You may be sure we cannot be happy."[22] By no means had their morbidness either begun or ended with Dr. Tennyson. Rather, he was at the center of it, caught between the instability that had touched his ancestors and the irrationality that surrounded him. According to Sir Charles Tennyson, many of Dr. Tennyson's antecedents were on the "verge of insanity." Dr. Tennyson's own father was a volatile and fretful hypochondriac who had the power to make life for those around him, in George Tennyson's own words, "if not miserable, quiet and grave."[23] Dr. Tennyson's brother and sisters were also susceptible to the black bloodedness. His brother Charles was "a great invalid and sufferer," who in 1809 broke down from "overwork and worry"; his sisters were hypochondriacs. Elizabeth, later Elizabeth Russell, was especially well known for her "nervous excitability," and Mary for her "morose and moody nature."[24] Moroseness was indeed part of the family tradition, even before the siblings of Somersby were born.

As time passed, the tradition continued. Morbidity was expected and, perhaps, subconsciously encouraged. Letters, sketches, and numerous medical texts belonging to the family libraries reveal just how frequently and how vociferously the Tennysons, for generations, defined themselves in terms of their morbidness and mental instability, a definition necessarily encouraged by the century's increasingly strong emphasis on inherited madness.[25] Tennyson's aunt, Elizabeth Russell, the hypochondriac, most clearly illustrates the family's sense of its shared hereditary curse. In a letter written to her brother Charles she shared her concern about their brother, Dr. Tennyson, who was displaying signs of mental derangement. Her words capture the family's traditional fears: "I fear our poor dear brother is a pitiable sufferer. . . . It is painful indeed to take a view either a home or perspective one of all the branches as well as the stems of our family" (28 July 1823).[26] Ten years later Alfred echoed this aunt's fears and joined in the family's practice of identifying itself as melancholic. When congratulating his aunt on the birth of a son, he wrote, "I hope for his own peace of mind that he will have as little of the Tennyson about him as possible" (10 March 1833).[27] His sensitivity to the curse surfaced again when he carefully, if not morbidly, watched his children, Hallam and Lionel, for any sign of its threatening presence. As Ricks points out, when the poet's son Hallam nearly died while away at school, his fear about the curse came to the foreground. The poet wrote, "God will take him pure and good, straight from his mother's lessons. Surely it would be better for him than to grow up such a one as I am."[28] Later these anxieties echoed in a poem for his grandson: "Laugh, for the name at the head of my verse is thine / Mayst thou never be wronged by the name that is mine!" ("To Alfred Tennyson My Grandson"). Alfred's wife, Emily, shared the Tennysons' fears. Like a hawk, she watched over the children, searching for signs of the inherited Tennysonian morbidness. Her letters to her sons and to a few friends occasionally contain references to her children's "over-sensitive nerves that may have descended to them." When Lionel went away to school, for example, she wrote to him, begging him not to overstrain himself: "as I have so often said to thee, beloved, that this overexercise exhausts the brain. So be warned in time." A few months later she confided to Edward Lear, "What is to be done with Lionel I do not know. He still stammers when overdone."[29] The Victorians viewed stammering as a sign of growing mental instability.

Alfred's sisters and brothers were also quite capable of thinking of themselves and each other in such morbid terms. Arthur and Horatio's Somersby sketchbook, for example, offers quite a striking instance of this capability. Among its many jottings, there is one particular sketch that Sir Charles Tennyson has reproduced in "The Somersby Tennysons." The sketch shows Alfred and Charles sitting down, heads bowed, looking very gloomy indeed.[30] Either Arthur or Horatio appropriately entitled the drawing "Brothers in Misery"—a title that would not have existed if their peculiar consciousness had not. Letters exchanged later in their lives show that this morbid consciousness did not die. None outgrew the tendency. Neither leaving the Somersby Rectory nor "growing up" released any of them from their "madness." For instance, in 1841,

Arthur wrote to Frederick: "God only knows one morning while in a state of all but maddening distress I cried—for a plain tale is soon told & without ornament—O God I am going mad, hear me, when the same soft kind firm voices spoke to me & said 'Be still & know that I am God' & then the high fever of anxiety & suffering fell instantly." Fifty years later, Arthur was again writing to Frederick: "What with my blinding eye & old age together I am my dear Frederick very much depressed at times I can only hope this distress may not be so considerably felt by you." Continuing the tradition of hypochondria and echoing Alfred's earlier fears of growing blindness, Horatio wrote to Frederick in July 1889: "What was the nature of your illness—indigestion? This I know will often affect the sight & with nervous temperament such as all of us have more or less, this dimness of sight may have seemed like a more chronic affair & likely to pass into blindness, whereas it may have been only the passing result of indigestion." Even as late as 1881, their sister Emily was still haunted by the specter of the family madness. In a letter to Frederick written after the death of Arthur's wife, she wondered, "What will become of poor Arthur now that Harriet is gone, she was his guiding star—surely he will be able to resist his old temptation, drink. If not, he will either soon die—a stroke of the palsy or go mad."[31]

Friends also occasionally recorded the Tennysons' willingness to identify themselves as mad or morose. There is, of course, the famous story that Dante Gabriel Rossetti told of Septimus announcing that he was "the most morbid of the Tennysons."[32] Another, quieter, yet just as striking, example comes from William Allingham's diary. Allingham was a frequent visitor to the poet's home at Farringford and during one of his visits Allingham recorded, with a smile, the reaction of Alfred's sister Matilda to the spectacle of her grown brother bounding about the grounds of his estate: "Wednesday June 13 1866. T. in the lawn and meadow running about bareheaded (for exercise). 'like a madman,' his sister says."[33] The phrase, "like a madman," might be uttered in jest, "Brothers in Misery" might be written rather wryly; "the most morbid of the Tennysons" might be thrown with bravado, but, as Ricks admits in reacting to the Rossetti story, the family's experiences with madness were anything but comic. In the end, looking at the family history, it is difficult to determine who really was the most morbid. Great-grandfathers, grandfathers, great-aunts, aunts, nephews, nieces, fathers, brothers, sisters, and sons were all vulnerable either to its reality or to its suggestion.

Many readers have the mistaken impression that Alfred's experiences with instability were confined to his family circle or to the Somersby Rectory.[34] That belief is limited and misleading. After Alfred left Somersby, marriage and friendship increased the circle's circumference. In

1836, his brother Charles, the brother closest in age and temperament, married Louisa Sellwood, the sister of Alfred's future wife. After their marriage, Louisa devoted herself to alleviating her husband's addiction to opium, initially prescribed by his doctor to relieve depression. But she did so at the expense of her own mental health. Only three years later, suffering a mental breakdown and feeling guilty for her husband's continued addiction, Louisa had to be placed under medical care away from home. The two did not resume a life together for nine years. As their life continued together, so eventually did their problems. Letters written by Charles and Louisa in the 1860s and 1870s are pathetic and give a vivid sense of what they must have suffered during their earlier years. In October 1878, for example, Louisa wrote a letter that graphically mirrors her instability and her sense of being responsible for Charles's difficulties.

> I am not strong enough; but from the depth of my iniquity; the corruption of a long life of wooing to the flesh which I was struggling or seeming to struggle to recover the fatal steps taken—Latterly I have become so much worse that I have no trace of what a Christian ought to have or to be. . . . This year it has been abominable beyond words. . . . I did not tell him [Charles] how worse I had become whilst I had been there my horrible ways there shocked his nerves so that his old pain returned & he grew worse—for his life's sake I was obliged to ask the doctor to remove me once more from him as by a doctor's orders I had been removed before.[35]

During that same month, Louisa received a comforting letter from her sister Emily, who by now was Alfred's wife. Notice that Emily relies on the concept of the "overworked brain" that she had used in her cautionary letter to Lionel: "October 27 1878: Doubtless, my sweetie, thou wilt accuse thyself of many things in the course of the fierce trial to him [Charles] and to thee but, all the more glory to God for the result, even if thy self-accusation were not mostly due to an overworked brain, overworked in doing what seemed to thee right.[36]

Emily was sensitive to her sister's troubles, for not only was she anxious about her sister and not only had she had reason to be anxious about Lionel's "overworked brain," but she also had reason to be most concerned about her own mental stability. Emily too was suffering—quietly. Before her marriage to Alfred in 1850, during their lengthy engagement (1838–1850), she had already experienced emotional difficulties. As the editor of her letters and her journal, James Hoge, rightly speculates, the tensions and frustrations accompanying this engagement affected her physically and mentally.[37] Later in her life Emily was to recall that "during my ten years' separation from him [Alfred] the doctors believed that I was going into consumption."[38] This physical reaction to mental anxiety was periodically to reemerge and was to keep the specter of mental illness very much on Alfred's doorstep. "Chronic spinal trouble," an elusive illness associated during her lifetime with hysteria and known to us through people like her friend Elizabeth Barrett Browning and her acquaintance Florence Nightingale, encouraged Emily to seek relief through homeopathic medicine and mesmerism. Her troubles also encouraged Alfred, shortly after their marriage, to learn how to mesmerize his wife to sleep. Throughout their life together he found its effect on Emily "really wonderful."[39]

Emily knew her problems were emotional as well as physical. She was aware that when her feelings were positive, she could get up and run with her children, and that when feeling depressed, she could not get herself to move. She once wrote to a friend, "You were very right, I was quite worn out body and mind."[40] She also recognized that she had affinities with the Tennyson family's black bloodedness. In a moment of candor, she wrote, "Between Ally and myself the sympathy is too intimate almost for us to help each other sometimes and we must rather be helped or hindered together" (15 September 1857). Emily's letters to Edward Lear, himself a manic-depressive and chronic sufferer, reveal just how aware she was of the depression hanging threateningly over her. When Lear wrote complaining of the "gloom and cloud" settling on him and of his despair resulting from severe asthmatic and epileptic attacks, Emily replied alluding to her own discomfort. On 7 December 1863, she wrote, "but then the days go and go and go and so at last one catches one on the wing of despair—may be the very worst." Earlier, on 7 April 1855, she had told him not to feel alone in his despair. That morbidness never entirely disappeared, even though she had tremendous inner strength and seemed to many to be emotionally strong and able to offer Alfred the support he needed. Suffering from overwork, in 1868 she confided, "my brain is too heavy."[41] In September 1874 she stopped her voluminous correspondence altogether, until 1877 when she resumed the responsibility of reading the hundreds of letters that came to the house and writing responses to them. During her three-year absence, she had kept to her invalid chair. Again between 1880 and 1882 all correspondence ceased and, once more, she remained confined to her sofa.[42]

Alfred must have also known that his wife's fatigue and chronic spinal trouble were hysterical. He was too aware of the symptoms not to know. The doctor he was consulting around the time of Emily's first breakdown was Sir James Paget, who, coincidentally, had published a series of lectures in *The Lancet* about the very same phenomenon. In the first lecture, published 11 October 1873, Paget declared, "One of the most frequent conditions in those whom the nervous mimicries occur is a singular readiness to be painfully fatigued by slight exertion. This is most marked in those with Spinal neuromimesis." He continues by explaining exactly what this "Spinal neuromimesis" or chronic spinal trouble is: "In these cases the patient complains of pain and tenderness of the back, to which one or more of the following symptoms may be superadded tending very much (to) mislead the medical or surgical attendant: —Pains in the limbs, especially in the lower limbs; a sense of constriction of the chest; involuntary spasms of the muscles; . . . a sense of weakness in the lower limbs, so that they are scarcely capable of supporting the weight of the body; and even actual paralysis." In the second lecture, Paget spoke of the overworked brain. In this lecture, as in the first, Paget unwittingly came very close to describing Emily's condition: "The brain is often wearied and rendered powerless by overwork; and the physician meets, daily, with cases in which 'there is no disease,' as the phrase so glibly runs, but in which there is, very obviously, the greatest distress. Inaptitude for work or rest, depression of spirits, with irritability of temper; a sense of weariness and hopelessness; frequent disturbance of general health; the digestion fails, the secretions are disturbed, and the man 'breaks down,' he is 'tired,' and what he wants is a 'rest.'"[43]

The fact that Alfred married the sensitive and vulnerable Emily and not Rosa Baring, who, as Ralph Wilson Rader says, was "not at all inclined to introspection or reflection—who took life pretty much as it came" is significant.[44] Throughout his life Alfred seemed to gravitate toward those who tended to be more introspective and to display signs of sharing the Tennysons' morbidity. From the very beginning, while living at Somersby, for example, Alfred had been drawn to his Aunt Elizabeth Russell and her hypochondria and nervousness. The two had carried on quite a correspondence about their respective ills and misfortunes. A portion of a letter written 10 March 1833 is typical and illustrates just how easily his aunt's morbidity and the subject of illness drew him toward her: "Is the 'fixed pain at the crown of the head' an entirely new symptom! I would beg of you not to distress your mind & consequently affect your health, by ruminating on the conduct of those who may be almost termed callous to all the kindlier sympathies, however they may cloak their deficiencies with the vesture of form." In that same letter, Alfred also spoke of his sister's illness. As the words suggest, his sister Emily and her continuing problems held a special place in her brother's mind: "Emily, whom you enquire after is here; she is not yet cured of the liver complaints, which sent her to Cheltenham—most probably it will cling to her all her life—at least have never heard of any one, who was cured by a serious derangement in that organ."[45]

Not only was he drawn toward his sister because she possessed a peculiarly sensitive and suffering nature, but because she was a living link between him and his closest friend, Arthur Henry Hallam, who had quite suddenly died away from home in Vienna on 15 September 1833. For that matter Hallam is another vivid example of Alfred's strong affinity for those who partook in his black bloodedness. Hallam was indeed a friend who shared with Alfred "the best and the worst," for like the Tennysons, Hallam was also subject to what his father termed "fits of mental depression."[46] As those who have studied the life and writings of Hallam have realized, this intimate friend had a most melancholic side to his otherwise "sanguine and hopeful" and rather rash nature. The "Blue Devils," periods of depression, plagued Hallam and frequently made life miserable. His juvenilia brim with depression. Moreover, letters written after going down from Cambridge show that his melancholic impulses continued. In 1831 and 1832 while Hallam was unhappily pursuing his law studies in London, lines from his correspondence offer graphic glimpses of these devils. Feeling miserable in April 1832, Hallam wrote to his Cambridge friend William Henry Brookfield, "I am groaning grievously under the burthen of London. I cannot get well, and the Blue Devils (not cholera), gripe hard." About three months later, he again wrote to Brookfield, explaining that his depression was not entirely a manifestation of his chronically high blood pressure: "When your first letter reached me, months ago, I was very unwell, and very wretched—not merely hypped, as usual, but suffering the pressure of severe anxiety which although past, has left me much worn in spirit. . . . I have been very miserable since I saw you: my hopes grow fainter and fewer, yet I hope on, and will, until the last ray is gone, and then—."[47] In December of that year, in a letter to Emily, Hallam recorded another despondent moment. In this letter he qualifies reports of his seeming gaiety by claiming his cheerfulness is purely superficial: "Poignant is the misery I often feel—or why say I, 'often'? It is *always* at my heart, smothered sometimes by force, yet there still, & withering all that otherwise might be pleasant—."[48]

Initially, part of Hallam's attraction to Alfred's sister was to her sorrowful and suffering nature. Like his friend, he too was drawn to morbid individuals. Hallam was conscious of this attraction. In an 1831 letter to Emily, he explains that it is not because of her carefree nature that he finds her attractive: "Is it to your gaiety, think you . . . and your festive smiles, and your playful humour that I have pledged my whole being?

Oh no—these are not my Emily; very dear are they to me, because they are parts of her; but there was something dearer yet, something more intimately herself; the musical sorrow, like the spirit of the nightingale's song; the dreamy desire of Beauty, only perfected through suffering."[49]

Likewise, Hallam's melancholic periods attracted Alfred to him. The poet was bound to feel an affinity with a person who could recognize in his own life as well as in others' the "darken'd mind" and the "impenetrable gloom"; who could read Cicero and recognize moments of "mental distress." How could Alfred not be drawn to Hallam, who in his 1831 prize essay on Cicero wrote:

> Others [Cicero's works] are the offspring of mental distress, and represent with painful fidelity that mood between contentment and despair, in which suffering appears so associated with existence that we would willingly give up one with the other, and look forward with a sort of hope to that silent void where, if there are no smiles, there are at least no tears, and since the heart cannot beat, it will not ever be broken. This is within the range of most men's feelings, and it were morose to blame Cicero for giving it expression.[50]

These lines from Hallam's essay reflect not only the author's despondency, but also the introspective side of many Cambridge undergraduates in the late 1820s and early 1830s when Hallam and Alfred were up at Trinity College. Without inviting a loss of perspective, it is intriguing to note how many of their friends and acquaintances were also caught between what Hallam recognized as this "mood between contentment and fear," who lived in a borderland of sanity and insanity. It is fascinating to note how many of them were either to remark at the time or to reflect on later their mental crises. Brookfield, Joseph William Blakesley, James Spedding, Richard Chenevix Trench, and R. J. Tennant were all, at times and in varying degrees, capable of speaking rather morbidly of themselves. Brookfield, Hallam's and Alfred's closest friend at Trinity, remembered this morbid tendency. He recalled that even Blakesley, whom Alfred singled out as a "clear-headed friend," had his despondent moments: "Yet over Blakesley, as over almost all brotherhood of sober enthusiasts, there hung a phantom cloud of melancholy, so that even his jesting was not spontaneous, but rather that of a 'kindlier, trustier Jaques.'"[51] Much of the brotherhood's melancholy was, of course, prompted by crises in their religious beliefs. They were part of what Walter E. Houghton has come to call "the age of anxiety."[52] Just before meeting Alfred in 1830, Trench, for example, had suffered through and survived several months of ill health and "low spirits"—a consequence of loss of faith.[53] The despair of Tennant, an intimate friend, was also prompted by grave religious doubts. Suffering from what Hallam euphemistically labeled "an unsettled frame of mind," Tennant wrote to Alfred about the "total despair" that was "always ready at hand to struggle and stifle" his spirit. He hoped that "by God's grace" he would "prevail." But, for Tennant, that grace did not always triumph. Once more he confided in Alfred:

> For darkness & weak doubts I strive to put my trust in the mercy of Almighty God, who promises peace & strength to all who seek it. . . . Often indeed the conviction of this fails me, when I try to fathom the depths of his counsels; he has through life afflicted me with the deepest sorrow and I am wholly unable to understand the merciful purpose of his afflictions, & when I trust on my understanding my faith fails,  & bitterness of unrelieved anguish expresses itself with such violence as cannot be conceived by those who have never felt as I have.[54]

Spedding was subject to similar doubts. Spedding's criticism of Alfred's "The Two Voices," a poem begun when they were undergraduates, reflects not only his own melancholic mood and doubts, but also comments on the familiarity of these experiences among his contemporaries. Reacting to the poem's despairing tone and its ambivalent posture of being caught between contentment and fear, Spedding observed that "the disease is familiar; but where are we to look for the remedy? Many persons would have thought it enough to administer a little religious consolation to the diseased mind; but unfortunately despondency is no more like ignorance than atrophy is like hunger; and as the most nutritious food will not nourish the latter, so the most comfortable doctrine will not refresh the former. Not the want of consoling topics, but the incapacity to receive consolation, constitutes the disease."[55]

With maturation, most found their peace. But one rather unpopular member of the Trinity brotherhood did not. Soon after he went down from Cambridge, Thomas Sunderland, immortalized in Alfred's "The Character," suffered from incurable delusions and acute mania. The person who had seemed to Alfred to be so "quiet, dispassionate, and cold" was vulnerable too. Apparently, even while at Cambridge, Sunderland had not always appeared as a stable figure. While at college another of the Trinity group, Richard Monckton Milnes, had reported home, "Sunderland has gone to the Isle of Man, to live there some time in perfect solitude, to expatriate himself as much as he can, he says, from human feelings, and 'be able to cut his father's throat, if necessary, in the good cause.' "[56] No wonder Alfred disliked Sunderland so much. His erratic behavior must have revived fearful memories and released fearful thoughts.

After the Cambridge years, peculiarly introspective people continued to surround Alfred and increase the circle of instability. During this period he became friends with Dr. Matthew Allen, the psychiatrist, and began visiting with more than ordinary inquisitiveness his private asylum near the Tennysons' new home at High Beech, Essex. Eventually, Septimus was put under the doctor's care.[57] Perhaps most dramatic of all are the several months the poet spent in hydropathic establishments in Prestbury, Birmingham, and Malvern—months that kept him in the constant company of nervous hypochondriacs, hysterics, alcoholics, and those with suicidal longings.[58] Between these water cures Alfred was staying with his nervous mother in London and was also keeping the company of Edward FitzGerald, Thomas Carlyle, and William Makepeace Thackeray—three valetudinarians.[59] FitzGerald had left Cambridge "a morbid hypochondriac" and was still displaying those tendencies. At times FitzGerald could become very morbid. To Alfred's oldest brother, Frederick, he wrote, "I don't think of drowning myself yet; and what I wrote you was a sort of safety escape for my poor flame. . . . It is only idle and well-to-do people who kill themselves; it is ennui that is hopeless."[60] FitzGerald, however, was not as melancholic as Carlyle, for Carlyle's despondency was chronic. As J. A. Froude, his contemporary biographer has noted, Carlyle's "mental juices were preying upon themselves" constantly. While FitzGerald was writing suicidal letters to Frederick, Carlyle was writing depressing entries in his journal: "May 3— Cold grey weather. All the world busy with their Industrial Exhibition. I am sick, very sad, and, as usual for a long time back, not able to get on with anything. My silence and isolation, my utter loneliness in this world, is lamed, bewildered, incapable of stirring from the spot in any good direction whatever."[61] That depression kept him a month in Malvern taking Dr. Gully's water cure—probably at Alfred's suggestion. The treatment, however, did not agree with him very well. A letter from FitzGerald alludes to its failure and, incidentally, allows another glimpse of the London friends' sensitivity to the instability surrounding him: "For the present here I am, at 19 Charlotte Street Fitzroy square, come up to have a fresh squabble with Lawyers, and to see an old College friend . . . who is gone mad, and threatens to drive his wife mad too, I think. . . . But I have seen Alfred once, Carlyle once, Thackeray twice; and Spedding many times. . . . Carlyle has been undergoing the Water System at Malvern, and says it has done him a very little good."[62]

Last, but not least, Thackeray was also experiencing problems. During the years Alfred was in London, Thackeray was preoccupied with his own wife's madness. Alfred was all too aware of the pain involved when Thackeray had to institutionalize his wife in 1842. Thackeray's suffering still haunted him years later. Once more Allingham's diary offers an in-

triguing insight into Alfred's character. The diary alludes to the fact that
three years after Thackeray's death, Alfred still talked about his friend's
troubles.[63] Notably, it was Thackeray's *Cornhill Magazine* that introduced Dr. James Hinton's ideas about suffering to the public. Hinton's
books, *Life in Nature* (1862) and *The Mystery of Pain: A Book for the Sorrowful* (1866), were to capture Alfred's close attention. He seems to have
been almost riveted to them, for the references to Alfred's avid interest
are multiple.[64] This interest is understandable, for whether Alfred was
aware or not, Hinton's life bore some painful resemblances to experiences in his own. As a young man, Hinton had suffered from severe
despondency. His doctors had advised: "The lad wants more mental oc-
cupation to keep his mind from feeding on itself." The advice was familiar. These earlier moments constantly threatened to return, and did.
In 1864 Hinton wrote to a colleague: "I have been dreadfully crushed
down and cramped and deadened lately, and I don't know how to raise
myself up."[65] In December 1875 the nervous tension was to become so
severe that he died of "acute inflammation of the brain"—a death that his
champions, Mr. and Mrs. Havelock Ellis, were to suggest was suicidal.[66]
Theirs was a judgment that would have resurrected painful memories of
Dr. Tennyson's end and of Arthur Henry Hallam, who died of similar
causes, of "a sudden determination of blood to the head."[67]

As Alfred's attraction to Hinton's works suggests, even after the London years came to an end in 1850 and he married, the poet still gravitated
to those who were despondent and self-consciously unhappy. No matter
how much less morbid he appeared after those years were over, minor
incidents, perhaps the most telling of all, reveal his captivation by morbid souls continued. One of his acquaintances in the years preceding his
marriage was Ludovic Colquhoun, a fellow patient at a hydropathic establishment near Birmingham. Once the experience was over, the two
determined to remain friends. Alfred wrote: "Our friendship com-
menced under hydropathic auspices. May it last when douches and sitz-
baths redden the spines and unhappy patients no more." The friendship
did last, and shortly after his marriage Alfred asked Emily to write to
the unhappy Colquhoun to visit when feeling despondent: "When we
have a house will you not come and let us try to cheer you a little and
nurse you into better health" (26 December 1850).[68] The Tennysons' desire to take in a suffering individual like Colquhoun is repeated throughout the rest of their lives.

Another minor incident illustrates their attraction. In June 1869 when
Alfred was away, his wife wrote with pride to him about their son Hallam, who had helped a boy with suicidal thoughts. She confidently pro-
posed inviting the boy to visit Farringford for two or three days so as

they could cheer him up.[69] This protective role was, of course, one that Alfred and Emily extended to their own families as well. Their home at Farringford and later at Aldworth became, in many ways, an asylum for suffering family members. For example, Alfred's sister Matilda, who had been dropped on her head as a baby, stayed with them almost constantly from 1865 until Tennyson's death in 1892. Occasionally her presence must have been exceedingly hard to take. Emily confided to her husband: "Tilly is, I am glad to say, better today so I hope she may be persuaded not to go to a London doctor; though, of course, if he will set her right more quickly she had better go being so nervous about herself as she is" (15 June 1870).[70] Even if family members did not come to them for help, they, in the form of letters, went out to them. For instance, during the particularly difficult times of her unstable sister's life, Emily wrote to Louisa daily offering what comfort she could. Friends were also given asylum or support. After Thackeray's death, for example, Alfred and Emily went to visit his daughters in London. When the daughters soon afterward came to live at Freshwater, the support continued. According to Sir Charles Tennyson, the daughters arrived late at night in bitter weather. "The fires were burning cheerfully and as they sat resting in the half light, they were suddenly aware of a tall figure standing at the window in heavy cloak and broad-brimmed hat. It was Alfred, who had walked down to give them in this way his silent sympathy. From that time until the poet's death there was no more frequent or welcome visitor at his home than Annie Thackeray."[71]

During his later years, not only did Alfred gravitate toward those who suffered, but also toward those who were involved with the suffering of others. His friendship with Dr. Allen is an early example. There were, however, other psychiatrists. The poet's long engagement with Dr. Robert James Mann was not only based on their shared interest in the microscope and the telescope, but was also rooted in Dr. Mann's profession as a psychologist. The two visited and carried on a considerable correspondence, especially following the publication of *Maud*. Dr. Mann was one of the poet's supporters when the public was unwilling to offer such support, and preferred to think of the poem, with the help of a critic, as "mud" or "mad."[72] In a letter to the doctor about *Maud*, Alfred refers to their mutual sensitivity to the nature of madness: "I seem to have the Doctors on my side if no one else, I have just received an article by a madhouse Doctor giving his testimony as to the truth to nature in the delineation of the hero's madness. Valuable testimony it seems to me" (9 October 1855). Other letters reveal that the two discussed "the delineation of the hero's madness" quite carefully.[73] The poet's willingness to receive Dr. Richard Maurice Bucke is another example of Alfred's fasci-

nation with psychiatrists. Undoubtedly it was the doctor's profession as
a psychiatrist as much as his letter of introduction from Walt Whitman
and his interest in parapsychology which prompted Alfred to grant this
American an interview on 9 August 1891.[74]

The fascination with madness was to remain just as the depressing
images of the poet's troubled father and the brothers and sisters "in misery" were to linger and haunt Alfred in later years. Neither his father's
death nor the move from the Somersby Rectory eradicated memories of
those images. The Tennysons were too immersed in their morbid identity to bury the past and too nervous to cease conforming to their black
bloodedness. Despondent moments in the lives of new family, friends,
and acquaintances kept the past in the present, and, in effect, allowed the
specter of madness to hover uncomfortably near. At times that specter
was most threatening to Alfred, for he felt its presence within him. That
presence was to make all the difference in his life and in his poetry.

## Chapter Three

# Tottering on the Edge
# of Madness

lfred Tennyson was not merely an observer of his friends' and his family's emotional difficulties, for rarely did he not feel anxious about his own instability. Believing he had inherited the Tennysons' morbid temperament and sensing his nervousness mirrored theirs, he thought himself as vulnerable as the most unstable of them. As Robert Martin points out, "There was no reason that Alfred could see why he might not inherit any or all the taints that seemed visited on his brother, and there was even the possibility that he had inherited the epilepsy that made his father's life such hell."[1] Tennyson often spoke of how his temperament "embittered his existence" and prevented him from knowing "what it was to feel well." At a particularly difficult time, he confided to Dr. Ker that he awoke from a night's sleep worrying "how am I to get through the day?"[2] Unfortunately that concern was all too typical. Throughout his life Tennyson was a hypochondriac. He never ceased to worry about his physical and mental health, even after he assumed the stable guise of England's laureate. Moreover, as Tennyson's question suggests, his hypochondria was complicated by moments of desperate depression. During those periods Tennyson lived in fear of going mad, of drawing too close to the edge and falling. That fear was always to be a haunting shadow that caused him to live life most cautiously.

Tennyson's emotional difficulties are visible in the 1820s when he lived under the rectory's manic-depressive atmosphere. There he was sensitive to his own moods, to the madness seething within himself, just as he was to his father's mania and to the troubles experienced by his brothers and sisters. He studied and watched himself closely and reacted to the surrounding emotional turmoil. For instance, two years before his father's death, Tennyson imagined himself going blind, and he despaired. He sought professional help—a pattern that he was to repeat. Thinking it a matter of "life and death," he traveled to London to consult Dr. Benjamin Brodie, one of the growing number of physicians sensitive to nervous diseases and disorders. Tennyson changed his diet and allowed himself to be cupped. However, like many treatments to come, neither eradicated his anxiety for long.[3] Shortly afterward, rumors flew around Cambridge that Tennyson would have to leave because of ill health.[4] The periodic depression continued and alarmed many, including Arthur Henry Hallam, who wrote to Frederick inquiring, "What can be done for him? Do you think he is really very ill *in body*? His mind certainly is in a distressing state."[5] The hysteria, mania, and melancholia at home were taking their toll.

Hallam's sudden death in September 1833, however, dealt one of the sharpest blows to Tennyson's tottering equilibrium. Initially Tennyson sought the seclusion of Somersby to work out and sometimes to feed on his bitterness and broken spirit. At times depression swamped him and he felt suicidal. The death, according to Sir Charles Tennyson, "struck at the very roots of his will to live."[6] Eventually, Tennyson regained his balance, but only to have it knocked about by other painful blows. The publication of his grandfather's will in 1835 caused Tennyson a terrible disappointment. The will offered him no hope of financial independence. Then, a few months later, he was once more subject to disappointment when Rosa Baring rejected him. Tennyson had apparently turned to her to try and fill the void left by Hallam's death.[7] Tennyson's despondency grew worse.

The years between 1836 and 1850 were undoubtedly the most traumatic for Tennyson. During that time he came as close as he ever did to realizing his worst fears. Continuing tensions emanated from his difficulties with Emily Sellwood. Not only did the Sellwoods disapprove of the engagement, but Tennyson himself doubted his ability to meet the responsibilities of marriage. Even though he had an extremely strong commitment to Emily, he apparently was troubled by his tottering emotional state. He felt he had to break the engagement, and so in 1848 he wrote to Emily that he had decided to "fly for my good, perhaps for thine, at any rate for thine if mine is thine."[8] His enigmatic words are mirrors of his confusion. Undoubtedly, in addition to the fear of passing on the Tennysons' black bloodedness, the all too vivid image of his brother Charles and his troubles after his marriage to Emily Sellwood's sister Louisa were terribly disturbing to Tennyson. While he was envisioning his life with Emily, he was also watching Charles's instability increase and, furthermore, ruin Louisa's mental health—eventually she had to be sent away and placed under a doctor's care. Feeling unstable himself Tennyson found it difficult not to identify his future with theirs. He must have worried that he too might crumble under the pressures of marriage, and that he might exaggerate his wife's already too sensitive nature—Emily was also having emotional problems. No wonder he felt he must "fly for my good, perhaps for thine." To compound his immediate fears, outside pressures existed to increase his doubts, to play on his nervousness, and to make him feel more obligated to break his engagement. These pressures came from the medical and popular opinion that marriage not only involved the possibility of passing on a mad inheritance to one's children but also that marriage exacerbated instability; hence neurotics—those with nervous disorders in their past or present—should not marry.[9] That view was stressed and echoed by many in the mid-nineteenth century, including Dr. Matthew Allen, who believed that marriage was at the core of many of his patients' problems. Allen insisted that the complications of marriage were "demons" that plagued "man's health and peace" and were responsible for causing "the most terrible forms of insanity."[10] Tennyson, of course, saw Allen frequently during these confusing years. Significantly, Tennyson and Emily married after Charles and Louisa resumed their life together.

Ultimately, however, Allen's views about marriage were to prove not nearly as threatening as his wood-carving scheme. Early in the 1840s, when Tennyson was visiting Allen's private asylum near High Beech, Essex, Tennyson became intrigued with the doctor's plan to make money through a mechanical device to carve wood.[11] Tennyson's letters to friends brim with enthusiasm for the scheme. "We shall go on swimmingly," he exclaimed to Rev. Rawnsley. In another letter he bubbled, "We have dropt the name 'Pyroglyph' as being too full of *meaning* . . . & call ourselves 'The Patient Decorative—Carving & Sculpture Company!'"[12] His ebullience is, in fact, somewhat disturbing. Because Tennyson felt such zeal he foolishly invested all his money (three thousand pounds) into the scheme. The results were disastrous. The plan failed; Tennyson lost all his money (that is, until he collected insurance after the doctor's death); and, as might be expected, his morale plunged to alarming depths. His London friends feared for his sanity. In 1844 FitzGerald wrote, "He looked and said he was ill: I have never seen him so hopeless."[13] Aubrey de Vere remembered that on 16 July 1845 Tennyson "seemed much out of spirits and said that he could no longer bear to be knocked about the world, and that he must marry and find love and peace or die. . . . He complained much about growing old, and said he cared nothing for fame, and that his life was all thrown away for want of competence and retirement. Said that no one had been so much harassed by anxiety and trouble as himself."[14] Tennyson spoke of himself as feeling "very crazy," and he asked himself, "Is life worth anything?"[15] A picture emerges of a terribly

despondent and confused person who must have recalled his earlier visits
to the asylum with horror, for the line between himself and the inmates
of Allen's institution was growing thinner and thinner.

As he had known, a decade before, after watching his father and, for
that matter, all his family, he realized again he needed to get away, to
separate himself from an atmosphere that encouraged rather than soothed
his anxiety and that would not let his mind be diverted from itself. In a
move pregnant with ominous memories, Tennyson entered a hydropathic establishment in Prestbury, near Cheltenham. Twenty years earlier his father had gone to Cheltenham to seek relief. For several months
in late 1843 and throughout 1844, Tennyson submitted himself to the
water cure at Prestbury. In late 1847, feeling once more overwhelmed by
his nervousness and feeling the effects of his tottering equilibrium, Tennyson spent yet more time at another hydropathic establishment, Umberslade Hall, just outside Birmingham. Later that year, continuing to
suffer, he moved to Dr. James Wilson and Dr. James M. Gully's famous
establishment in Malvern, where he remained for several weeks. In 1848
he returned to Malvern for more treatment. Malvern too was a place that
must have held a morbid and, most certainly, poignant attraction for
Tennyson since Malvern was the place where Hallam had rested in September 1829 after his recuperative tour of Europe—even before Wilson's
and Gully's time its waters were famous for their "unequalled purity."[16]
Hallam had been there to help rid himself of his depression and ease his
hypertension. Ironically while he was there he had written a poem and
mailed it to Tennyson—a poem about a visit to a madhouse in Malvern.
In the second stanza, Hallam addresses Tennyson and describes a young
lady whom he observed locked within a cell.

> Alfred, hadst thou been here, thine eye
>     Would scarce have seen for very tears,
> And well I know, no more than I,
>     Would'st thou forget the still despairs
> That almost learned a joyous look
> On one poor maiden's face, whose sight I could not brook.[17]

The sympathetic treatment Tennyson received at Malvern, though,
softened these poignant associations. Dr. Gully, especially, was a person
of great sympathy for someone with Tennyson's temperament and tal-
ents. For instance, before Gully became involved in hydropathy, he pri-
vately circulated his "Lectures on the Moral and Physical Attributes of
Men of Genius and Talent."[18] Later he was again to demonstrate his attraction to such individuals when he not only took a special interest in

Tennyson, but also made a point to invite the suffering Carlyle to spend a few weeks with him at Malvern.

Tennyson, however, was not always to be so fortunate as he was at Malvern under Dr. Gully's guidance. His earlier stays at Prestbury were not at all pleasant. The hydropathic methods there were harsh and arduous. Indeed, Tennyson's willingness to tolerate the treatments offered at Prestbury and his willingness to keep faith in those methods are a monument to his despair. His endurance offers a most graphic insight into the depths of his despondency. To bear with the terrible discomforts, months at a time, Tennyson must have feared he was coming very close to the edge, that he was following the family's morbid tradition far too closely.

Sir Charles Tennyson is sensitive to the more rigorous nature of the Prestbury cure. In his biography, to support his view he prints a portion of a letter Tennyson wrote to FitzGerald on 2 February 1844, in which he complained that "of all the uncomfortable ways of living, sure an hydropathical is the worst: no reading by candlelight, no going near a fire, no tea, no coffee, perpetual wet sheet and cold bath and alternation from hot to cold."[19] Ricks, in his biography, includes the most telling portion of that February letter. The selection carries important clues as to the exact character of Tennyson's rougher experiences at Prestbury.

> I am in an Hydropathy Establishment near Cheltenham (the only one in England conducted on pure Priessnitzan principles). I have had four crisises [*sic*] (one larger than had been seen for two or three years in Gräfenberg—indeed I believe the largest but one that has been seen). Much poison has come out of me, which no physic ever would have brought to light. Albert Priessnitz (the nephew of the great man) officiates at this establishment, and very quick and clever he is and gives me hopes of a cure in March: I have been here already upwards of two months.[20]

The great man Tennyson refers to is Vincent Priessnitz, the founder of the internationally famous hydropathic establishment in Gräfenberg. So well known was this man and his institution that by the early 1840s Gräfenberg became, unofficially, the international headquarters of the cure. Interested doctors from England and other parts of the world gathered there to learn Priessnitz's principles and to observe his treatments and miraculous cures. One of Prestbury's directors, Richard Beamish, was such a disciple. In 1843, the year Tennyson was confined to Prestbury, Beamish published a book describing the cure, *The Cold Water Cure as Practised by Vincent Priessnitz at Gräfenberg, in Silesia with an Account of Cases Successfully Treated at Prestbury, near Cheltenham*.[21] The book helps to clarify the character of the "four crisises" mentioned in Tennyson's letter to FitzGerald.

Depending on the patient's needs, Priessnitz and his followers offered a variety of hydropathic treatments. Many adherents copied the principles and treatments incorrectly, and many like Dr. Gully used the methods with modifications. Beamish and others at Prestbury, as Tennyson points out in his letter, followed the great man most literally. Beamish outlines the various treatments.

> The mode in which water is applied as a curative agent may be seen,
>
> 1. In the wet hand-rubbing; 2. Wet sheet (*leintuch*); 3. Dripping-sheet (*abreibung*); 4. Tepid bath (*abgeschrecht*); 5. Cold bath (*wanna*); 6. Hip bath (*sitz*); 7. Foot bath (*fusz*); 8. Head bath (*kopf*); 9. Stimulating wet bandages (*erregender umschlag*); 10. The *less* stimulating wet bandage (*weniger erregender*); 11. The soothing wet bandage (*kühlender umschlag*); and 12. the Douche. To these is added, 13. The dry blankets, or sweating process.[22]

The treatment was absorbing, lasting all day and touching on every activity. Some treatments began as early as five in the morning. After the assistant woke the patient, he wrapped him in wet sheets and led him to a cold bath. At Prestbury this meant water between thirty-three and fifty-five degrees Fahrenheit. After the patient had been in the bath several minutes, the attendant rubbed him down with either cold, wet hands or dripping-wet, cold sheets. Immediately, the attendant returned the patient to bed, wrapped him in blankets, and offered him a breakfast of bread and cold water. After breakfast, the patient exercised and then took a *sitz* or hip bath (thirty-three to fifty-five degrees Fahrenheit) where he might remain from anywhere from fifteen minutes to one hour. Sometimes the doctors chose to give the patient a foot bath, which involved placing the feet in cold water and rubbing them vigorously. On other occasions, the doctors chose to immerse the patient's head in cold water, one side at a time. As the patient improved and his tolerance for the cold water increased, the doctors prescribed a douche (shower) which, like the other dousings in cold water, was always followed by a massage. All this activity, unbelievably, took place before noon. After a bland meal and drinks of cold water, the whole process was usually repeated, and again after the evening meal. No wonder Tennyson had time neither to read nor to think!

So far the methods administered at Prestbury might not seem that different from those very briefly outlined in Elizabeth Jenkins's account of Tennyson's relationship with Dr. Gully.[23] The reason for this similarity is that the establishment at Malvern was based on Priessnitzan principles. Moreover, so far the methods, although time-consuming and momentarily shocking, might not seem that uncomfortable. Because the immersions were followed or accompanied by massages or by wrapping in warm, dry blankets, the resulting sensations could be as pleasurable as Jenkins implies. As proof of their potentially pleasurable nature, a patient of Dr. Gully's wrote an article for *Fraser's Magazine* dispelling the notion that these baths were uncomfortable. The patient explains that after being wrapped in the blankets "in ten minutes or less, a sensation of delicious languor stole over us: in a little longer we were fast asleep. . . . Body and mind are soothed into an indescribable tranquility; the sensation is one of calm, solid enjoyment."[24]

Such "solid enjoyment" might have been a reality for some at Dr. Gully's establishment. Neither at Presbury, nor later at Umberslade Hall, however, does Tennyson allude to any such feelings. Obviously, Tennyson's nervousness and depressed state are partially responsible for his lack of enjoyment, but they are not entirely to blame. A much-publicized aspect of Priessnitz's treatment is also responsible. Priessnitz named this aspect the "crises." In addition to a cure involving baths, sheets, a bland diet, and exercise, Priessnitz and many of his followers encouraged crises: excessive sweating, feverish attacks, convulsions, diarrhea, vomiting, rashes, and boils. These crises were the means by which the patient, as Tennyson writes in his February letters, expels the "poison" out of his system, and, thereby, restores the proper balance to the body. To encourage these crises and thus rid the body of its impurities, the attendants wrapped the patient in cold, wet, coarse linen sheets (*erregender umschlag*), sometimes as frequently as every twenty minutes during the day. The "stimulating blankets" were long enough to pass three times around the body, and wide enough to wrap the patient from the armpits to below the abdomen. The attendants wet one-third of the sheet, passed the whole bandage around the body, and waited until the patient began to expel the impurities upsetting his circulatory, digestive, and nervous systems. Although sweating, fever, vomiting, and rashes were common results, the most publicized form these crises took was the eruption of boils over large areas of the patient's body. Priessnitz, especially, encouraged these boils, for they were excellent visual proof that the poison was being abstracted away from the diseased system and was seeping out of the body. For this reason, the boils were encouraged to remain open. At Prestbury, boils were so common that they became synonymous with the word *crises*. Beamish's explanation of treatments at Gräfenberg and Prestbury illustrates the equation of boils with crises: "By a steady application of the various hydriatic appliances . . . the humours of the body are brought to the surface, pass off by insensible perspiration, or are thrown out in boils, called crises; the time which is taken to accomplish this varies very much. . . . The rising of these boils usually produces fever, and sickness of the stomach."[25]

Tennyson's February letter to FitzGerald makes it quite clear that these "crisises" were an important part of his treatment at Prestbury. Not only were they important to the treatment, but they were also a source of pride for Tennyson. He seems pleased that he has had "four crisises (one larger than had been seen for two or three years in Gräfenberg—indeed I believe the largest but one that has been seen)." Tennyson does not explain what these four crises are. If we combine the evidence offered in the letter with the evidence offered by Beamish, there is little doubt that they were large boils. Beamish's book describes the kinds of crises or boils that Tennyson had in mind when he compared his to one seen in Gräfenberg. Beamish's description gives modern readers a rather grim sense of what Tennyson was experiencing, voluntarily, in the early months of 1844. The description comes in a case study of a woman whom the doctor "directed to go to bed, to apply erregendere umschlage from the breasts to below the hips, and round the calves of her legs, and to change them every half hour during the day, and as often as possible during the night. This treatment had the desired effect. . . . In four weeks a tremendous auschlag, or crisis, appeared on her body, larger than anything [Vincent] Priessnitz had ever before witnessed, and, as I was informed, scarcely to be comprehended. This continued open for *four months and a half*. . . and her cure was accomplished."[26]

As unpleasant as this case description is to read, the discomfort to Tennyson must have been considerably greater. His willingness to tolerate and even take pride in these crises is remarkable. Not only is it a powerful reminder of the depths of his unhappiness during this period, but it is also an emblem of his faith in the water cure to save him from "the perpetual panic and horror."[27] After a relapse in July, Tennyson still clung to that faith. That month he wrote to Edmund Lushington, "It is true I had ten crisises but I am not cured, tho' I do not doubt the efficiency of the treatment in most cases, having *seen* most marvellous cures performed."[28]

The practices to which Tennyson subjected himself were not acceptable to everyone. Many distrusted the cure, for they feared it was yet another form of quackery, or, worse yet, a plague imported from foreign lands. An article in the *Athenaeum* expresses this distrust: "Hydropathy is, in fact, but one head of the great hydra Quackery,—and is sprouting up at the expense of its scotched sisters, Mesmerism, Phrenology, and

Homeopathy. They are all the offspring of the same stock—phantasies of overwrought German abstraction; which, long after they have ceased to trouble the parent mind, are imported at second-hand for the amusement of us in English."[29] Hydropathy's association with mesmerism, phrenology, and homeopathy would not scare away Tennyson.[30] Rather his fascination and limited practice with the first two and his wife's willingness to try homeopathic potions (however "murderous" she thought they were) would make the treatments that much more valid and attractive. Tennyson, however, might have been more sensitive to the major criticism directed against Priessnitz's methods of encouraging boils. These crises placed the water cure's reputation in jeopardy, caused fright to many contemplating the treatment, and prompted a rush of books weighing the pros and cons of the treatment.

Significantly, two of the cure's most vociferous and successful champions were Dr. Wilson and Dr. Gully. In 1843, reacting against the growing scepticism of the public and the medical profession, these two physicians published *The Dangers of the Water Cure*, which took to task each criticism and each "danger" associated with the various treatments. The criticism to which they were most sensitive was that launched against the crises or boils. In a section entitled "The Crises Induced by a Water Cure Is Dangerous," [*sic*] they argued that the criticism in their case was invalid. At their establishment at Malvern only twenty-two of five hundred patients experienced boils, and those erupted naturally. Throughout the section, Wilson and Gully not only displayed impatience with the method of stimulating boils, but also distinguished themselves from practitioners, like Priessnitz, who insisted on using such methods. The physicians explained: "Let it be understood, however, that we by no means class ourselves with those practisers of the Water Cure who appear to consider *a crisis of boils* essential, and who, therefore, are much given to stimulate the system without precise measurement of its capabilities."[31]

Not only did Wilson and Gully underplay the necessity for boils in effecting a cure, but they also underplayed the side effects of such boils. Once more the physicians distinguished themselves from those like Beamish who maintained that "the rising of these boils usually produces fever, and sickness in the stomach." In contrast to such claims, Wilson and Gully maintained that in their hands "there is no disorder of the tongue nor, by any chance, any vomiting: and delirium and fainting are circumstances altogether unknown in its history. If any of the patients treated by us at Malvern, who have had the crisis of boils, will assert that any one, or all of these symptoms . . . accompanied such crisis in their person, we are ready to give up the point."[32]

Although these Malvern doctors were conservative about stimulating boils, they were not entirely against the principle of crises. For them, some form of "throwing off" the disease was important and necessary. Critical sweating, feverish attacks (most frequent in cases of long-standing hypochondria), eruption of pimples, and diarrhea were all positive for they threw off disease and nervousness in a natural way. These crises were also necessary, for they helped to prevent insanity. Almost warning those who might resist these milder crises, Wilson and Gully wrote, "It is true also, that nervous patients will prefer a feverish attack, which terminates their torments in health, to the aggravation of their disorder, and its conversion into insanity." No doubt, fearing such a conversion, Tennyson was willing to continue with the cure. In fact, most of the hydropathic establishments were filled with those who were on the verge of losing their minds and packed with treatments designed to prevent patients, like Tennyson, from sliding over the edge into his brother Edward's asylum. The descriptions of cases treated at Prestbury and Malvern reveal those who are not ready for the asylum, but, if allowed to continue without the treatments, would soon be locked away. The establishments were as much concerned with alleviating physical suffering as giving asylum to a patient's nerves, "the internal sources of a patient's torments."

Although Tennyson would leave these cures feeling more hopeful about himself, it would not be long before his anxiety and nervousness would return, and he would be wondering "how am I to get through the day." According to FitzGerald, in the autumn of 1848, Tennyson was more bound up in himself than ever, taking iron pills and worrying more about "his bowels and nerves than about the Laureate wreath."[33] In the end the lasting effects of these water cures seem to have been minimal. About the only effects to remain were Tennyson's habit of taking several baths a day and his belief in exercise.[34] The regime's insistence on the restorative powers of exercise stayed with Tennyson, so even as an old man he would walk as far as fifteen miles a day. Allingham's diary is full of breathless comments recorded as if trying to catch the conversation as Tennyson bounded over Farringford's fields and cliffs. Neither, however, was enough to guard Tennyson permanently against his morbid tendencies.

Many biographers and critics breathe a sigh of relief over Tennyson's marriage, for in their mind Emily brought stability and was the healer and the end of all his problems.[35] Indeed, following his marriage in 1850, Tennyson was considerably less morbid than he had been during the horrendous 1830s and 1840s. "Cheerfulness" did, as Palgrave noted, "break through."[36] It should not be forgotten, however, that marriage did bring its difficulties, and that Tennyson could still be morbid and be plagued by relapses, hopelessness, and despair. Recollections of walking tours offer glimpses of this continuing instability. Three years after his marriage, Tennyson toured Yorkshire and Scotland with F. T. Palgrave, who described his companion's behavior as "often meditative, sometimes depressed in tone"—a behavior, according to Palgrave, Tennyson attributed to his "'black blood,' which he said, 'half-smilingly' was his 'inheritance.'" Again in the middle of August 1859 the two traveled. This time Palgrave wrote how the hot sun of Portugal released Tennyson's hypochondria and made him more morbid than ever.

> This so wrought upon & disturbed T, in a manner with which many English travellers to Italy during the heat will be unpleasantly familiar, that he [always an alarmist from sensitiveness about health], now began gravely to talk about leaving his bones by the side of the great novelist Fielding who died & was buried at Lisbon in 1754. This idea had in fact been in Ts mind during our voyage; as we steered into the harbour he mentioned it; & hence when one day soon after our arrival we drove past the Cemetery, I managed to divert his attention to the other side of the road way. Now, we were both anxious: but one dose from an English doctor set him right. Prescribing for himself,—a common case,—had been three-fourths of the evil.[37]

One year later Thomas Woolner accompanied Tennyson and Palgrave on a holiday in Cornwall. Allusions to Tennyson's health again play a memorable role in recollections of the trip—no trip was complete without allusions to Tennyson's physical and mental state. With a sense of relief Woolner wrote that Tennyson was "physically better" and that "he was perpetually grumbling and making jokes at the expense of Palgrave, or at mine—and taking long walks, and swimming, and not smoking much and drinking scarcely any wine; so you may consider all this as flourishing."[38] Drinking apparently was a danger signal, particularly given Tennyson's family history of alcoholism.

At home Tennyson's moods also swung between cheerfulness and despair. His wife's letters trace this manic-depressive pattern. Sometimes she could write to their sons, "Papa has been fairly cheerful of late," and she could tell them about "Papa running up and down with his two pitchers of bath water to water the lawn or making a great rain from thy bedroom window, falling before that in which I sit."[39] (The episode is almost a manic parody of his experiences at the hydropathic establishments.) At other times, Emily confided to Lear, "Ally" is "in a lower state of body and mind than is his wont."[40] As in the past, anxiety brought on physical reactions. Up until his death, "solar plexus" (a nervous disease of the stomach), palpitations, severe eczema on his legs and back, creeping paralysis, and his fear of going blind troubled him. In February 1871 Emily wrote about his problems with eczema, problems precipitated by the death of his close friend John Simeon: "poor Ally has had a dreary 8 or 9 months from eczema. He is better but not well. Much more languid than I like to see him. He has never got over our loss in May."[41] Although Emily disagreed, doctors attending Tennyson shortly before his death were familiar enough with his nervousness that they were more than willing to attribute his decline in health to "nervous exhaustion."[42]

As they had before his marriage, all these diseases preoccupied and depressed Tennyson. His letter diary during the 1860s reveals just how preoccupied he could be. Many entries revolve around his consultations with numerous doctors and references to the people who helped to cure him. The diary records how dinner guests were subjected to discussion of his ailments, especially when the guest happened to be a physician as in the case of a French doctor who visited Farringford on 29 June 1863. The doctor apparently did not respond sympathetically enough to the reaction Tennyson was having to a vaccination. Tennyson grumbled in his diary: "A French doctor a man of great & growing celebrity here saw my leg last night—as he was going to dine here so I thought he had better have a look at it & said it did not matter, was very annoying and gave me some directions to follow." Tennyson was much more pleased with a lady who came to nurse the infected leg and whom he found to be "very civil," because she doctored and bandaged him "day & night." The hypochondriacal Tennyson demanded sympathy and constant attention.[43] Moreover, as in the past, Tennyson's anxiety about his health sent him away from home in search of relief. In the autumn of 1861, for example, Emily wrote to her homeopathic friend, Margaret Gatty, "I am grieved to tell you that my husband has been nearly three weeks in town under doctor taking chlorine baths, etc. He has not yet returned, neither is it certain when he will be allowed to return."[44] After his brother Charles's death in 1879, Tennyson suffered badly and left home again. This time, echoing Dr. Tennyson's attempts to get better, Tennyson traveled to Venice to divert his mind from itself, and from silence, the "perpetual ghostly voice" that literally and alarmingly haunted him.[45]

Because Tennyson was so cautious about himself and so watchful, he was aware of the roots of his problems. His choice of doctors indicates that he recognized how acutely the mind and the body influenced each other, especially how the mind could influence the body. His choice also mirrors how aware he was of his family's hereditary instability and the role it played in determining his condition. As a young man he had consulted Brodie, who understood that many diseases had their true origin in "mental anxiety." Brodie believed that nervous disposition was hereditary and that "it prevails in particular families, and that having been once established in the system, it is never totally eradicated."[46] Later, of course, his experiences with Priessnitz, Gully, and Paget supported Brodie's opinions. All recognized that it was nervousness that could turn people into hypochondriacs. Paget was keenly sensitive to imaginary diseases, and Gully was very much aware that hypochondria was "essentially" the "deeply-rooted irritation of the whole of the nerves."[47] Whether it was Brodie, Paget, Priessnitz, or Gully, the rationale affecting Tennyson's choice seems consistent. The recognition that his suffering was as much a result of anxiety or hereditary instability was the common denominator in his seemingly endless search for relief. Tennyson knew his palpitations were as much the flutterings of his heart muscles as they were what Emily once called "the flutterings of the nerves."[48]

Given Tennyson's understanding, H. D. Rawnsley's story about Tennyson attributing his "fits of melancholy" to the gout is not truly representative.[49] Admittedly, there was a part of Tennyson that wanted to believe that his moods had their origin in physical ailments (probably the same part that enjoyed Paget's statement that eczema was not a nervous disorder); but there was also the part that knew better. A remark offered to another Farringford visitor rings truer: "'If I had to choose life over again I wouldn't be a poet, I'd be a pachyderma.' Then, seeing me [Herbert Warren] smiling, 'I don't mean a hippopotamus,' he went on, 'I mean I'd choose to be a thick-skinned fellow with no nerves.'"[50]

But if Tennyson could have chosen to live his life over, he would probably have refused to be a "thick-skinned fellow with no nerves." He would have elected to cast off the protective armor, because too much of his personal and poetic identity depended on those "nerves." To begin with, Tennyson's morbidity was a source of pleasure for him—a most human trait. He was more than capable of indulging in his suffering. There were moments when he found a peculiar pleasure in lapsing into and then wallowing in his depression—a proclivity that seems to have caught his friends' attention, for on occasion they were known to remark on his willfulness and self-pity, even when the threat of going mad was at its worst.[51] Tennyson was also aware of this proclivity. For instance, when he brought the lotos-eaters to life, he acknowledged this tendency to bask pleasurably in self-pity and suffering. He knew enough about himself to recognize the lushness of the lotos-eaters' brooding. Like them, he too was tempted

> To lend our hearts and spirits wholly
> To the influence of mild-minded melancholy;

> To muse and brood and live again in memory,
> With those old faces of our infancy
> Heaped over with a mound of grass,
> Two handfuls of white dust, shut in an urn of brass!
>
> [ll. 108–13]

The poem's seductive lines draw in their readers just as Tennyson felt drawn to the dubious pleasures of "mild-minded melancholy."

Undoubtedly there was a certain enjoyment in yielding to rather than overcoming his morbidity. But, for Tennyson that pleasure was always to be qualified by the ugly fear of madness, and, moreover, that pleasure was minimal compared with the more complex satisfaction he experienced when he chose to leave the land of the lotos-eaters, when he ceased to feed off his "black blood," and instead fought against it. The ensuing struggle was a real and lasting source of pleasure for Tennyson. It was the source of a vitality which helped him shape not only his life, but also his art. In an early sonnet, "Conrad! why call thy life monotonous?" he wrote, "We live but by *resistance*, and the best / Of Life is but the struggle of the will" (ll. 9–10). Here he expressed a view that was to be essential to his struggle to survive. Later he translated these lines into the image of the person who picks up the oar and rows against threatening currents.[52] Tennyson was a person who worked hard at pulling that oar. Like Ulysses, even in the most depressing moments when neither the present nor the future promised bliss, Tennyson could not stay still for long. He had to cling to the belief that he must be "strong in will / To strive, to seek, to find, and not to yield" ("Ulysses," ll. 69–70). He could not wallow forever. He too had to take up the oar and struggle forward and thereby survive. For instance, when he felt suicidal after Hallam's death and during the horrendously difficult times with his finances, his family, the Sellwoods, and his tottering equilibrium, Tennyson did not elect to feed entirely off his morbidity; he also worked hard revising and writing his poetry; he set up a schedule of study, and he survived.[53] Work was one means of resisting his moods. At the hydropathic establishments Tennyson often felt hopeless and low because he was not permitted to compose, or as he put it, "even to think." Letters Tennyson wrote to his publisher, Edward Moxon, are reminders of how necessary work was to Tennyson's sanity. In many letters Tennyson begs Moxon to visit him and keep him in touch with his work. From Umberslade Hall, for example, he wrote, "come down on Saturday and see me here. . . . Here is a hall in a pleasant park & you would be all the better for a Sunday's mouthful of fresh air. We can give you a bed here & you should do just as you like. I want to talk with you. I find it very difficult to correct proofs under the treatment, but you shall have them all back with you on Monday." The letter concludes with "come!" repeated several times.[54] Tennyson continued to find idleness lethal later in his life. Emily was aware of her husband's need to keep working and would write to people like Woolner asking for stories that would stimulate Tennyson to write. Her sensitivity to the problem comes through in a letter she wrote to Woolner on 12 December 1861, "What you say about work for sensitive minds—Idleness to them *is* far the hardest work, it saps the very roots of life."[55]

Within Tennyson there seems always to have been a tension similar to the conflicting impulses that are present in "The Lotos-Eaters." Self-pity pulled against his desire to struggle; idleness vied against action. Tennyson's posture is ambiguous, for at once he was caught in the self-indulgent pleasures of melancholy and in the desire to fight against that indulgence. His willingness to enter and take the treatments offered by the hydropathic establishments serves as an extraordinary emblem of this ambiguity. He was attracted to these institutions because they massaged and indulged his sickness, and yet simultaneously they offered him a means of escaping his sickness. This ambiguous posture extended beyond Tennyson's personal life into his poetry and created a whole body of work which has caught the critics' attention because it has forced them either to wind through the ironic patterns of the poems or to come to terms with "the strange diagonal" holding the competing impulses of the poems together. This posture has created a number of poems like "The Two Voices" and "The Lotos-Eaters," which capture the moment that Hallam recognized between contentment and fear. It has created puzzling poems like *The Princess*, which sets one competing theory about female education against another, and it has caused one critic to remark that Tennyson's poetry "totters on the edge of madness."[56]

Ultimately, though, it is not the tottering, ironic voice that predominates—although recent criticism emphasizes that aspect of the poet's verse. Rather, it is the voice of a survivor which speaks more loudly.[57] Like his life, his poetry is primarily a history of his survival. It measures and traces the steps of his ceaseless struggle against the madness without and the instability he feared was going to catch up with and destroy him. His poetry celebrates that struggle. It takes its cue from its creator's "nerves," and it takes its shape from Tennyson's attempts to order the threatening chaos.

# Chapter Four

# Why I Am I

s we have seen, between 1822 and 1830 Tennyson was composing poems that reflect his father's instability and its unbalancing effect on the Somersby household. These poems, however, were not to be the last to address such instability. No matter how vehemently Tennyson vowed "never to search my Father's groves" ("The Outcast"), he continued to do so. Even after the passing of time and his leaving Somersby, his need to write about these experiences remained. Striving to find his way through those groves and their twisted paths, by the end of his life Tennyson had composed over seventy poems. Many of these poems are about his precarious equilibrium; others feature mad personae from history, mythology, and literature. All hover about his work as the instability they reflect clung to his consciousness.

Early on in his efforts to riddle these encounters and to wrestle with his instability Tennyson wrote poems that express his personal anguish. Superficially, many of these poems appear to be no more than youthful rehearsals of Romantic conventions. Indeed, many are indebted to Tennyson's enthusiasm for Romantic verse, particularly to Lord Byron's, and to his enthusiasm for anything Gothic. But, as might be expected, these poems are also indebted to the manic-depressive atmosphere plaguing the Tennyson household. For instance, "Memory (Memory! dear enchanter)" owes its despairing tone both to Byron's melancholic verses and to the gloom clinging to the Tennysons.[1] Consequently in the poem, when Tennyson complains that memories of past hopes make the present seem unbearable, he is not merely imitating his literary mentors; rather, he is endeavoring to share his own melancholic mood that was prompting him to wonder, "Where's now that peace of mind."

However, Tennyson was not always content to let the Romantic topoi register his despair. Neither was he content to wallow in his despondency and simply write confessional poetry. Rather, from the beginning Tennyson felt compelled to step back from himself and analyze the black moods and riddle their meaning. Because he was a "survivor," it was not enough to describe the gloom or the despondency. To live through his encounters with instability, he believed he must not only confront them but also, in a sense, dissect them. To accomplish this end he frequently observed these encounters from a variety of perspectives. Robert Martin has briefly commented on this tendency to look "at the emotions from more than one point of view" and remarked that the effect on his poems is "binocular."[2] The effect on the poems, however, is more than binocular. It is also clinical, for Tennyson's need to observe the emotions also encouraged him to approach his mad subject matter in ways that are reminiscent of the case studies written by nineteenth-century mad doctors who in their attempts to understand madness closely studied the progress of their patients' illnesses and recorded in accurate detail their patients' distinguishing characteristics. Tennyson's poems are also clinical in that their vocabulary and structure often reflect the scientific studies of the mind which were available to him. It is not unusual to find Tennyson's poems borrowing vocabulary and ways of understanding madness from scientific texts. That Tennyson would be influenced by these texts and write poems in which he adopts the posture of a scientific observer is not surprising, for even though he, perhaps, was never more accomplished in his scientific studies than "an intelligent amateur," he had "a decided penchant for factual accuracy," and from an early age he had a wish to understand the "mechanics of the mind." This inclination to learn what he could about human behavior set him off on a lifelong quest to study character and to pose the troublesome questions found in his 1827 poem "The 'How' and the 'Why'": "How you are you?" and "Why I Am I?"[3]

One result of Tennyson's quest was his decision in the 1820s and early 1830s to compose a series of character poems: "Claribel," "Lilian," "Isabel," "Mariana," "Madeline," "Adeline," "Amy," "Marion," "Lisette," "Mariana in the South," "Eleänore," "Fatima," "Margaret," and "Kate." These are an extraordinary group, for they exhibit a Tennyson who in his attempts to understand these characters is being what Paul Turner identifies as "almost clinical."[4] In a manner approaching that practiced by the century's mad doctors when they wrote their case studies, Tennyson identifies significant physical characteristics and distinguishing qualities of mind which determine how each of his subjects perceives the world around her and controls the way others react to her.[5] For instance, in "Claribel" he notes how Claribel's solemn ways affect the landscape so that it too seems to suffer from an "inward agony"; in "Lilian" he considers his subject's "airy fairy" ways and how they simultaneously charm and frustrate him; in "Madeline," he concentrates on this person's subtle range of facial expressions, which mirror her "ever varying" nature and unbalance those around her; in "Marion" he defines "the peculiar charms of a very ordinary person"; and in "Adeline" he dwells on his subject's mysterious smile, half earthly and half divine, which makes him wonder "what ails her." In other poems Tennyson explores the idiosyncracies of those like Margaret, whom he finds "no less divine, but more human than Adeline." In others Tennyson focuses on the characters' distinguishing physical traits: for instance, he looks at Eleänore's large, dark eyes and "bounteous forehead" and marks how they display her mind's "luxuriant symmetry," a quality that enchants him.

Of all the character poems, however, the most vivid examples of Tennyson's interest in being clinical are the Mariana poems. The most popular of these is, of course, "Mariana," a poem in which Tennyson, in a manner still resembling the physicians' case studies, charts a frustrated woman's loneliness and increasing despair. Throughout the poem he follows the progress of her mind while she waits despondently through the night for her absent lover. When the lover fails to come and night approaches once more, Tennyson marks how her despair plays on her mind and distorts her perceptions: Mariana sees "old faces," hears voices, and exaggerates sounds so that even a mouse "shrieks." In the end, her mind is as trapped in its despair as the plaintive refrain is caught at the end of each verse: "I am aweary, aweary, / I would that I were dead!"

Because "Mariana" is popular and because it appears by itself in anthologies, readers often forget it has a companion piece, "Mariana in the South." In this companion poem Tennyson continues to chart Mariana's plight, but with a difference, for this time he demonstrates how a southern climate alters Mariana's response to her frustration. For instance, he dwells on the region's heat and how it encourages the intensity of Mariana's despair. In addition, he alters the refrain so that Mariana in the south, instead of repeating "I am aweary, aweary, / I would that I were dead!" keeps petitioning "Our Lady" and frequently moans, "Madonna, sad is night and morn." All these alterations are most consciously carried out. They vividly demonstrate Tennyson's willingness to examine and experiment, quite scientifically, with a character and to explore how that character alters according to the circumstances in which it finds itself. Just how consciously this experimentation was done is made clear in a letter Arthur Henry Hallam sent to W. B. Donne. In the letter Hallam stresses the fact that Tennyson "intended" the poem to be "a kind of pendant to this former poem of *Mariana*, the idea of both being the expression of desolate loneliness, but with this distinctive variety in the

second, that it paints the forlorn feeling as it would exist under the influence of different impressions of sense."[6]

There is no such explicit record of there being another pendant to
"Mariana," but another character poem written in the early 1830s qualifies and further illustrates Tennyson's inclination to be clinical. "Fatima"
does not bear the name, but it does share the plight of the Mariana poems.
It too is a case study of desolate loneliness. Like the Marianas, Fatima is
also waiting and despairing for her lover. Her words echo their refrains.
Her words, though, are not exactly theirs, for, of course, Fatima's frustration is subject to the influence or circumstance of a more aggressive
passion, one that compels her to roll among the flowers, crush them to
her breast and her mouth, and make her wish to die "clasped" in her
lover's "embrace." The poem, indeed, displays a Tennyson who is continuing to "dissect" and to study how different circumstances affect behavior.

Tennyson's interest in approaching these characters in a clinical manner
is significant, for it mirrors the way in which he was personally attempting to answer the questions "How you are you? Why I am I?" It is clear
from surviving correspondence that at the same time Tennyson was
composing these character poems, he was also involved in studying the
minds of his family. Indeed, the poems might be considered as extensions
of this study. The care with which he was observing his family emerges
in a letter he wrote in 1835 to his Uncle Charles about Septimus, who
was becoming as despondent as Edward. Note the letter's clinical tone,
and how carefully Tennyson analyzes his sick brother.

I think it is my duty to inform you of Septimus' state of mind. My
grandfather talks of letting him stop at home two or three months
longer—if this be acted upon I have very little doubt that his mind
will prove as deranged as Edward's, although I trust that his intellect may yet be preserved by getting him out into some bustling,
active line of life *remote from the scene of his early connexions.* I have
studied the minds of my own family—I know how delicately they
are organized, and how much might be done in this instance by
suddenly removing Septimus from all those objects and subjects
with which he has been familiar and upon which he has been ac-
customed to brood, into some situation where he might be enabled
to form his own friendships with those of his own age and to feel
that there is something to live and care for—but this, if done, should
be done immediately, because every hour which he wastes at home
tends to increase his malady. At present his symptoms are not un-

like those with which poor Edward's unhappy derangement began.[7]

The letter reflects the Tennyson family tradition of talking, at length, about each member's nervous disorder and, more important, its practice of consulting medical texts. This practice later caused Tennyson to confess he had spent so much time reading the numerous medical texts in his father's library that he imagined, like a medical student, he suffered from every disease he read about.[8] In the reading of these texts Tennyson found ways of understanding and solving the riddle of his family's sickness, for these texts were not exclusively devoted to physical diseases. What needs to be emphasized is the fact that in these texts considerable space was also devoted to the definition, causes, and cures of madness. For instance, books in Dr. Tennyson's library like Van Sweiten's *Commentaries*, William Buchanan's *Domestic Medicine*, and Richard Reece's *The Domestic Medical Guide* discuss madness and prescribe cures. Other texts in the library helped too. Most certainly Tennyson's clinical perspective on human behavior was encouraged by his early reading of the library's scientific books. Of course, many critics have rightly noted the youthful Tennyson's immersion in the study of biology, geology, chemistry, and electricity.[9] They have failed, however, to notice how these studies also offered him insights into the workings and aberrations of the mind. They have neglected to note, for example, that an early standard like Erasmus Darwin's *Zoonomia* includes discussions of madness, the "Production of Ideas," and the phenomena of dreams; they have also overlooked the fact that the library's physiology texts offered him explanations about all types of human behavior, particularly that connected to the nervous system. Another source that helped foster Tennyson's clinical bias are the library's philosophical texts. These texts encouraged the clinical posture because by listing definitions of madness they also offered Tennyson a way of observing insanity. In Tennyson's copy of a philosophical dictionary, for example, there are exhaustive definitions of madness, hysteria, and melancholia. Not to be forgotten is the library's copy of Burton's *Anatomy of Melancholy*, a text that Tennyson later deemed important enough to read out loud to Emily shortly after their marriage.[10]

All of this reading, talking, and "dissecting" could not help but influence the way in which Tennyson approached the subject matter of his poetry. In addition to encouraging him to analyze character, his studies also encouraged him to use a vocabulary that, at times, could be quite scientific or clinical. In the early poems Tennyson often punctuated lines with self-conscious technical references to the brain, the nerves, the fibres, the veins, and the blood's circulation.[11] Phrases like "shattered nerves," "human brain," "quick and healthful blood," and "store of nerve and fibre" are not uncommon; even though some of them sound like commonplaces, they belong to nineteenth-century texts that are defining human behavior and are trying to solve the questions Tennyson poses in "The 'How' and the 'Why.'" For instance, one particularly transparent reference to these texts comes in the 1832 "Palace of Art" when Tennyson paraphrases Friederick Tiedemann's concept discussed in Van Swieten's *Commentaries* that "the brain is moulded" four times within the womb.[12]

These early studies of madness and the brain, however, involved Tennyson in more than occasionally injecting scientific phrases into the poetic line. These studies also involved Tennyson in exploring how ideas begin and end. Sections of the dream poems offer examples, for in these Tennyson is never content to jump directly into the dreams and describe them. As in the character poems, he prefers to analyze or dissect the experience, and so he takes the reader step by step through the dreamers' waking thoughts and demonstrates how these enter the brain and form the dreams' images.[13] For example, reflecting contemporary scientific theory that dreams repeat waking sensations,[14] Tennyson in his 1832 poem "A Dream of Fair Women" shows how images from the legend the narrator is reading and his reaction to them come together, after he falls asleep, to shape his dream. And, once more borrowing from contemporary dream theory, Tennyson, at the end of the poem, documents how a noise outside the dream steals "into the brain" of the narrator and dissolves his dream.

These early attempts to be clinical stayed with Tennyson. As a result, when he left Somersby he chose not to give up his quest to riddle the "how" and the "why." Indeed, rather than satisfying his need to understand "Why I am I," these early studies provided the impetus for him to begin a lifelong quest for an even more precise understanding of human behavior—a journey propelled by his continuing instability and by the ever-expanding circle of madness surrounding him. Among other consequences, this search prompted his friendship with psychologists like Dr. Matthew Allen and Dr. R. J. Mann and with scientists like John Tyndall and Herbert Spencer who, caught up in the implications of their research, studied the scientific use of the imagination and the psychology of human development. Later in life these efforts to gain insights into human nature moved Tennyson to make more formal contacts with others possessing similar concerns. In 1877 he became a founding member of the Metaphysical Society, originally named the Psychology Society. This group kept him in touch with the pressing issues concerning the mechanics of the mind and brought him closer to leading psychologists

of his day. One of its members was the editor of the *Asylum Journal*, Dr.
John Charles Bucknill, and another was Dr. James Sully, a psychologist
whose interest in human nature led him into a study of the relation between genius and insanity.[15] Even Tennyson's membership in the Society
for Psychical Research (1881) helped to preserve his clinical bias, for the
society emphasized providing evidence to support the claims about the
spirit world and published accounts of its findings.

Because this quest to solve the riddles of the "how" and the "why"
continued, Tennyson persisted in writing poetry that is as clinical as his
earlier attempts. It is not surprising, therefore, to find the wife in the
1860 poem "Sea Dreams" comforting her husband by carefully analyzing
his disturbing dream and explaining that it originated in his knocking a
glass over, "breaking that, you made and broke your dream: / A trifle
makes a dream, a trifle breaks" (ll. 139–40). Her words echo those in the
earlier poem "A Dream of Fair Women." Tennyson also persisted in ex-
perimenting with character by subjecting it to different circumstances.
In a manner approaching the one he had used in the Mariana poems,
Tennyson composed "Despair," an 1881 poem about an elderly couple's
attempted suicide. The poem itself is not as overtly clinical as others, but
the impulse behind it is. When Tennyson wrote "Despair," he consciously tried to reconstruct what the feelings of a "would-be-suicide"
might be "in this latter half of our nineteenth century." Choosing a vocabulary that reveals his scientific bias, Tennyson explained that he had
"hypothesized" his subjects' feelings.[16]

Few, if any, critics have recognized this clinical posture in the poetry.[17]
Several, however, have felt its presence enough so that they speak of
Tennyson as an "accurate" poet. As early as 1831 Tennyson's friend Hallam singled out this quality when he glowingly reviewed Tennyson's
first volume of poetry, *Poems, Chiefly Lyrical*, and called the public's attention to Tennyson's genius that captures "moods of character" with
"extreme accuracy."[18] Many reviewers have followed Hallam's lead. For
example, immediately after *Maud* appeared in 1855, Dr. Bucknill expressed his admiration for the poet's "vivid truthfulness," and Dr. Mann,
equally impressed by the poem's truthfulness, wondered "where can this
unprofessional psychologist have acquired his accurate insight into the
phenomena of insanity?"[19] Recently a critic has repeated that question by
showing his amazement at the "realistic" portrait of the mad mother in
"Rizpah."[20] There is a difference though. When Mann wondered where
Tennyson acquired such accuracy, he was being rhetorical, for Mann knew
the poet too well not to be sensitive to Tennyson's quest to understand
madness. The critic, however, is showing his insensitivity to that quest.
Furthermore, he is disregarding a trait in Tennyson's character that es-

caped few of Tennyson's friends. This trait is his compulsion to be accurate. In his memoir, Wilfrid Ward recalls how annoying this compulsion could be: he remembers that Tennyson's "accuracy as to quite trivial matters was ever scrupulous. If a story were told with the slightest inaccuracies of detail he would spoil it by repeated interruptions, rather than let them pass." Tennyson's need to be "accurate" also caught the attention of another friend, who recorded in her diary that the poet once apologized for making mistakes in a poem of his. He was upset that he had written a line that was inaccurate. As he explained to his friend, it was impossible for there to be a "crimson coloring" in "the middle moonlit nights." [21]

Not surprisingly, this compulsion to be accurate complemented Tennyson's clinical impulses and encouraged him to compose several poems that are more ambitious than many of his other poems in their attempts to analyze the mechanics of the mind. Two of the most rigorous of these are among Tennyson's lengthy studies of madness: these are "The Lover's Tale" (1827–1829) and *Maud* (1855), both of which reflect Tennyson's close studies of character and his scrupulous attention to detail.

"The Lover's Tale" is like the Mariana poems, for it too charts the breakdown of a lonely and frustrated lover. The early sections, parts one through three (1827–1829), are spoken by Julian, a sensitive young man who since his childhood has loved his cousin Camilla. So obsessed is he by his love for her that he can speak of little else. Camilla, however, does not share his passion, so she allows herself to be wooed away by Julian's rival, Lionel. When the news that the two are to be married reaches Julian, it throws him into confusion, and, as the marriage day approaches, the devoted lover has trouble holding on to reality. Eventually he is too broken to carry on. Like "The Lover's Tale," *Maud* is also similar to the Mariana poems. In many ways it reads like a rehearsed version of the earlier poem, for in a series of tightly controlled lyrics, Julian's plight comes to life again. Once more there is the growing instability of an obsessed and thwarted lover, and once again there is madness. *Maud*, however, is not completely like "The Lover's Tale," for references to contemporary social scandals, to the Crimean War, and to grievances of Tennyson's early life ground the poem in the familiar world of the 1850s. The opening lyrics immediately place the poem in this world. For example, when the hero speaks of his father, whom he fears committed suicide after being wronged in a business deal by Maud's father, "that old man now lord of the broad estate and the Hall" (l. 19), he is alluding to Tennyson's bitter memories of his father, who was denied his inheritance by the great man of the Hall and who consequently drank himself to death. As Ralph Rader has conclusively proved, these memories are also bound up with Tennyson's personal frustration over his thwarted relationship with Rosa Baring. Like the lover who is cut off from Maud's society because of his inferior position, Tennyson was denied Rosa Baring's. This frustration opens *Maud*. In part one the hero, who already is unbalanced by an obsession for Maud, anxiously awaits her arrival after a long absence abroad. As the hero waits, he recalls the childhood they had shared, the promise that one day they should marry, and he wonders nervously how she will regard him. He fears she will be cold and say, "let me alone." When the carriage carrying Maud drives by, he studies her face and attempts to determine her mood. From then on, he does little but watch, wait for, and study Maud—often from a distance. At times her coyness and blushes disturb him; at others, her behavior makes him feel confident that she loves him. Occasionally the two exchange glances, even words, but always hovering around them are his fears, suspicions, and anger, and, worse, there is Maud's arrogant brother who opposes their union. Added to these obstacles is an emblem of the materialism that ruined the hero's family, a "new-made Lord," whom the hero fears is winning Maud's favor. As the poem progresses so does the hero's instability. His obsession causes his moods to waver between anger and despair, exaltation and lyrical anticipation, until finally they get the better of him. In a garden outside the Hall, he waits for Maud. She comes and they talk, but the brother and the rival discover them. They duel and the brother dies when the hero fatally wounds him. Haunted by Maud's cries and his awful deed the hero flees. Eventually news reaches him that Maud died shortly after her brother. In part two, more distressed than ever and pursued by guilt, bitterness, and mad hallucinations, the hero is locked in an asylum cell. In the final section, part three, time has passed. The hero remains in his cell, but his mood has changed. He is less manic but still scarred by his experiences. Believing himself to be whole and to embrace "the purpose of God," he now desires to bury his crazed self by devoting himself to some great cause. He ends the poem championing the Crimean War and proclaiming: "It is better to fight for the good than to rail at the ill."

In both "The Lover's Tale" and *Maud* the emphasis is on the lovers mastered by a passion or obsessive love that envelops and destroys them and holds them not only to the past where there was promise of fulfillment but also to the present where there is injustice and disappointment. Their *idée fixe* traps them between these poles of past and present. This stress on the lethal power of tyrannizing passion partially belongs to the importance medical thought places on the *idée fixe* as one of the distinguishing qualities of madness. Tennyson's lovers and their single-minded preoccupation with the objects of their affections conformed to the numerous descriptions of monomaniacs that crowded the treatises on insanity. Like the monomaniacs in Van Sweiten's *Commentaries*, in Tennyson's philosophical dictionary, and in the writings of Allen and Mann, these lovers suffer from a "long fixing fancy upon one sort of thoughts," from "much application to one set of ideas," and from "violent and long continued passions."[22] Moreover, like these "madmen," Julian and the hero of *Maud* labor under their obsession for years. They resemble those monomaniacs, who, according to one doctor writing for the *Quarterly Review*, sometimes have their thoughts "immoveably intent upon one and the same object" for "twenty or thirty years"—a detail that suggests that when Tennyson prolongs his lovers' dilemma, he is being as much accurate as dramatic.[23]

It is not, however, so much Tennyson's emphasis on the lover's *idée fixe* which demonstrates his obligation to the medical world as it is his indebtedness to that world's studies of what happens to individuals laboring under a "long continued passion." For example, in "The Lover's Tale" Tennyson, following his scientific mentors, quite clinically charts Julian's progress as his errors or fancies gradually envelop him until nothing "is"; things only "seem." From the beginning Julian, like the monomaniacs, confuses fancy with fact. The more his preoccupation with Camilla persists, the more it distorts his perception: he transforms a murmuring brook into a roaring flood and the moonlight into a phantom; he confuses weddings with funerals; his morbid imagination goes wild. Sounds and sights become so confused that eventually Julian becomes delirious, and his "mad" hands tear "the bright leaves of the ivy screen." These errors weaken his judgment and Julian is left with little knowledge of reality. He deteriorates into a maniac. The narrator of *Maud* suffers a similar fate. Although some critics claim that his love for Maud helps him temporarily gain sanity, the opposite seems to be true.[24] His love entangles him further in his sense of past wrongs and in his obsession for Maud. The result is that the more he dwells on Maud, the more he commits errors and the more reality slips away. He loses his sense of time, and he has such difficulty distinguishing between substance and shadows that, for example, when he hears people talk about him, neither the time nor the occasion is clear. He is forced to wonder: "Did I hear it half in a doze / Long since, I know not where? / Did I dream it an hour ago, / When asleep in this arm-chair?" (1: 285–88). Despairing, he cries out "O let the solid ground / Not fail beneath my feet." However, his despair weakens his resolve and the errors increase. His morbid imagination distorts his understanding of Maud's brother so the brother's slightest move seems exaggerated. Even though there are moments of sanity, as when he stands back, looks at the seashell (2: 106–18), and exercises a clinical detachment, they do not last. Eventually, the delicate balance tips. Violent images pass through his head and his pulse beats too loudly. Hanging on to one last "spark of will," he wonders: "Am I to be overawed?" That spark is not enough to fight his weakened mind, and the living death comes. He is committed to an asylum, where his erroneous mind resembles Mariana's. Like her he exaggerates sounds and watches as Maud's "cold and clear-cut face" grows and fades before him.

The increasing intensity of the lovers' confusion has its parallel in the commonplaces describing monomaniacs. Van Sweiten's *Commentaries*, for example, warns that "an increasing melancholy may degenerate into mania."[25] Some years later Allen subscribes to the commonplace, and so does George Man Burrows, who suggests that this mania comes only "when interruption, or opposition be given to his cherished and fixed delusion."[26] Burrows's observation can easily be applied to Julian and to the hero of *Maud*, for it is only when Camilla chooses Lionel and when the "new-made Lord" and the brother interfere with the lovers' obsessions that the images become fevered, angry, and destructive.

Other details charting the lovers' fall reflect those prominent in contemporary discussion of mad humanity and continue to demonstrate Tennyson's compulsion to be accurate and analytical. To begin with, Tennyson acknowledges what many physicians also realized—that breaking away from the destructive "errors of mind" is an enormously difficult task. Recognizing this difficulty, nineteenth-century doctors frequently prescribed traveling or the waters in the hope that the change might separate their patients from their errors.[27] The Tennysons, of course, were familiar with this prescription. In "The Lover's Tale" and *Maud* Tennyson exhibits his sensitivity to the problem by showing how hard, or even impossible, it is for either Julian or the narrator of *Maud* to escape from their "errors." So trapped are they by their obsessions that they keep feeding off their distorted visions. For a fleeting moment Maud's lover recognizes that it would be wise "if I fled from the place and the pit and the fear" (1: 64), but he is trapped even as he wishes to escape. He sees the workmen at the Hall, a sight that stimulates his memories of Maud and that, consequently, counteracts any desire he might have to flee.

This power of memory to ensnare an individual in his obsessions belongs to nineteenth-century theories of madness. Although the phrase "mad memory" is no stranger to literary depictions of madness and is certainly no stranger to Tennyson's early "Romantic" verse, it also finds its place in the physicians' insistence that memory is destructive, for memory keeps old habits and grievances alive.[28] Throughout "The Lover's Tale" and *Maud* Tennyson exhibits a keen awareness of memory's power to exacerbate madness. Tennyson is eager to show a Julian who in the opening 570 lines is so overwhelmed by his memories of Camilla, that his mind becomes a "granary" bulging with kernels from the past. Initially these kernels are sweet, but after Camilla's rejection they turn sour. Memory now feeds "the soul of love with tears" and increases the darkness growing within him. The hero of *Maud* is also haunted by bitter and sweet remembrances of the past. Unfortunately these memories mingle with the "errors" of his mind and create monstrous inaccuracies that exacerbate his insanity. Tennyson's psychiatrist friend Mann, in his review of *Maud*, was quick to blame memory for its role in creating "further fancies" and for producing "the most grotesque and incongruous interminglings of delusion and truth."[29] For him as for other doctors, memory when mixed with delusion yields insanity.

As might be expected, however, memory as a culprit pales next to the inordinate passions that hasten the lovers' decline. Tennyson gives special prominence to the lovers' excessive grief, jealousy, lust, and fears. He stresses Julian's excessive passions: his inordinate regard for Camilla, his jealousy of Lionel, and his great disappointment when he learns that Camilla and Lionel are to be married—the shock is such, in fact, that for Julian it feels like the splitting of an iceberg (ll. 591–93). In *Maud* Tennyson emphasizes similar monsters: his hero speaks of the shock following news of his father's "suicide," his subsequent loss of fortune and pride, his excessive love for Maud, and his equally irrational jealousy of the "new-made Lord" he sees riding at Maud's side. All these conspire to hurl him toward his asylum cell. He is fully aware of how lethal these passions are: "Down with ambition, avarice, pride, / Jealousy, down! cut off from the mind / The bitter springs of anger and fear" (1: 375–78). Continuing the commonplaces of madness, these words identify the passions and accuse them of causing insanity, an act that complemented the nineteenth-century belief in moral insanity. Because of the idea's popular acceptance, a reader could pick up any book on insanity available in Tennyson's lifetime and find variations on Dr. John Johnstone's statement that the disposition to madness lies dormant until it "is called into action by different circumstances during the progress of life—by passion inordinate, by love, by ambition, by avarice, by jealousy, and by intemperance of every kind."[30] One variation occurs in Haslam's popular book on insanity, published in 1809. Haslam blames "grief, ungratified desire, religious terror, disappointed pride, fright, anger, the habitual indulgence of any passion whatever, and any sudden and violent affection."[31] In 1848 William Willis Mosely echoed Haslam by identifying "excesses of excitements of joy, sorrow, watchfulness, weariness, unexpected losses,

. . . the excitements of love, mortified ambition" and "pride" as the "predisposing causes of madness." [32] The familiar words bounce back and forth through the century and throughout Tennyson's poetry.

Physicians in the nineteenth century were quick to blame the passions but not to let the entire responsibility remain with them. They were also eager to identify another predisposing cause of madness which threatened Tennyson as much as the passions and their destructive force. These physicians emphasized the role of an inherited "nervous disposition" in bringing on madness. Among many to hold such an opinion was Dr. Alexander Crichton, who directed the institute to which the Tennysons sent Arthur when he was drinking excessively and showing signs of nervous disorder. Crichton believed that it is not so much the passion of love itself which causes insanity; rather, it is the effect this passion has on a person who is already prone to suffer from "a considerable degree of nervous disposition." He talks about how "both the exalted state of the imagination and the increased sensibility of the body" work together to increase the passion and leave the individual "fancying himself to be violently in love." [33] Crichton's words find their parallel in *Maud*. Because Tennyson is often talking about himself and his fears in the poem, it is only natural that inherited madness is one of the most potent forces working against the hero's sanity. Tennyson portrays a hero who is sensitive to his hereditary curse and fearful of it. When the hero speaks of his father and becomes feverish, he exclaims: "What! am I raging alone as my father raged in his mood? / Must *I* too creep to the hollow and dash myself down and die" (1: 52–53). Later he worries that his love "may bring a curse," and fearfully asks, "Do we move ourselves, or are moved by an unseen hand at a game" (1: 127). Such a question nagged nineteenth-century physicians as well.

Yet another cause widely publicized throughout the century preys on the lover in *Maud* and propels him toward his tragic end. This cause originates in the belief that conditions of the age are guilty of producing a nation of nervous dispositions. As the historians of British psychology Hunter and Macalpine point out, in the early decades of the century "there developed an interest in what is today called social psychiatry—the influence of society, its culture and organization, institutions, beliefs, habits, deprivations, and calamities on the mental ease and disease of its members." [34] In the physicians' minds, one of the greatest threats to people's "ease" was the country's incredibly fast growing wealth. Accompanying this wealth was not only the figure of avarice but also the possibility of a sudden pecuniary embarrassment. These were responsible for a national sickness. Even before he becomes entangled in his monomaniacal regard for Maud, the hero is engaged and weakened by mammonism.

At the beginning of the poem when he speaks of his father's suicide, he rages against England, which is becoming a nation of pickpockets, "each hand lusting for all that is not its own," and shows his horror at the contemporary scandals involving greedy acts. Thomas Carlyle used these scandals in his diatribes against the mammonism of the age: one involves the baker who for the sake of an extra profit used chalk, alum, and plaster to fill out the bread he sold to the poor; another includes mothers who in desperation over poverty kill their babies "for a burial fee." In thinking about these acts, the hero works himself into a frenzy almost equal to what he is trying hard to avoid. To make matters worse for him, his sense of well-being and stability have already been undermined by his father's sudden change in fortune.

Not all the details describing the lovers' fall come from Tennyson's interest in contemporary scientific thought. Many also originate in his knowledge of historical attitudes toward madness and melancholia. For instance, when he dwells on Julian's heated brow, when he places *Maud*'s hero in a raging, red landscape, and when he has Julian complain of his blood creeping "like marsh drains" through all his "languid limbs," Tennyson is paraphrasing any number of historical descriptions of madmen and madwomen which equate manic behavior with fevers and heated blood and speak of the melancholic's pulse as "small, weak, slow, and rare." These details were familiar to him through the literary conventions and through his reading of *The Anatomy of Melancholy*, a text that Tennyson often seems to have in mind. The emphasis Tennyson gives the lovers' tyrannical and maddening obsessions is very much like Burton's. For instance, quoting one of his authorities, Aelian Montaltus, Burton insists that if a melancholic's passion becomes too intense it must necessarily lead to madness, particularly when accompanied by days of "continual meditation and waking."[35] Burton's warnings about the dangerous passions, especially about the disastrous effects of jealousy, also find their way into "The Lover's Tale" and *Maud*. Quoting Vives, Burton cautions that jealousy "begets unquietness in mind, night and day," and works on the melancholic so that he "pries into every corner, follows close, observes to a hair" and "hunts every word he hears, every whisper, and amplifies to himself (as all melancholy men do in other matters), with a most unjust calumny of others."[36] The result is that the melancholic misrepresents "everything [that] is said or done." Maud's lover and Julian share many of the melancholic's characteristics: their suspicious and jealous natures make life hellish for them and they easily misconstrue the world around them. Maud's lover, particularly, observes everything "to a hair." Throughout the poem, he lurks in corners, waiting for glimpses of her; he "hunts" her every word, hears every "whisper," and catches every syllable of the ballad she sings, even as she stands at a distance. He also amplifies each phrase and gesture, so that the slightest change in expression takes on a greater significance than it should.

The correspondence between the poems and Burton's text is not surprising, for not only did Tennyson own a copy of *The Anatomy* but so did many others.[37] The text was in vogue; people read it with care. Its historical ideas did not seem as quaint, even comic, as they do now, for the text's definitions of melancholia and madness blended easily with their own. Indeed, so acceptable were its ideas that nineteenth-century physicians often quoted the text as an authority. They subscribed to a majority of the causes and cures of madness discussed in *The Anatomy* and held on to such dated phrases as the "spleen," "thick juices," "vapours," and "humours."

The similarities between Tennyson's lovers and Burton's melancholics are also indebted to the fact that Burton's text is composed of ideas that had already shaped literary conventions of madness. One vivid example of this practice is apparent in the drama of John Ford, a Jacobean dramatist whom Tennyson admired. Ford was not only sensitive to the literary conventions associated with madness but he was also well acquainted with Burton's text. For Ford, *The Anatomy* served as "a kind of psychiatric textbook" to help him structure his characters and pose his play's dramatic problems.[38] For instance, to create the melancholic Prince Palador and to write the masque exposing the prince's "symptoms" in *The Lover's Melancholy*, and to create the mad Penthea and jealous Bessanes in *The Broken Heart*, Ford consulted Burton. Indeed, Ford let Burton serve a function that Tennyson was later to let Burton and all the scientific authorities on madness serve. Both wished to be accurate and both were sensitive to the literary conventions associated with their depictions of madness.[39]

For Tennyson the wish to be accurate and the desire to keep in touch with the literary conventions were not impossible goals because scientific and literary depictions of madness often reinforced one another. It should be clear to any reader of either "The Lover's Tale" or *Maud* that not all details charting the lovers' fall come from scientific texts. Many come from an enduring literary convention involving madly obsessed lovers. Tennyson's emphasis on the lovers' obsessions, their being lost in the "mists of error," and their being destroyed by their excessive passions is as much indebted to classical and biblical depictions of madness, to Jacobean drama, Romantic verse, and to Gothic fiction as it is to the articles on madness featured in nineteenth-century scientific journals. Contrary to expectations, however, the two worlds complement one another, for both share the assumptions that madness comes from excessive grief, jealousy, and lust, and that madness involves distortion and error and the loss of self. Because of these shared assumptions about the dangerous passions, Tennyson when composing "The Lover's Tale" and *Maud* could borrow what he needed from either the literary or the scientific world. From the literary world he could use images of nineteenth-century melodramas featuring unstable lovers standing by the seashore in the moonlight and brooding about lost loves; he could take the tenacious images of feverish, anxious lovers pursued by "mad memory"; and he could recall the many ancient and contemporary literary examples of heartbroken lovers who go mad, kill, or commit suicide. What is significant is that he could freely borrow from that tradition without being disloyal to contemporary scientific thought that also spoke of those laboring under a tyrannical passion. At times, this correspondence between the two worlds was such that scientific concepts of madness could help even Tennyson fill out the more clichéd or conventional literary figures to form a more accurate, and for Tennyson a more satisfying, portrait of madness. Clinical case studies encouraged Tennyson to analyze his lovers' obsessed minds in a way that literary conventions of madness would not have made so possible. These conventions tended to rely almost exclusively on stock characterization and clichés. Undoubtedly, the physicians' case studies pressed Tennyson to go beyond the conventional idea that the mad get lost in the "mists of error" and to trace, more precisely, the "errors of the mind" and the consequences of those errors.

This blending of literary and scientific thought, however, was not always to be so graceful. Occasionally a dry medical phrase counteracts the thrust of the lyrical Shelleyan lines of "The Lover's Tale." For instance, in the first part of the poem the phrase "the first moved fibres of the brain" tugs against the context, which is a rich, almost mythic evocation of a happier past. Another instance comes when Julian speaks of waking from a trance as life entered the "avenues of sense" and passed "through into his citadel, the brain." Nowhere, though, do the visionary and clinical elements pull more strongly against each other than in the sequel to "The Lover's Tale." The sequel, based on a tale in Boccaccio's *Decameron*, is called "The Golden Supper" and was written in 1869, over forty years later.[40] Its tone differs considerably from the earlier sections. One reason is that because Julian is "overcome," a narrator must tell the tale. He begins by speaking of Julian's despair and describes the time, several months after the wedding, when Julian refused to honor his need to leave his home so full of sad memories, and followed, instead, an internal "whisper" that cautioned him to "Go not yet." While remaining at home, he learns that Camilla has died. Julian, still mastered by his passion for his cousin, goes to the family vault. Once there he discovers the meaning of the whisper, for when he leans down to kiss Camilla and claim her as his own, he feels her heart beating. The excited Julian rushes her home to her mother, and after helping to nurse her, leaves to travel in the wastelands until he receives the news that she has given birth to Lionel's child. The last and most elaborate portion of "The Golden Supper" is a lush description of the banquet that Julian and the narrator have arranged to stage the melodramatic reunion of Camilla with Lionel, who, believing she is dead, has disappeared. At the banquet the veiled Camilla and her baby make a dramatic entrance and walk among the guests who are amazed and confused, for they, like Lionel, believe she still lies in the family vault. No one knows of her "resurrection." In the last lines of the poem Julian looks wildly on as Camilla, Lionel, and the baby come together and form a family circle. The sight is too much for the unstable Julian. He leaves the hall and he leaves his native land once more, this time "for ever."

Obviously there are problems in "The Golden Supper" because Tennyson wrote it so long after the earlier sections. One is that the sequel is not quite in tune with the first three parts. Many of its problems, however, are related to Tennyson's continuing wish to work within a literary and a scientific context. In the sequel, unfortunately, the two worlds do not complement each other as effectively as in the earlier sections. Instead, the two worlds tend to bring two sets of expectations which compete with one another and create ambiguity. One set of expectations originates from the strong mythic or otherworldly quality in "The Golden Supper," arising from Camilla's miraculous resurrection. Working to enhance this quality are several mythical allusions and the lush language of the narrator. For instance, when the narrator describes what Julian sees when he enters Camilla's tomb, the words echo Keats's "The Eve of St. Agnes" and evoke a mystical, if not Gothic, scene. He saw

> His lady with the moonlight on her face;
> Her breast as in a shadow-prison, bars
> Of black and bands of silver, which the moon
> Struck from an open grating overhead
> High in the wall, and all the rest of her
> Drowned in the gloom and horror of the vault.
>
> [4: 55–61]

The other set of expectations comes from the pointed and nagging reminders that Julian is "overcome" and therefore cannot continue. Throughout the sequel Julian suffers from feverish seizures, acts and reacts excessively, drinks too much, wanders into an unhealthy, melancholic wasteland, and ends his journey in a hostel resembling the scandalous private asylums of Tennyson's age. There Julian raves in the attic and looking like a skeleton becomes an image of his living death.

The problem is that on the one hand the mythic elements of the sequel encourage the reader to trust the narrator's story and believe that Camilla has really been "resurrected," and that on the other hand pointed reminders of Julian's instability elicit quite the opposite reaction. Knowing how accurate Tennyson liked to be, it is difficult not to wonder whether Tennyson intended for the reader to perceive Camilla's return as no more than an hallucination created by Julian's morbid mind. To complicate matters, Tennyson hints that the narrator is not entirely reliable; he too is unstable, for he has traveled through the unhealthy marshes and has come to the "asylum"; he also identifies strongly with Julian. At the end of the sequel he addresses him as "my Julian" and the two leave for the wastelands together. Moreover, the narrator's descriptions can be disturbing. For example, his account of the family reunion unsettles the reader's trust for at first it seems to belong to a legendary splendid world where such experiences are possible and full of happiness, but a second look reveals a reunion replete with images of death: there are kisses that are "half-killing"; there is the cry uttered when Camilla and Lionel come together which "seemed / For some new death than for a life renewed"; there are feelings of "fright" not happiness. Therefore, it is madness, not health, which colors the ending, but not enough to allow the reader to know exactly whether Tennyson intended Camilla's return from the grave to be understood only as a figment of Julian's and the narrator's "errors of mind." The reader is left somewhere in between myth and fact.

*Maud* also has its "ambiguity."[41] Though *Maud* is a tighter poem than "The Lover's Tale," it causes confusion and attracts controversy. The problems originate in the final section in which the lover, now institutionalized, claims he has "awakened, as it seems to the better mind." Because of the hero's claims, a majority of readers are inclined to believe that he has regained his sanity, and they tend to cling to Tennyson's passing claim that at the end of the poem the hero emerges "sane but shattered." They quickly forget he is still "shattered."[42] Among those who wish to believe the hero cured are the nineteenth-century psychiatrists Bucknill and Mann. They consider him recovered and believe he speaks words of "reason." Those like Bucknill and Mann are most willing to think of the hero as being reasonable, but on the other hand are most unwilling to trust what he says. They feel uncomfortable with his words championing the bloody and unpopular Crimean War, and they cannot understand how the peace-loving Tennyson could give the hero such thoughts. Because many critics take the hero's championing of the war literally, they often attack Tennyson and question his intentions.[43] These readers are left feeling ambiguous about *Maud*.

Opposing this majority are a few who believe the hero to be more shattered than sane at the end of the poem. Recently Paul Turner reopened the debate over the championing of the war and joined the few. In making his case, Turner reminds the majority of a letter Tennyson wrote to Archer Gurney on 6 December 1855. In the letter Tennyson speaks of the hero's continuing madness and ridicules those who are not sensitive to this and who think that when the hero speaks "with so little moderation" he is speaking for Tennyson: "I wonder that you and others did not find out that all along the man was intended to have an hereditary vein of insanity, and that he falls foul on the swindling, on the time, because he feels that his father has been killed by the work of the lie, and that all through he fears the coming of madness. How could you or anyone suppose that if I had to speak in my own person my own opinion of this war generally I should have spoken with so little moderation."[44]

The letter to Gurney is helpful in resolving the ambiguity of the ending, but it is not necessary to depend on the letter. Tennyson offers enough clues in the final section to guide the reader and let him understand that the hero is still unstable and is therefore not to be completely trusted. Unlike "The Golden Supper," the ending of *Maud* can be understood in the context of Tennyson's studies of madness and his inclination to be accurate. Here there is no mythic dimension pulling against Tennyson's clinical impulses. Here the clinical impulses are purposefully strong and help direct the reader.

From the beginning of the final section, Tennyson wants his readers to think of the hero as being unstable. Because the hero's mood is changed and because he no longer raves, many have mistakenly thought he has regained his reason. The opposite is true, however, for he still suffers, although quietly, and continues to be irrational. The shift in the hero's mood is typical of many observed by nineteenth-century physicians who, like Allen, pointed out that this shifting is "the most striking characteristic of the insane."[45] To reinforce the sense that his change of mood is not one that catapults the hero back into the rational world and out of his mad cell, Tennyson places this change "at a time of year / When the face of night is fair on the dewy downs, / And the shining daffodil dies, and the Charioteer / And starry Gemini hang like glorious crowns / Over Orion's grave low down in the west" (3: 4–8). According to Allen, who was one of several psychiatrists subscribing to the idea that an alteration in the season affects the patient's mental health, this time of year was fraught with danger, for it "excited" the melancholy "anew . . . especially if the patient has long been worn down."[46] Tennyson is quick to remind the reader that such is the case: the hero "has crept so long on a broken wing / Through cells of madness" (3: 1–2).

Because the lover continues to be unstable, irrational thoughts crowd around him. Among these is his dream of a war—a marvelous war that will support the "glory of manhood," end all tyranny, and bring back a noble world where there is peace, no lusting for money, no misspent ambition. This dream, of course, creates a world that contradicts the one in which the lover has lived and continues to live. It is a world that is free of the greed that ravaged him and his father and that liberates him from his rage. Furthermore, it is a world that resurrects the memory of Maud and her "chivalrous ballad-song" that had praised "men that in battle array, / Ready in heart and ready in hand, / March with banner and bugle and fife / To the death, for their native land" (1: 169–72). The lover longs for that world as he had yearned to be one of those valiant men and to be glorified by Maud.

When the dream ends, he hears the cannon "booming from the battle-ships at Sole," and his morbid mind mistakenly associates the dream's glorious and chivalrous battles with the Crimean War. Longing so for peace of mind and for a nation not overrun by Mammon, the hero imposes the expectations created by his dream on the war and champions it. His ecstatic description of the Crimean War is an elaborate example of what many psychiatrists called "castle building." It is one of many hallucinations that characterize the unstable; it is spurred on by faulty associations and mad memories. These "errors of mind" create an ending that is illusory, still "mad," and despairing.

As the convention of madness allows, however, madmen speak truth. Therefore, there is as much truth inherent in the lover's desperate act as there is illusion. The truth is that the lover is meant to be correct in castigating the materialism of the age. As we have seen, Tennyson had little patience with the scandals featured at the beginning of the poem, and he felt bitter toward the greed that had affected his family; consequently, he uses the hero to attack these enemies. Tennyson also meant for there to be a flicker of truth in the lover's championing of war as a purge. So despairing is Tennyson of the moral climate that he shares the lover's exasperation; he, too, wonders if the present climate does not create a scene more warlike than war itself; he shares the hero's hope, however unrealistic, that war will elicit in Englishmen a stronger sense of solidarity with, and of responsibility toward, one another and so lead them to eliminate these evils. But there is a difference. Tennyson is not content, as some critics would have him, to remain with the lover here and wish for a "war with a thousand battles, and shaking a hundred thrones." Unlike the lover, he knows that these are the dreams and words of a morbid individual and therefore must be qualified. They are not the absolute truth. Readers must not let the shadows of truth cloud their vision nor believe the hero too much. Readers must not forget that even though the hero is less manic at the end, he is, like Julian, an outsider, and, like Julian, he will probably travel through the melancholic landscape again. Indeed, Tennyson was to journey there again. The wastelands and madness in "The Lover's Tale" and *Maud* reappear in the *Idylls of the King* and in poems that continue to study character and explore others tyrannized by ruling passions. Throughout these poems, Tennyson's clinical and poetic impulses still are present and are working together to help him portray the mad personae.

## Chapter Five

# Madness as Metaphor and the *Idylls of the King*

any of Tennyson's contemporaries were convinced that they were living in a country and in an age literally madder than all others. In the popular mind England and insanity were all too frequent companions. The physician Alfred Beaumont Maddock was one of many to register alarm. In 1854 he wrote that "in no other country, compared with England, do we find such numerous and formidable examples of this extensive scourge."[1] Later Tennyson's Dr. Matthew Allen also remarked on the nation's poor health. Alluding to the common belief, he wrote: "It need scarcely be mentioned, that the present constitution of society is not in a healthy state. . . . Discord and disseverment prevail to an extent which seem to threaten its decomposition and destruction."[2] For all of these believers the metaphor of madness touched a sensitive spot and must have seemed as much a reality as a poetic device.

Of all the poems demonstrating Tennyson's sensitivity to his contemporaries' sense of England's unhealthy state, none illustrates it more thoroughly and indeed more anxiously than the *Idylls of the King*. Here Tennyson resurrects the legendary Camelot to expose simultaneously the forces threatening contemporary England's moral fiber and the excesses enslaving the minds of the nation's inhabitants. Because of the link he sees between personal and national aberrations, Tennyson deliberately chooses not to reproduce any of the king's twelve grand battles. Rather, he chooses to reconstruct the smaller, grittier, nastier, internal battles that propel Arthur's kingdom toward destruction. The blows of these battles are blows to the head, to the mind. The battles are personal and internal as well as national.[3] Throughout the poem, therefore, Tennyson confronts those excesses that created the monomaniacal lovers, the obsessive and tyrannical fathers, the revolutionary mobs, and, worst of all, civilizations mastered by lust. Also before him is his understanding of madness and how it attacks the mind. That knowledge serves as a paradigm for analyzing the collapse of the nation's health. Camelot is, in fact, a macrocosm of a mind laboring under the tyranny of one idea. Conversely, the morbid mind is a microcosm of a diseased England.

To describe England's unhealthy state Tennyson does not depend only on his scientific understanding of madness. He is also aware of the heritage of the madness metaphor. This metaphor and this heritage give him a means of addressing his fears and of writing about sexual excesses, wild enthusiasts, and people driven mad by ambition. Moreover, the metaphor reinforces the tragedy of the fall of Camelot and exposes those responsible for it. These are the people who are not only subject to their passions but also subject to their deceitful dreams, which cause them to misapprehend the world. Finally, the metaphor of madness serves as a vivid emblem of the nation's increasing moral inadequacy.

It is not surprising that when writing the *Idylls* Tennyson utilized the metaphor of madness as well as his clinical knowledge of it, for as we have seen Tennyson could never regard madness solely from a clinical perspective. Throughout his poetry madness is literary as well as clinical. For example, in *Maud* the hero is at once a patient belonging to a nineteenth-century case study and a mad lover belonging to a literary tradition that often featured those who suffer from a thwarted, single-minded adoration. Because Tennyson was familiar with literary portraits of madness, he could not overlook their metaphoric function. Even in a poem as clinically accurate as *Maud*, the madness is not merely present for its own sake; rather, it allows Tennyson to describe the horrors resulting from the nation's unhealthy regard for Mammon and the travesties attached to the sheer "lunacy" of sacrificing children, love, and moral principles to greed. And, as it had for innumerable writers in preceding generations, madness underscores the hero's tragic confusion.

*Maud*, of course, is not the only poem in which Tennyson shows his sensitivity to madness as a literary metaphor. In "The Flight" (1836), "The Wreck" (1855), and in "Aylmer's Field" (1862), for instance, madness functions metaphorically to expose and heighten the suffering of those tyrannized by Mammon-worshipping parents, who for the sake of an economically and socially advantageous marriage deny their children love and disrupt the moral order. Before going on to discuss at length the function of madness in the *Idylls*, it will be helpful to review Tennyson's use of the metaphor of madness in these shorter poems. In "The Flight" and "The Wreck" Tennyson demonstrates the wickedness of arranged, mercenary marriages by letting their victims speak of the immorality and suffering that result. They speak of mercenary fathers who are tyrant vassals "of a tyrant vice" ("The Flight," l. 25), and they speak of their own madness, their burning temples and their "oft-wandering mind" ("The Wreck," l. 130). The madness in these poems not only magnifies the tragic consequences of the parents' failings but also punishes those parents for their immorality. The most extreme and melodramatic example of this madness comes in "Aylmer's Field" when Tennyson uses insanity to dramatize and damn Sir Aylmer's greed, a greed that drives his daughter Edith mad, causes Lionel, her socially inferior lover, to commit suicide, turns his wife into an hysteric "confined to a couch of fire," and in the end drives himself, raving, into an asylum—a fitting punishment given the metaphorical context and the continuing literary tradition that prompted many of Tennyson's contemporaries to castigate such offenders by driving them mad.[4]

The metaphor in these poems, however, has a value for Tennyson beyond its conventional task of mirroring despair and disorder and of doling out punishment. The metaphor also offers Tennyson the opportunity of safely encountering reality. In the poems mentioned above, for instance, it allows him to speak of his own traumas suffered at the hands of those who discriminated against him because of their regard for Mammon. And it also allows him to speak of these matters without risking writing a poem that is either too autobiographical or too removed from his readers' experiences. The metaphor diffuses the private nature of the poem by attaching his experiences to those of many who were familiar with the metaphor and who, like Carlyle, felt threatened by a pervasive and inordinate regard for wealth at the expense of moral principles.

That these poems are personal should be clear from earlier discussions of Tennyson's emotional difficulties. Because of the circumstances surrounding his father's disinheritance, Tennyson, at times, felt as desperate and as thwarted, and indeed as maddened, as the confused lovers in these poems. He, like his father, was affected by the disinheritance. Because he lacked position and wealth, he too was subjected to those who champion Mammon. For example, as Ralph Rader and, more recently, Robert Martin have pointed out, Tennyson suffered considerably when Rosa Baring's father put an end to their relationship because of the Tennysons' inferior financial and social status.[5] In addition, there is evidence that Tennyson also felt angry and chaotic when Arthur Henry Hallam's father opposed his family's relationship with the less prosperous Tennysons. Experiences like these, especially in the early 1840s, brought Tennyson close to a breakdown. These traumas were so pressing that they necessarily formed the subject matter of these poems about greedy parents, thwarted love, and subsequent breakdowns. Since Rader's discussion of *Maud*, for example, it is clear that Tennyson's frustrations over his affair with Rosa Baring served as a nucleus of that poem and, by extension, "The Flight" and "The Wreck." The affair and the Barings' resistance to the union, though, are only implicit in these poems. The metaphor protects the privacy by offering Tennyson a ready-made vocabulary and structure in which to address the affair and to encounter the subsequent periods of depression and hysteria. Moreover, the very conventional nature of the metaphor allows him to move these intimate and painful interludes into the public arena with little fear of exposing his personal difficulties with the Barings or his own chaotic state of mind. Paradoxically, then, the metaphor simultaneously exposes the personal instability and shelters it. Personae emerge which originate in Tennyson's own traumas but which, because they are transposed into the familiar by the metaphor, cease to be purely personal. They are instead a unique blend of scientific fact, literary convention, and personal and national traumas.

Naturally, madness as it functions metaphorically in Tennyson's poetry addresses more than his impatience with people's dangerous regard for Mammon. Building on perhaps the most familiar and certainly the most tenacious of the literary conventions associated with madness, Tennyson often couples insanity with "unbridled passion" and lust. "Lucretius" (1868), a poem based on the legend of Lucretius's death, offers an example of this coupling. In this poem Tennyson charts in detail the deterioration of Lucretius's mind after his frustrated wife gives him a love potion that is more powerful than she expects. It arouses the beast within him and kills any power he might possess to subdue or rule the resulting sexual passion. In the end, disgusted and unbalanced by his overwhelming lust and believing he can never find "passionless tranquility," Lucretius commits suicide. Even though there are moments in the poem when Tennyson satisfies his need to be clinical and consequently describes how the wife's love potion "confused the chemic labour of the blood" and "made havock among those tender cells" (ll. 20–23), there are many more moments when Tennyson satisfies his compulsion to explore the metaphorical function of Lucretius's instability. Tennyson uses madness so he can dramatically display Lucretius's fall and the rise of the unchecked brute brain. He uses madness to express his utter disgust at the power of the bestial nature to overthrow the noble Lucretius. As it had for him in *Maud*, the metaphor allows him to express his disgust in a public and acceptable idiom. His contemporaries, of course, were well versed in the ancient image of "unbridled passion" and immersed in their own practice of linking dissipation to madness and suicide. Victorian novels and melodramas were all too well populated with characters in a frenzy or a stupor because of an overwhelming, reckless passion.[6]

It is important that Tennyson have this metaphor, for sexual passion, particularly for him, was fraught with an anxiety far surpassing that attached to his fears concerning Mammon worship. As several critics have noted, one of the most active forces governing Tennyson's life and work is his distrust of the flesh, of human sexuality, a distrust so strong that in the guise of Lucretius he can do little more than gasp at the sight of the lustful satyr, "I hate, abhor, spit, sicken at him." Tennyson was convinced that given an opportunity, the bestial nature would rise to the surface and quickly disturb a person's equilibrium. He was all too willing to equate the satyr with sexuality and madness. Because of these fears, throughout his life he found it difficult to feel comfortable with any sort of passion or sensual pleasure. For example, as a youth he wrote "The Passions" (1827) and uneasily explored the passions' power to enslave and destroy. That uneasiness never disappeared, for later he dramatized the decline of victims of sensual excess like the sailors in "The Lotos-Eaters" (1832) and the dissolute company in "The Vision of Sin" (1842). Much later he couched his unease in the comical "Spinster's Sweet-Arts" (1885) by creating the portrait of a happy, eccentric spinster who, because she has not given in to her "brute brain," has avoided the tragic end that the passionate and sinful "Black Sal" met.

With this sensibility it is not surprising that Tennyson was so often attracted to the moralistic melodramas and novels of his period and to Ann Radcliffe's cautionary words from *The Mysteries of Udolpho*, words that would stick in his mind and preface his early poem "The Passions": "You have passions in your heart—scorpions; they sleep now—beware how you awaken them! they will sting you even to death." Tennyson must have remembered these words when a series of national acts exacerbated his anxiety and verified his sense of a growing, unhealthy sexual freedom. These acts authorized the establishment of the divorce courts in 1857 and the attempts, beginning in 1866, to legalize marriage with a deceased wife's sister. These acts went hand in hand with numerous studies on prostitution in the 1830s, with the success of Swinburne's sex-centered *Poems and Ballads* (1866), and with the popularity (beginning in the 1830s) of what was known as "the literature of prostitution." This literature had caught the attention of those anxious about "unprofitable reading" and those whom Walter E. Houghton identifies as being acutely aware of "unbridled sensuality."[7] Tennyson referred to that literature as "the thoughts of Zolaism" ("Locksley Hall Sixty Years After," l. 145).

As might be expected, because the metaphor of madness helps Tennyson address moral dilemmas, it also aids him in writing his political poems. The phenomenon is not surprising. As can be discovered in a survey of literary madness, throughout the history of literature writers have often called on madness and its accompanying confusion to capture the chaos of civil strife, the frenzy of battle, the lawlessness of revolution, and the foolishness of lawmakers and leaders. Consequently, when Tennyson injects phrases like war's "mad blasts" into his poems and when he speaks of the "maddening strife" and "maddening shouts" of battle, he is participating in a well-practiced convention. However, there is a difference, for he is employing the metaphor at a time when his reading public is more sensitive than usual to its truth. Well versed in the classical tradition with its practice of equating war and political chaos with madness, and all too familiar with Swift's use of madness to satirize political follies, Tennyson's contemporaries were already attracted to the metaphor and used it to address their growing concern over their nation's faltering mental health. In fact, such was the metaphor's popularity that cartoons in *Punch* and newspaper accounts of disturbing national events and deviations from the status quo frequently drew on it.

Tennyson shared fears about the nation's health, and, like others, tended to blame much of the nation's insanity on the behavior of individuals. Convinced that one could not exist without the other, he stressed the interrelation between personal and national aberrations. Part of his willingness to see this connection came from the support he received from those like Maddock and Allen, but much of it also came from the literary metaphor that set a precedent for it. The Jacobean drama, for instance, to which Tennyson was attracted, is full of examples of intertwined personal and national madness. Tennyson had only to recall the madness and mad masques in *The Duchess of Malfi*, *'Tis Pity She's a Whore*, and *The Changeling* to find examples.

Because Tennyson is sensitive to the interrelation between personal and national aberrations, he sees the mad excesses of the French Revolution and the wild behavior of the rick-burning peasants terrorizing the Cambridge countryside as extensions of personal appetites which have not been checked but have been allowed to gain the upper hand. In a manner that finds its parallel in the equation of political chaos and madness in Charles Dickens's *Barnaby Rudge* and in Thomas Carlyle's *The French Revolution*, Tennyson in "The Vision of Sin" parallels the company's sensual liberties and destructive actions with the frenzied actions of the civil libertarians who are "roaring" for freedom. In "Aylmer's Field" he suggests a similar parallel when he equates the tyrannical personality of Sir Aylmer and the resulting horrors of the chaos and tragedy during the reign of terror: Sir Aylmer with his "hoary" hair and ravenous greed is as much a wolf as those wolves said to have prowled on the shores of France, eating the revolution's victims. The parallel continues when Tennyson writes that the only marriage left to the dead Edith and Lionel is one similar to those shocking unions left to dead men and women who during the Reign of Terror were tied naked together and wrapped in "ghastly" sacks. "Lucretius" also draws a parallel between personal and public excesses. In this poem, Tennyson asks the reader to regard the wife's action and its effect on Lucretius as being similar to those vile actions of an undisciplined democracy. Both bring anarchy and madness. The inferior wife's careless act and her wish to master the noble Lucretius are analogous to a frightening democracy in which the base "crowds that in an hour of civic tumult" overthrow "the best and stateliest of the land."[8]

Not only did Tennyson find precedents for the parallels in the literary metaphor of madness, but also in his preoccupation with and the Victorians' fear of monomania, a fear that also complemented the metaphor. In Tennyson's mind England is similar to those fictional lovers and sinners who are tyrannized by a mastering passion. England is just as clogged by its tyrannical passions and accumulated poisons. The mad city or kingdom and the mad man are inseparable. For example, in the germ of *Maud*, "Oh That 'twere Possible!" the city's yellow choking vapors are more than a picture of the smoke coming from the factories—the monuments to Mammon. They are also those internal vapors (associated with melancholy in Burton's *Anatomy*) which clog people's organs and pollute their minds, trapping them in a "yellow" or melancholic mood—a mood, of course, which quickly alters its character and becomes monomaniacal.

Tennyson's sense of a nation suffering from monomania was encouraged not only by the definitions of madness but also by the increasing interest of psychiatrists and the informed public in mob psychology. They were fascinated with epidemics of madness and the power of the mob or violence to capture the mind. They translated French studies on the epidemics of the Middle Ages and they investigated the revolutions of their own time. At the turn of the eighteenth century, Benjamin Rush's studies on the behavioral consequences of the American Revolution and Philippe Pinel's studies on the excesses of the French Revolution caught people's interest.[9] More and more people agreed with their conclusion that revolution and political upheaval caused insanity. They agreed with Pinel that the storm of revolution stirred up the "corresponding tempests in the passions of men, and overwhelmed not a few in total ruin of their distinguished birthright as rational beings."[10] By 1828 these conclusions were acceptable enough for George Man Burrows to announce confidently: "Great political or civil revolutions in states are always productive of great enthusiasm in the people, and correspondent vicissitudes in their moral condition; and as all extremes in society are exciting causes, it will occur, that in proportion as the feelings are acted upon, so will insanity be more or less frequent."[11]

Because Tennyson shared in the public's fear that England and its subjects had lost control and had become slaves to their passions, it is not surprising that when he wrote the *Idylls* he made use of madness in his characters, and its infectious spread through the kingdom, as a metaphor for the breakdown of order and as the fatal genesis of that collapse. Madness is to be expected in a poem that anxiously explores the ruin of the nation's morality and, thus, its sanity. It is also not surprising that in the *Idylls* he uses madness as he does in his other poetry to mirror despair, disorder, inordinate passion, and civil chaos. Indeed the metaphor of madness is most appropriate, for not only is there precedent for it in Tennyson's poetry and in the treatises concerning the nation's "insanity," but also in the public's familiarity with the metaphor. For them as well as for Tennyson madness was familiar as a metaphor of disorder and as a real threat. Madness is a most appropriate gauge of the fall of Camelot.

Because madness plays such a vital role in Tennyson's vision of the fall, and because it allows him to link his fears to his sense of the nation's distress, it emerges as a binding, central force in the *Idylls*.[12] As a result, the *Idylls* is Tennyson's most extensive inquiry into madness as a reality and madness as a metaphor. With such a concentrated use of the metaphor, contrary to what many might expect, the *Idylls* exceeds even *Maud* in its exploration of madness. The madness in the poem as it appeared in its final, published form (1883) should be considered at length.[13]

Significantly, when the *Idylls* opens, madness belongs to the past. For the moment, it is conquered, and all is held in balance. Soon, however, as the realm begins to deteriorate, all kinds of madness appear and infect the inhabitants of Camelot. The insanity extends far beyond that usually associated with Lancelot, Balin, and Pelleas. In the end it seems even to reach King Arthur. He leaves Camelot in "confusion."

The first idyll, "The Coming of Arthur," opens with multiple and conflicting accounts of the king's birth, the variety of which immediately suggests that the king is born with a multiple inheritance: he is born of anger, passion, bitterness, sweetness, nobility, and love.[14] With this inheritance, he emerges as a person who contains within him the bestial and the noble passions. He is at once baseborn and sublime or "more than man." Initially as king he unites and controls these warring elements so that he and his kingdom are balanced. He and "his knighthood for a space / Were all one will" (ll. 514–15). They draw in "the petty princedoms" so that all function harmoniously. Moreover, because he can balance these passions, he is able to transform the "great tracts of wilderness / Wherein the beast was ever more and more, / But men less and less" (ll. 10–12) into an orderly society. No longer do the wolves roam his land and devour children; no longer do the children fall victim to the beastly and excessive passions of their forebears. To complete the harmony, Arthur marries, an act that is necessary in the minds of Tennyson and his contemporaries who, despite certain fears for those with a predisposition to madness, maintain that few are whole without marriage and without uniting the masculine and feminine elements of their character.[15] The marriage as a representation of this wholeness, however, cannot last long in the *Idylls*, for already the seething passions are surfacing and tyrannizing the kingdom and the citizens. Even in this first idyllic section there are hints of the evil lurking below and the madness waiting to break out, for Gawain bursts into song and wildly dashes about while Modred eavesdrops hoping to find a means of overthrowing the king (ll. 319–24).

In the second idyll, "Gareth and Lynette," order continues to dominate, but the challenge posed to that order or sanity by the bestial passions becomes slightly more visible. As yet, though, neither the individual inhabitants of Camelot nor Camelot itself is overwhelmed and maddened by the baser instincts as Lucretius was. The mood throughout the idyll is idealistic. It is replete with allusions to a fairy-tale world where wishes come true and with proclamations or evidence of Gareth's faith in King Arthur's court. Gareth's innocence within such a world allows him to overcome potentially treacherous moments. Later, however, Tennyson will tip Gareth's innocence upside down and place his faith within the context of a fallen world that does not even have the benefit of the virtues and illusions belonging to the fairy tale.

This second idyll opens with affectionate banter between Gareth and his mother and with his telling the story of the goose and the golden eggs. Through the telling of the story, Gareth disarms his mother's objections to his leaving home for Camelot. In leaving, Gareth turns his back on a life of idleness (his weak father's life), always so dangerous in Tennyson's mind, and goes forward. When Gareth comes to the gates of Camelot his companions are frightened. Armed with his innocence and idealistic faith, Gareth is not bothered by the shadowy, illusory movements that meet him as he enters Camelot, or by the riddle of the king's birth that has no answer (ll. 184–231). He enters "with all good cheer." Believing in Arthur's order of the Knights of the Round Table, he willingly takes the difficult vows "Of utter hardihood, utter gentleness, / And, loving, utter faithfulness in love, / And uttermost obedience to the King" (ll. 542–44). By believing in and becoming a vassal to Arthur's order, he is able to combat the excessively proud and nasty prodding of Lynette, to overcome the four destructive knights, to survive his journey through the maddening mire, to save the baron, and, in the end, with Lancelot's help, to save the "blooming boy" from a death in life. He controls pride, despair, savagery, doubt, peril, lawlessness, insanity, the passions, and the temptations met in the various stages of life. His victories over the "wronger of the Realm" are the conquests of Arthur's ideal soul. They mirror the king's judicious hold over the realm which Gareth has witnessed in Arthur's court. Gareth's victories are analogous to Arthur's victories over himself, for even he must control his base inheritance (he is "baseborn") which periodically threatens to unseat him. For example, when the widow of Arthur's enemy requests his aid, the king's tense reply reflects his inner turmoil. Control, however, wins:

> "We sit King, to help the wronged
> Through all our realm. The woman loves her lord.
> Peace to thee, woman, with thy loves and hates!
> The kings of old had doomed thee to the flames,
> Aurelius Emrys would have scourged thee dead,
> And Uther slit thy tongue: but get thee hence—
> Lest that rough humour of the kings of old
> Return upon me!"
>
> > [ll. 363–70]

This power, though, is possible only in an innocent, fairyland setting. As Tennyson knew only too well, the shadows and riddles of one's inheritance always threatened to disrupt even the best situations.

Beginning in the next idyll, "The Marriage of Geraint," the ideal state begins to totter. The wise Merlin's warning that Gareth is passing into a city where "the King / Will bind thee by such vows, as is a shame / A man should not be bound by, yet that which / No man can keep" ("Gareth and Lynette," ll. 265–67) contains truth. These vows are the ideal, and, in reality, they are impossible. People are normally more vulnerable than Gareth was. As people and a nation progress in life, from their morning to their evening, they are going to meet with conflict; they fall into battle with the mire of despair, lust, pride, anger, and anarchy; and many are going to become victims of these vices. It will not always be possible to rescue the child from death or madness; to save the innocent or nobler self from the darker, deadlier self. It will not always be possible to fall and laugh as Gareth has done:

> And Gareth crying pricked against the cry;
> But when they closed—in a moment—at one touch
> Of that skilled spear, the wonder of the world—
> Went sliding down so easily, and fell,
> That when he found the grass within his hands
> He laughed.
>
> > ["Gareth and Lynette," ll. 1191–95]

In the future idylls madness will become a more immediate and ominous threat. It will not be dismissed as quickly as it is in this second idyll, where madness is a word used lightly and where it is as illusory as the knight who is the Star of Evening. Gareth's fight with that "madman" is long, but Gareth wins. In the future such struggles with madness will be harder. Once a person is touched by its lawlessness, rarely will he regain order. Balin will return to the court and be reprieved, but his sanity is only to be temporary. The nation too will not recover from its infliction. From "The Marriage of Geraint" on, Tennyson describes how many lose these battles, how many tumble and become lost in the mire of their tyrannizing passions. Neither the people nor the nation can break their habits and release their saner selves.

The long, hot summer, the season for madness and the heat of excessive passion, begins in the next two idylls, "The Marriage of Geraint" and "Geraint and Enid," when Lancelot's and Guinevere's sexual passion for one another has begun to gain control. No longer can their affair be kept secret. Rumors spread, and with those rumors corruption extends from the two lovers to many in Arthur's court. Their effect on the court is very much tied to Tennyson's discomfort with and distrust of sexual passion. No passion is as contaminating as theirs; it too easily destroys the mind's and the nation's delicate balance, too frequently rouses the monster madness from its sleep. Because Lancelot and Guinevere have not repressed their lust, they and others will weaken and become more vulnerable to other excesses. Geraint is the first to be sullied and victimized by their affair. Before learning of their "guilty love" (ll. 24–28) Geraint has exhibited "exceeding manfulness / And pure nobility of temperament" (ll. 211–12), but afterward he fears he is effeminate, dashes madly into the wilderness, and distorts what he hears. He has lost control of the delicate relation between his masculine and feminine qualities, which, of course, the ideal King Arthur exhibits. Now the knowledge of Guinevere's and Lancelot's passion transforms Geraint's moments of splenetic behavior (as when he shouted at the armorer and "flashed into sudden spleen") into a prolonged, mad fury; it transforms his effeminate tendencies (his wearing of the long purple scarf with the gold apple dangling from it) into impotency; and it turns his scrupulous attention to his wife's deportment and clothing into a dangerous obsession, and, finally, into a sexual fantasy. Because of Guinevere's sin, the fear envelops him "lest his gentle wife, / Through that great tenderness for Guinevere" (ll. 29–30) become as tainted as she. Like the mad lovers in case studies and those belonging to the literary convention, Geraint's mind is seized by one mastering thought, causing him to distort all that goes on around him. To give a sense of just how deeply Geraint is trapped by his unhealthy obsession, Tennyson repeats phrases and locks them into an obsessive pattern. For example, when Geraint madly refuses to leave Enid's side, Tennyson uses the trapped syntax to speak of the consequences. Geraint grows

> Forgetful of his promise to the king,
> Forgetful of the falcon and the hunt,
> Forgetful of the tilt and tournament,
> Forgetful of his glory and his name,
> Forgetful of his princedom and its cares.
>
> [ll. 48–54]

The consequences of Geraint's monomania are almost fatal. His excessive anger, pride, jealousy, and fear fight to rule him. Under their domain, losing his grip on reality, Geraint mistakes his wife's motives, deceives King Arthur, talks to himself, and babbles to others. He is an example of those who "Do forge a life-long trouble for [themselves], / By taking true for false, or false for true" ("Geraint and Enid," ll. 3–4). Geraint's excesses lead him to those "Gray swamps and pools, waste places of the hern, / And wildernesses, perilous paths" (ll. 31–32)—wild places that complement the chaos, danger, and barrenness of his sick mind. Like any truly sick person he vacillates between wrath and despair, between irrationality and rationality. In the more rational moments, Geraint and Enid come to a smoother landscape, a meadow cared for by mowers. But even there Geraint displays excessive behavior—an indication of his continuing unbalanced state. Without realizing it he ravenously consumes all the mowers' food; and then, when he understands what he has done, he overpays them "fifty fold." Later he pays the host with "five horses and their armours," a payment that the amazed host admits is equal to five times the cost of a room at his inn.

Geraint's appetite and payments are as out of proportion as his judgment. His monomania affects not only his "appetite" but also his sense of the world around him. He rides "as if he heard not"; he hears only half, as when waking from his sleep to catch the last few words of his wife's speech. Sometimes he neither hears nor sees. Enid must do that for him. She says: "I hear the violent threats you do not hear, / I see the danger which you cannot see" ("Geraint and Enid," ll. 420–21). In the end, lawlessness nearly overwhelms Geraint. His excesses lead him to the Earl of Doorm's wasteland. Here the "wild Limours" attacks "all in a passion uttering a dry shriek." Although Geraint stuns this mad lover, he receives a terrible wound. He totters. Losing his balance, he falls from his horse. The struggle with Limours, though, is a turning point for Geraint. He begins to find a way out of his living death, to release himself from the lawless lord's estate—a realm resembling an asylum. Among its inhabitants are a man-at-arms "half whistling and half singing a coarse song" and another "flying from the wrath of Doorm / Before an ever-fancied arrow" (ll. 522–32).

It is logical that Limours unbalances Geraint, for Limours's excessive passion for Enid mirrors Geraint's and, furthermore, comments on Guinevere and Lancelot's affair. His fate mirrors what Geraint's might have been if Enid had not kept her husband in touch with reality. Limours has become "wild" because he is completely subjected to his own sensations. There is no one to help him hear or see, he says, except "Enid, the pilot star of my lone life, / Enid, my early and my only love, / Enid, the loss of whom hath turned me wild—" (ll. 306–8). Geraint survives only because he is cared for by Enid, a person who shields her head from the sinful sun and the fires of madness, who shuns "the wild ways of the lawless tribe." Governed by moderation, she refuses to eat and partici-pate in Geraint's lawless appetite, and can therefore protect him. Even-tually with Enid's help Geraint's manliness and balance return. The earl slaps Enid, and her cries for help awaken and arouse Geraint's masculin-ity. He takes his sword, an emblem of Arthur's order, and "with a sweep of it / Shore through the swarthy neck" of the Earl of Doorm. The taking of the sword is an act by which Geraint simultaneously regains his sanity and his masculinity.

With harmony restored, Geraint and Enid can now mount the same horse and ride together back to King Arthur's court, where the king's reigning order promises to nurse Geraint back to health. In the court an image of restored inner harmony awaits them. Edyrn, who had believed himself "well-nigh mad," is now, in Arthur's words, "One of the no-blest, our most Valorous, / Sanest and most obedient" knights (ll. 909–10). Unfortunately, though, the court is no longer a perfect place. The restored harmony is not secure. Experience has broken the innocence, and Enid realizes that governed passion may soon erupt to tyrannize once more. When she meets Edyrn and remembers his former, destructive self, she cannot help shrinking "a little." As Tennyson adds: "In a hollow land, / From which old fires have broken, men may fear / Fresh fire and ruin" (ll. 820–22)—an autobiographical statement from Tennyson, who periodically had seen madness break out and threaten to consume him and his family; and, moreover, a poignant statement for his contempo-raries, who had feared that the horrors of the French Revolution and the chaos of brutal democracy might break out on English soil and upset the nation's delicate balance.

Enid fears more than Edyrn. She also lives in horror of the "bandits scattered in the field." Although Geraint seems to be whole again, and although the Earl of Doorm is dead, the earl's lawless followers, like the rumors of Guinevere and Lancelot's affair, are very much alive, although scattered. Geraint too is suspicious. He can "never take again / That comfort from" Enid's and Guinevere's "converse which he took / Before the Queen's fair name was breathed upon" (ll. 948–50). Shadows also hover over the king's justice. There is still a belief that man and nation can "repent," but now that belief is qualified. Significantly, Arthur is not blind to the difficulties:

> "The world will not believe a man repents:
> And this wise world of ours is mainly right.
> Full seldom doth a man repent, or use
> Both grace and will to pick the vicious quitch
> Of blood and custom wholly out of him,
> And make all clean, and plant himself afresh.
>                                     [ll. 899–904]

All these fears, suspicions, shadows, and qualifications seem to be Tennyson's attempt to show how easy it is to doubt. Like Arthur, Tennyson worries about that doubt. He wants people to hold on to their idealism and beliefs, for without them the Limours and the lawless bandits of Doorm will turn civilization into a wild place. Doubting brings people closer to their madness. It causes people to neglect the task of weeding out their evil passions. Like Yniol, Enid's father, they stand idly by allowing their kingdoms to topple over from disuse; they stand there in old and rusty arms, tyrannized like Edyrn, who if only given the chance to live under Arthur's order can be made sane again.

The hot summer and the fevers of madness continue to blast through "Balin and Balan." They bring with them a confusion more perilous than that in the previous idylls. People's doubts, wrath, pride, and lust are more lethal than ever. Moreover, what Enid and Tennyson had feared comes true. The old fires break out afresh and consume. Only for a while does Balin find inner harmony, but all too soon the anger and "outer fiends," which his brother Balan had begged him to control, rage. He cannot recover his sanity as Edyrn and Geraint had. In "middle May," the season of madness, Balin fights "hard with himself" to repress his moods but cannot. He vows, "I will be gentle," but fails. He kills his brother and falls into despair, crying "My violences, my violences!"

Throughout this idyll Balin's struggle to control his violence is his quest. He desperately wants to heed his brother's warning, so he accepts Arthur's invitation to "walk with me, and move / To music with thine Order and the King" (ll. 72–74), and he tries to "learn what Arthur meant by courtesy, / Manhood, and knighthood" (ll. 155–56). Neither the invitation nor the lesson is strong enough to destroy the disorder threatening Balin's stability. Already the king's order is slipping away. Balin ends up going on a journey that takes him the very opposite of where he wishes to go. Ironically, instead of keeping him within Arthur's promised order, Balin's quest leads him away from Camelot into the chaotic wilderness filled with hallucinations—a sure sign of insanity. His flight from court horrifyingly echoes the maddened figure in the previous idyll, who stumbled through the lawless woods "flying from the wrath of Doorm / Before an ever-fancied arrow" ("Geraint and Enid," ll. 530–31). Balin's madness is similar:

> He felt the hollow-beaten mosses thud
> And tremble, and then the shadow of a spear,
> Shot from behind him, ran along the ground.
> Sideways he started from the path, and saw,
> With pointed lance as if to pierce, a shape,
> A light of armour by him flash, and pass
> And vanish in the woods; and followed this,
> But all so blind in rage that unawares
> He burst his lance against a forest bough,
> Dishorsed himself, and rose again.
>
> [ll. 316–25]

Eventually he falls under the power of King Pellam, the enemy of order, who will not pay tribute to Arthur's court. Balin can no longer bridle his passion, so his horse does not carry him back to Camelot as Gareth and Enid's had. Instead it crushes him. When Balin falls from his horse there is no laughter. That was possible only in Geraint's fairy-tale world. Death replaces not only laughter, but also marriage and the future promise concluding the previous idylls. Balin and Balan die tyrannized by madness. As Balin admits, "My madness all thy life has been thy doom, / Thy curse, and darkened all thy day; and now / The night has come" (ll. 608–10).

Once more Guinevere's and Lancelot's lust has tipped the balance, for Balin lost control after the shock of overhearing the queen and her lover's amorous conversation in the garden. The shock of his discovery unleashes his madness. He gives in to its fury, blaming his inheritance from an angry father, and turns his back on Arthur's court.

The queen's guilty passion, however, is not the only root of Balin's madness. Despair and unwillingness to have complete faith in Arthur's order also unbalance him. Both conspire to destroy his trust. Balin fears: "Too high this mount of Camelot for me: / These high-set courtesies are not for me" (ll. 221–22). Like his anger, his doubts distort his judgment. He chooses to follow not only shadows, as Geraint did, but also shadows of shadows. Believing that to become one of Arthur's knights is "beyond

*my* reach," he mistakenly and single-mindedly champions Guinevere as
an image of purity and order: "'No shadow' said Sir Balin 'O my Queen, /
But light to me! no shadow, O my King, / But golden earnest of a gen-
tler life!'" (ll. 202–4). His delusion and his single-mindedness bring their
own madness, creating more confusion. Despite Sir Garlon's scorn of
Guinevere's purity, Balin insists she is the "fairest, best and purest." Later,
despite Vivien's blatant distortion of Guinevere and Lancelot's garden
conversation, Balin believes her account is the truth. Vivien's "truth" is
yet another blow to his chaotic mind. Once more the shock excites his
madness. Emitting a "weird yell, / Unearthlier than all shriek of bird or
beast" (ll. 535–36), Balin goes wild. His brother believes the shriek to be
that of the "wood-devil I came to quell." In a moment of utter chaos the
brothers do not recognize each other and attack. Indeed Balin has momentarily turned into a wood-devil: "his evil spirit upon him leapt, / He
ground his teeth together, sprang with a yell, / Tore from the branch,
and cast on earth, the shield" (ll. 529–31). But his death is not the death
of the demon in the woods. The real demons are left to scatter like the
lawless lords, "to dwell among the woods" and bring destruction and
madness closer to the center of Arthur's order. Vivien with her "truth"
is the real wood-devil, not Balin. From this moment on, the survivors
are the destroyers.

In the next idyll, "Merlin and Vivien," Balin's disorderly world creeps
closer to Camelot, for despair, passion, and madness attack Merlin, the
very architect of the order. Like a cancer, the warring passions are mul-
tiplying and gradually overtaking the individual's healthy soul and that
of the nation. In this idyll Vivien is a demon driven by her lust and pride.
She pursues Merlin into the woods, where she wears down his resistance
to her sensuous touch and entangles him in his own lust and weaknesses.
She leaves him trapped within the walls of a hollow tower, locked within
the cells of madness, useless, and tyrannized by his passion. Merlin has
allowed "the meanest" to have power "upon the highest." In the end,
Merlin is "lost to life and use and name and fame." His end is prophetic
of Guinevere's. She too will be locked within the convent's hollow walls,
useless and barren.

Merlin's fall comes because he is first melancholy's victim.

> Then fell on Merlin a great melancholy;
> He walked with dreams and darkness, and he found
> A doom that ever poised itself to fall,
> An ever-moaning battle in the mist,
> World-war of dying flesh against the life,
> Death in all life and lying in all love,

The meanest having power upon the highest,
And the high purpose broken by the worm.
[ll. 187–94]

In this warped state he is most vulnerable. He has little power to resist
Vivien's wiles. He despairs too easily; therefore he gives in too easily.
His fall is a pessimistic image of what Tennyson considers is happening
to his country, and it is also a reminder that the wisest and the cleverest
are as vulnerable as their inferiors. As Tennyson once commented, "Some
loyal souls are wrought to madness against the world. Others, and some
among the highest intellects become the slaves of the evil which is at first
half disdained."[16]

As the heat of summer continues, so madness continues to gauge the
passions' assault on the ideal order. In "Lancelot and Elaine," madness
comes to and from those whose minds are as trapped as Merlin's. They
too are held in hollow towers, tyrannized by their lust. The story in this
idyll centers on Elaine, who, like her family, lives apart from Arthur's
realm and is therefore unsullied by its moral erosion. Corruption comes,
however. This time it is neither Guinevere nor Vivien whose sensuous
touch destroys; it is Lancelot's which brings death and confusion.

Before Lancelot's arrival in her father's kingdom of Astolat, Elaine is
an innocent "lily maid." After he comes, however, and she catches a
glimpse of his guilty love, Elaine's innocence disappears. Lancelot's
"mellow voice" arouses her and unbalances her mind. Immediately her
infatuation distorts her perception and sets her off on a destructive quest
to gain Lancelot's love. She begins by misinterpreting his courteous ways,
mistakenly thinking "all was nature, all perchance, for her." Then, in a
manner reminiscent of Tennyson's tyrannized and maddened lovers, she
dwells "all night long" on Lancelot's face. Sudden flashes of wild desire
govern her, and she impetuously offers her red sleeve, a symbol of her
passion, as a favor to Lancelot to carry with him to the tournament he
has left Camelot to attend. Foolishly Lancelot accepts and gives her his
shield. So wrapped up is he in his passion for Guinevere that he is not
sensitive to Elaine's. After he leaves for the tournament, Elaine climbs to
her tower, takes the shield, and "there kept it, and so lived in fantasy."
She is now like all those before her whose passion has possessed them
and trapped them in a hollow, barren world. Nothing now exists for her
but her passion and her false idea of Lancelot's intentions. After the tournament, when she is nursing the wounded Lancelot, she immoderately
exclaims: "I have gone mad. I love you: Let me die." Lancelot will not
and, worse, cannot give his love, for he is bound by his passion for the
queen. Therefore, denied his presence and his love, Elaine once more

retreats to that mad tower and mixes "Her fancies with the sallow-rifted glooms / Of evening, and the moanings of the wind" (ll. 995–96). Now, so lost is she in her delusion, that she cannot recognize truth. Her self-deception echoes Balin's, for she does not believe the rumors her father tells her about Lancelot's affair.

> "Sweet father, all too faint and sick am I
> For anger: these are slanders: never yet
> Was noble man but made ignoble talk.
> He makes no friend who never made a foe.
> But now it is my glory to have loved
> One peerless, without stain.
>
> [ll. 1079–84]

In the end, like a hysteric, she wills her death. As she dies, so separated is she from her true and saner self that her father barely recognizes her: "So dwelt the father on her face, and thought / 'Is this Elaine?'" [ll. 1023–24].

Elaine's loss of self parallels Lancelot's. Because he cannot break the hold of his lust, he too loses his way and himself. Angry with himself, yet still drawn by his desire for Guinevere, he decides to attend the king's tournament rather than remain in Camelot pretending to the king to be suffering from an unhealed wound (ll. 88–159). His journey to the jousts, like his warring mind, is not straightforward. It is impetuous and chaotic.

> Then got Sir Lancelot suddenly to horse,
> Wroth at himself. Not willing to be known,
> He left the barren-beaten thoroughfare,
> Chose the green path that showed the rarer foot,
> And there among the solitary downs,
> Full oft lost in fancy, lost his way.
>
> [ll. 158–63]

Lancelot is as lost in his fancy as Elaine is in hers.

Throughout the rest of the idyll Lancelot progressively loses his grasp on his sanity. Periodically the anxieties stemming from his divided loyalty to Guinevere and to Arthur, his battle between his sense and his conscience, spur the madness seething within him. At times he appears very much like Balin, for he becomes another demon of the woods: "His mood was often like a fiend, and rose / And drove him into wastes and solitudes / For agony, who was yet a living soul" (ll. 250–52). Lancelot's disguise at the tournament is yet another manifestation of this loss of self. By pretending to be a "stranger knight," he is acting out, maybe even acknowledging, this loss; furthermore, he is courting death. After the tournament he lies almost fatally wounded. Like his madness, his existence is a living death. The disguise and the wound at once echo and reverse Gareth's harmless, innocent, and advantageous charade as the kitchen knave. In that early idyll, before corruption had spread, Gareth's noble nature showed through the disguise. The charade did not bury his true self. Indeed it permitted Gareth to find himself. Now, however, in a disorderly and maddening climate, deception is evil. It is a means by which Lancelot strays further from his nobler nature. In fact, that nobler nature is so weakened that people at the tournament do not, at first, see through his disguise. After the tournament Lancelot has so little moral strength that he is unable to rescue Elaine, to help her "from herself." Moreover, he has little drive to save himself. While he is recovering from his wound he resolves to give up Guinevere. But, as the narrator knows too well, after Lancelot's physical health returns, his passion will also revive to war with and tyrannize his conscience once more.

> Yet the great knight in his mid-sickness made
> Full many a holy vow and pure resolve.
> These, as but born of sickness, could not live:
> For when the blood ran lustier in him again,
> Full often the bright image of one face,
> Making a treacherous quiet in his heart,
> Dispersed his resolution like a cloud.
>
> [ll. 873–79]

Elaine's and Lancelot's lust and their resulting loss of self find their parallels among other figures in this idyll. Gawain and Guinevere are two examples. Gawain comes to Astolat on a quest to find Lancelot and give him the tournament prize, but being more enthralled with Elaine and lost in his desire for her, he forgets his mission. Elaine asks him:

> "O loyal nephew of our noble King
> Why ask you not to see the shield he left,
> Whence you might learn his name? Why slight your King,
> And lose the quest he sent you on, and prove
> No surer than our falcon yesterday,
> Who lost the hern we slipt her at, and went
> To all the winds?"
>
> [ll. 648–54]

Gawain's lust crowds out any remaining loyalty to the king's order. Guinevere's passion distorts her judgment and turns her into "the wild Queen." She cannot recognize the truth, that Arthur is human, that he has "a touch of earth." Her jealousy when she learns of Elaine is completely out of proportion, and she acts rashly, throwing the tournament's prize into the water.

In all cases this madness is barren, a living death. The king's description of Lancelot at the end of the idyll as "a lonely" person and "heirless" is also true for Elaine, Guinevere, and Gawain. All are lost to their passion and consequently themselves. Arthur, whose personal order is ideally balanced and whose will controls his passion, knows better than those whose lives become a living death, and he realizes that freedom can come only with control, with limits. As Arthur tells Lancelot, "Free love, so bound, were freest." Excess binds rather than liberates. It locks people into hollow towers.

As in "Lancelot and Elaine," much of the emphasis in the first half of the *Idylls* is on the destructive excesses of pride, anger, despair, jealousy, and desire, and on their challenge to the individual's as well as to the nation's sanity. Throughout this half, those excesses have spread and have come close to overwhelming Camelot. They have surfaced as madness, an emblem of the order's unbalance, but for the most part that madness has remained outside the kingdom's gates. Given Tennyson's and his contemporaries' concern for England's sanity and their fear of immoderation, however, it is inevitable that this chaos enters those gates. In the idyll "The Holy Grail," the madness that had once been held outside the realm in exile—like Balin—is now within. Arthur's absence in this idyll signals the entrance of disorder, and perhaps more significantly the people's growing disbelief in his order.

In "The Holy Grail" Tennyson concentrates on the distortion and insanity found in the quest for the spiritual and nonmaterial, a quest that held Tennyson's close attention. This idyll reflects his anxiety concerning England's religious crisis. Like England, Camelot is an unbalanced state suffering from a loss of faith. Tennyson watches nervously as its subjects, damaged by doubt, worn down by the excesses of the previous idylls, and lacking the benefit of any clear vision, attempt to fill the existing void with a meaning and a faith which, in his mind, take people further and further away from religious faith. These attempts send them on quests that increasingly distort their understanding and allow them to fall deeper into their personal quagmires. As Tennyson said to his son Hallam: "Faith declines, religion turns from practical goodness and holiness to superstition. . . . These seek relief in selfish spiritual excitement."[17]

Tennyson's concern for false religious visions was topical as well as personal. In the nineteenth century not only were there numerous investigations into the physical and emotional sources of apparitions, but there was also a clinical interest in religious enthusiasm and hysteria. With few exceptions physicians easily linked these apparitions or "delusions" with insanity. In 1824, for instance, Alexander Morison talked about an insanity that comes from "excessive devotion, and contrition or remorse of conscience," and he identified doubt in religious doctrines "previously professed" as one source of madness.[18] Four years later George Man Burrows recognized, as most Victorians did, the danger of "exuberance of zeal on any subject," and he, like many others, found religious enthusiasm the most dangerous exuberance of all. He writes: "excess of religious enthusiasm, unless tempered by an habitual command over the affective passions, usually and readily degenerates into fanaticism."[19] To this distrust was added the fear of mass hysteria. Sensitive to the contagious nature of passion, people were all too aware that religious experiences can be no more than a form of hysteria. Mesmerism also undermined the validity of religious enthusiasm, for it had popularly demonstrated the power of suggestion and the power of one individual over another.[20]

Tennyson has these concerns very much in mind throughout "The Holy Grail." He parades one false vision after another. Time and time again he illustrates how the defining qualities of character and people's expectations and excesses trap and deceive them.[21] He also demonstrates how dangerous such religious delusions are; how they can, as the physicians claimed, quickly arouse hysteria or insanity, spread from person to person, and tyrannize not only minds but nations.

The first to see the Holy Grail is the nun. She is a religious hysteric,[22] a figure familiar to nineteenth-century readers. In the past, frustrated by "blunted" love, she had thrown all her "fervent flame," her thwarted passion, into religion and had given herself "to fast and alms." Now, in this idyll, news of Guinevere and Lancelot's affair arouses in her that frustrated lust and excites her zealousness. After denying herself food and following a strict regime of prayers, she suddenly awakes in the "dead of night" to a vision. The combination of her thwarted passion, zealous fasting and praying, and the delusive night would be enough to warn most of how erroneous her vision of the Holy Grail is. Her description of the cup, however, confirms just how impure and deceptive this revelation is. The cup is "rose-red with beatings in it, as if alive." Her frustration colored and shaped it.

The nun's hysteria is contagious, for it soon entangles the whole court. First it mesmerizes Sir Galahad. Sir Percivale watches, fascinated, as "this Galahad, when he heard / My sister's vision, filled me with amaze; / His eyes became so like her own, they seemed / Hers, and himself her brother more than I" ("The Holy Grail," ll. 139–42). When she speaks to Sir Galahad, her words are sensuous and hypnotic. She weaves her words in the way she had woven her belt with crimson threads. His will soon

becomes her servant, as Merlin's had become Vivien's: "and as she spake /
She sent the deathless passion in her eyes / Through him, and made him
hers, and laid her mind / On him, and he believed in her belief" (ll. 163–
65). Not heeding Merlin's example, he sits in the fallen wizard's seat,
whose inscription warns, "No man could sit but he should lose himself."
Thus, contrary to his belief that by becoming the nun's disciple he will
"save himself," he, like those before, falls. Possessed, he cannot speak,
except "in a voice shrilling." The deluded knight now held in the hysteric's control sees visions of the Holy Grail as crimson as the nun's lust.
Caught in her hysteria, he tells Percivale:

> "And never yet
> Hath what thy sister taught me first to see,
> This Holy Thing, failed from my side, nor come
> Covered, but moving with me night and day,
> Fainter by day, but always in the night
> Blood-red, and sliding down the blackened marsh
> Blood-red, and on the naked mountain top
> Blood-red, and in the sleeping mere below
> Blood-red."                                    [ll. 468–76]

Sir Galahad is overwhelmed by his enthusiasm. Hence, he cannot find
his way back to Camelot. His eyes, now as mesmeric as the nun's, capture Percivale. Percivale speaks: "While thus he spake, his eyes, dwelling
on mine, / Drew me, with power upon me, till I grew / One with him,
to believe as he believed" (ll. 485–87). These lines frighteningly echo
those describing the nun's hold over Galahad. Wanting to see the Holy
Grail too, Percivale follows Galahad. Percivale's ensuing vision is colored by the nun's and Galahad's hysterical, crimson passion. The vessel
he sees hanging over his head is "redder than any rose." Its hue gives "a
rose-red sparkle to the city." Percivale, though, is not as blindly zealous
as either of them. Doubts tug at his mind to prevent him from coming
as close to the spiritual city as they do. Subject to the absent king's warning, "This Quest is not for thee" and fearing he was following "wandering fires," Percivale cannot make Galahad's spiritual leaps. The bridges
that knight crosses to reach the spiritual city crumble before Percivale.
Beneath, Percivale sees a quagmire filled with his doubts. He fears them
as much as the unconditional belief waiting for him on the other side.
He is one of many in the nineteenth century caught between the sensuous
and the spiritual worlds, comfortable in neither. He lacks what the monk
recognizes as "the warmth of double life." He literally cannot bridge the
two. Thus, when Percivale sees the vision it is at a distance.

Once more, state of mind has shaped the vision. The experience has had little to do with spiritual reality. Rather, the appearance of the Holy Grail is nothing more than a mirror of the person's expectations and a measure of his own weaknesses. Lancelot's inability to see the Grail clearly or to benefit from its healing qualities is similar. His "grief and love" block his journey to the spiritual heights. To begin with he has "small heart" to pursue the quest. Then, when he sees the Grail, it reflects nothing of a true spiritual world. Its heat reflects only his own madness and the sordidness of his excessive lust.

> "Then in my madness I essayed the door;
> It gave; and through a stormy glare, a heat
> As from a seventimes-heated furnace, I,
> Blasted and burnt, and blinded as I was,
> With such a fierceness that I swooned away—
> O, yet methought I saw the Holy Grail,
> All palled in crimson samite, and around
> Great angels, awful shapes, and wings and eyes.
> [ll. 838–45]

Frightened and perhaps knowing better, he leaves, exclaiming, "this Quest was not for me." Sir Bors also sees the Holy Grail "according to" his "sight." To Bors, who is more selfless, who "scarce had prayed or asked it for myself," an unexpected, sweeter, more delicate vision comes. This time the crimson and the rose-red tint of the vision is pink: "—O grace to me— / In colour like the fingers of a hand / Before a burning taper, the sweet Grail / Glided and past" (ll. 689–92). Yet another knight in search of the Grail falls prey to his character. Following his nature, Sir Gawain predictably forgets the quest. He is the very antithesis of Galahad who loses himself in a false, spiritual world and cannot find his way back to Camelot. Gawain is so weighed down by his sensuous concerns, that he cannot even move from the silken pavilion with its "merry maidens" to search for a spiritual light.

Each of these knights has sadly proved King Arthur correct.[23] They have followed "wandering fires" and have become lost in the quagmires of themselves. Their hysteria has taken them away from Camelot and allowed them to indulge in their weaknesses and to maintain neither personal nor national order. The resurgence of their personal disorder is reflected in the ruin and waste of their kingdom. On their return to Camelot the wearied knights find "horses stumbling as they trode / On heaps of ruin, hornless unicorns, / Cracked basilisks, and splintered cockatrices, / And shattered talbots, which had left the stones / Raw, that they fell from" (ll. 713–17). England's traditional symbols of order have fallen. Moreover, the city with its four zones, each representing progress from the bestial toward the spiritual ideal, has crumbled. The cracks in the city's foundations are the consequences of the inhabitants' passions, untempered by Arthur, who if he had not had to quell the spreading evil would have moderated these passions and prevented the knights' hysteria. The closing description of Camelot reflects Tennyson's fears that England is a country cracking under the weight of such enthusiasms, excesses, doubts, and materialistic concerns; that it has lost sight of the true spiritual values; and that it is filled with those who, like Percivale, are caught by their doubts and cannot make the spiritual leap.

The remaining idylls follow the cracks as they spread through and shatter the foundations of Arthur's realm. In two short idylls, "Pelleas and Ettarre" and "The Last Tournament," the fall comes quickly. These two idylls reverse all that Camelot has ideally represented.[24] A new generation of knights reigns and revives the ascendancy of bestiality which Arthur had fought and controlled. Pelleas, a new knight "to fill the gap / Left by the Holy Quest," and Tristram are among this new generation. They are the inheritors of the unhealthy state. They move about in a kingdom where the sensuous Gawain and the evil Modred are becoming more visible. Until now this evil pair has been lurking in the background.

To illustrate this reversal, Tennyson continues to use the image of madness. Pelleas's madness is a sad image of the breakdown of any control or law. The supremacy of the will, desired so by the nineteenth century, is not his. Deluded by false splendor, deceptive dreams, and his passion (which he mistakes for true love), and a slave to "the pleasure of the blood," Pelleas becomes a vassal to the proud, deceitful, and lustful Ettarre. Blindly he rejoices: "Behold me, Lady, / A prisoner, and the vassal of thy will" (ll. 232–33). He is now held by yet another demon of the woods, a woman who is more willing to dally with the sensuous Gawain than with Pelleas, a knight who aspires to be Arthur's true follower, and a demon whose excesses attack her until she loses herself in her "ever-veering fancy."

Because Pelleas's will is possessed by a demon, any self-control he might have easily evaporates. Such is the case when he discovers Gawain and Ettarre sleeping together. In a manner reminiscent of the maddening King Lear reviling his eldest daughter, Pelleas loses all control and screams maniacally at Ettarre:

> "O towers so strong,
> Huge, solid, would that even while I gaze
> The crack of earthquake shivering to your base
> Split you, and Hell burst your harlot roofs

Bellowing, and charred you through and through within,
Black as the harlot's heart—hollow as a skull!
Let the fierce east scream through your eyelet-holes,
And whirl the dust of harlots round and round
In dung and nettles! hiss, snake—I saw him there—
Let the fox bark, let the wolf yell. Who yells
Here in the still sweet summer night, but I—"
                    ["Pelleas and Ettarre," ll. 454–64]

He continues his harangue by echoing the maddening speaker of "Locksley Hall," who longs for a savage nation where there is no insanity and
lust: "O great and sane and simple race of brutes / That own no lust
because they have no law!" (ll. 471–72). Pelleas's breakdown is complete
after he learns of Guinevere and Lancelot's impurity. He falls into a deep
depression and loses not only his faith in the order, but also all sense of
self—he has "no name." Now suicidal, he asks Lancelot to slay him. His
sword, which had been for Pelleas an image of his belief in Arthur's vows
and a symbol of the king's order, is also no longer with him. Those
idealistic values and the sanity it represents are gone. Like the sword
Pelleas has left lying on the sleeping bodies of Gawain and Ettarre, those
values and that harmony are now mingled with and overwhelmed by the
bestial passions. Leaving the lawless realm, the broken knight returns to
Camelot with no will, no name, and no sword. He goes into darkness.

                    And he, hissing "I have no sword,"
Sprang from the door into the dark. The Queen
Looked hard upon her lover, he on her;
And each foresaw the dolorous day to be:
And all talk died, as in a grove all song
Beneath the shadow of some bird of prey;
Then a long silence came upon the hall.
                    [ll. 590–96]

This silence signals that Modred's time to upset the order has come.
    This idyll has reversed the action of the second idyll, "Gareth and
Lynette." In that earlier, healthier time, Lynette's scorn of Gareth, the
new knight, was not destructive. When Arthur's order was more secure,
and Guinevere and Lancelot's sin had not upset its balance, Gareth's power
to counteract the evil forces remained with him. He could conquer Lynette's taunting; he could master her pride, battle the four knights, and
travel through the mire. There Gareth can defeat death and "a blooming
boy / Fresh as a flower new-born" can step out of darkness (ll. 1371–74).
    In "The Last Tournament" any semblance of order has disappeared.

There are no knights who even hope to follow Arthur's example. Passion, violence, and discord predominate. Red colors all. Freedom is lawlessness; fools are wise; the mad fight the mad; Lancelot, the sinner, rules, and not the king; and the lustful Tristram, not the pure knight, wins the tournament (appropriately called "The Tournament of the Dead Innocence"). Throughout this idyll Tennyson emphasizes Lancelot's madness to give a sense of this horrifying disorder now tyrannizing the center of Camelot. Trapped and worn down by his lust, Lancelot is powerless to stop the lawless tournament. Paralleling those idle and useless leaders who have watched their kingdoms fall apart, Lancelot listlessly officiates.

> But when the morning of a tournament,
> By these in earnest those in mockery called
> The Tournament of the Dead Innocence,
> Brake with a wet wind blowing, Lancelot,
> Round whose sick head all night, like birds of prey,
> The words of Arthur flying shrieked, arose,
> And down a streetway hung with folds of pure
> White samite, and by fountains running wine,
> Where children sat in white with cups of gold,
> Moved to the lists, and there, with slow sad steps
> Ascending, filled his double-dragoned chair.
> ["The Last Tournament," ll. 134–44]

Once more disorder and madness reign because Arthur is not there to control them. As in "The Holy Grail," the king is outside his city attempting to block this spreading evil. He is pursuing his former champion, Pelleas, now named the red knight because Pelleas's madness and rage so inflame him. In the ensuing struggle Arthur, ever in control of himself, allows Pelleas to defeat himself, as madness will. But, even though Arthur remains unscathed, his company does not. The discord is now as pervasive and as infectious as the religious hysteria. Arthur cannot restore harmony. In a terrifying scene Arthur's knights, excited by Pelleas, turn manic and destroy Pelleas and the village. Their conduct mirrors the horrible disorder.

> Thus he [Pelleas] fell
> Head-heavy; then the knights, who watched him, roared
> And shouted and leapt down upon the fallen;
> There trampled out his face from being known,
> And sank his head in mire, and slimed themselves:
> Nor heard the King for their own cries, but sprang
> Through open doors, and sording right and left

Men, women, on their sodden faces, hurled
The tables over and the wines, and slew
Till all the rafters rang with woman-yells,
And all the pavement streamed with massacre.

[ll. 466–76]

The anarchy is national and personal, for at the same time, Tristram is dallying with Queen Isolt—an adulterous relationship full of blatant disloyalties and excesses that magnify Guinevere and Lancelot's sin. Arthur sees the massacre and returns to see his "Queen's bower was dark." He knows the end has come.

The end comes rapidly in two short idylls: "Guinevere" and "The Passing of Arthur." From this moment on, Vivien and Modred are more powerful than ever before, for the evil that was lurking in the background has come to the front. There is no longer enough will to battle Vivien's wiles and Modred's sins. The madness has spread too far. Weakened by his bestial passion, Lancelot can now do little more than "pluck" the scheming Modred by the heels and throw him into the dust. Weakened by his knights who have either defected or lost themselves, King Arthur cannot survive. In "The Passing of Arthur" the king has enough strength left to kill Modred but not enough to withstand Modred's final blow to his head. Arthur's life begins to slip away. Camelot is no more. Before the king dies, however, he asks Sir Bedivere to return Excalibur to the lake, and he pleads with Sir Bedivere to take him to "the level lake"; to take him beyond the chaotic landscape that surrounds him.

"My end draws nigh; 'tis time that I were gone.
Make broad thy shoulders to receive my weight,
And bear me to the margin; yet I fear
My wound hath taken cold, and I shall die."

. . . . . . . . . . . . . . . . . . . . . . . . . . . . . . . . .

But, as he [Sir Bedivere] walked, King Arthur panted hard,
Like one that feels a nightmare on his bed
When all the house is mute. So sighed the King,
Muttering and murmuring at his ear, "Quick, quick!
I fear it is too late, and I shall die."

[ll. 331–34, 344–48]

The urgency of the second request is significant, for it shows how fearful Arthur is of dying among the "barren chasms" and "bare black cliffs" that "clung" around him. His urgency suggests how closely the ideal soul comes to losing itself, as the king's knights have done, in that chaotic landscape. In fact, so powerful is the chaos at the end that the king barely escapes it. Eventually, though, with Sir Bedivere's help, the king does reach the smooth way and dies on the barge as it travels down the peaceful waters.

> And the barge with oar and sail
> Moved from the brink, like some full-breasted swan
> That, fluting a wild carol ere her death,
> Ruffles her pure cold plume, and takes the flood
> With swarthy webs. Long stood Sir Bedivere
> Revolving many memories, till the hull
> Looked one black dot against the verge of dawn,
> And on the mere the wailing died away.
>
> [ll. 433–40]

Throughout the *Idylls* King Arthur has seldom spoken—even though his presence has always been felt. In "Guinevere," however, Tennyson does give Arthur his chance. For 165 lines the king lectures the queen, reminding her of his humanity, his love for her, the need for moderation, and, of course, her sins. The lecture is a curious mixture of compassion and severity, and a powerful one. Many readers, especially twentieth-century readers, have experienced difficulties with the king's speech. Many have been annoyed by its self-righteous tone.[25] They find his words too high-minded. They are annoyed with his moralistic posture because they claim that he has no right to be so critical. They claim that he is not "blameless." These readers want to blame "the blameless King" for Camelot's fall. Certainly the many references scattered throughout the *Idylls* to the impossibility of the king's vows encourage such thoughts. However, the blame does not lie with him or with his naïveté. It rests with the individuals, the citizens of Camelot, and not with the king. As Tennyson once said, "Take away the sense of individual responsibility and men sink into pessimism and madness."[26] Such is the problem in the *Idylls*. The fall belongs to those individuals who are unwilling to believe in or to follow the king's vows. Camelot would have survived had people not only continued to believe in the ideal, but had they also, through moderation, maintained a harmonious balance.

Tennyson's contemporaries would have had little difficulty with the king's lecture. They would have found him "blameless," for they too believed in moderation, and they too were involved in the battles of the *Idylls*. They knew that to keep order they must fight their bestial forces; that they must not lose sight of order and must exercise their wills. For a public that felt threatened by the passions and constantly searched for new ways in which to govern themselves and their nation, the effects of madness in Tennyson's *Idylls* were all too familiar. For these reasons the public would have also been most sensitive to Tennyson's praise of Prince Albert in the dedication preceding the *Idylls*. Tennyson lauds the prince for many qualities:

> And indeed He seems to me
> Scarce other than my king's ideal knight,
> "Who reverenced his conscience as his king;
> Whose glory was, redressing human wrong;
> Who spake no slander, no, nor listened to it;
> Who loved one only and who clave to her—"
> Her—over all whose realms to their last isle,
> Commingled with the gloom of imminent war,
> The shadow of His loss drew like eclipse,
> Darkening the world. We have lost him: he is gone:
> We know him now: all narrow jealousies
> Are silent; and we see him as he moved,
> How modest, kindly, all-accomplished, wise,
> With what sublime repression of himself,
> And in what limits, and how tenderly;
> Not swaying to this faction or to that;
> Not making his high place the lawless perch
> Of winged ambitions, nor a vantage-ground
> For pleasure; but through all this tract of years
> Wearing the white flower of a blameless life,
> Before a thousand peering littlenesses,
> In that fierce light which beats upon a throne,
> And blackens every blot.
>
> [ll. 5–27]

The praise mirrors Arthur's speech to Guinevere and suggests an equation between Arthur and Prince Albert. Both "loved one only" and, more important, both exercised moderation—both were "blameless."

Buried among the praise is the curious phrase "sublime repression"—a phrase that has puzzled many.[27] However, in the light of the public's fears and the *Idylls*'s concerns, the phrase is not so puzzling, but is clearly appropriate. To survive personally and to survive as a healthy nation, people must repress their doubts and their excesses. And in Tennyson's mind, given the necessity and the difficulty of this task, this repression is indeed "sublime." Tennyson suggests that his audience follow Albert's and Arthur's example: the audience must themselves exercise "sublime repression." They must be more aware of how the bestial forces constantly bombard and erode the will, upsetting the delicate balance, sending them and their nation headlong into madness. The *Idylls* is indeed an example not only of the sublime nature of repression, but of its necessity. The fall of Camelot is the fall of "sublime repression."

## Chapter Six

# Sublime Repression
# and the Pursuit of Sanity

hen Tennyson championed sublime repression in the *Idylls of the King* he was subscribing to his contemporaries' preoccupation with the absolute necessity of exercising such repression if they and their nation were to be sane. In addition, he was reflecting his own conviction of its necessity if he, personally, were to be whole and not subject to the terrifying danger of being overwhelmed either by his black bloodedness or by the destructive passions. Because of this conviction Tennyson joined his contemporaries in emphasizing the need for moral management and the will's power to control the passions. For him and for the majority of Victorians, the will was central to physical, spiritual, and psychic harmony. This belief in the supremacy of the will was, in fact, one of the shaping forces of Victorian culture, and as such helped direct the course of education, government, religion, philosophy, psychology, and the arts.[1]

Tennyson's trust in the concept of the will's power to prevent destruction and immorality was encouraged by psychologists interested in madness, by those like John Barlow, who writing in 1843 declared that "to educate a man in the full and proper sense of the word is to supply him with the power of controlling his feelings, and his thoughts, and his actions."[2] This trust was also encouraged by Daniel Noble, who emphasized the importance of energetically exercising the will in resistance to unwonted ideas, and by John Charles Bucknill, who in 1856 asked: "What is the condition to which insanity, mental alienation, unsoundness, derangement is opposed?" Bucknill's answer might have been Tennyson's: "It is that condition of the mind in which the emotions and instinct are in such a state of subordination to the will, that the latter can direct and control their manifestations."[3] Bucknill's words were later echoed by William B. Carpenter, a physiologist from the University College, London. In 1874 Carpenter continued to contribute to the notion of sublime repression when he published the *Principles of Mental Physiology*, in which he strongly suggested that the one way to overcome monomania or "delusion of the intellect" is to cultivate the will. Carpenter subscribed to the Victorians' belief in moral management and therefore insisted that the strength of that will "mainly depends upon the *constancy with which it is exercised.*" [4]

Because Tennyson firmly believed in the supremacy of the will, or to use another contemporary idiom, "self-government," he frequently expressed his opinion that without either, any tyranny is possible, national or personal. Without that power corruption spreads just as it did through Camelot, bringing with it lustful visions that multiply and destroy the order. Without the will, noble souls like Lucretius are destroyed or destroy themselves. Tennyson's opinion is most audible in the 1855 poem dedicated to the will. There it is easy to hear his awe of the person who is blessed with the power: "O well for him whose will is strong! / He suffers, but he will not suffer long; / He suffers, but he cannot suffer wrong" ("Will," ll. 1–3), and it is easy to hear his despair for the person who "bettering not with time, / Corrupts the strength of heaven-descended Will, / And ever weaker grows through acted crime, / Or seeming-genial venial fault, / Recurring and suggesting still!" (ll. 10–14).

The strength of these opinions affected Tennyson so that he felt a compulsive need to control himself and his art. Because of this need he tended to glorify those who exhibit order and manage themselves well. For example, in his poetry he frequently praises the forces of order: he praises the future wife of the Lord of Burleigh (in "The Lord of Burleigh"), who will "order all things duly"; he approves of the "thinking men of England," who "loathe a tyranny" and oppose the lawless powers (in "Suggested by Reading an Article"); and he extols the virtues of the Duke of Wellington, whose strong will keeps Britain "sane," frustrates the "tyrant powers," and hence keeps chaos and anarchy at bay (in "Ode on the Death of the Duke of Wellington"). Because the will is imperative to maintaining order, Tennyson not only praises those who possess it but also damns those who neglect it. Most of all Tennyson fears those who give in to idleness, an act that weakens the will's supremacy. Throughout his poetry that involves a search for order Tennyson often alludes to the dangers of being idle. For example, in the *Idylls* he paints the devastating portrait of Gareth's weak, useless, idle father, and in *The Princess* he criticizes the prince for giving in to "fancies hatched / In silken-folded idleness" (4: 48–49). This protest against idleness is most vehement in "The Islet," a short poem published in 1864. The poem summarizes Tennyson's fearful vision of the dangers lurking in the paths of idleness. The poem opens with a wife begging her husband to go to an Eden where

"Waves on a diamond shingle dash,
Cataract brooks to the ocean run,
Fairily-delicate palaces shine
Mixt with myrtle and clad with vine,
And overstreamed and silvery-streaked
With many a rivulet high against the Sun
The facets of the glorious mountain flash
Above the valleys of palm and pine."

[ll. 16–23]

But knowing better, the husband recalls the dangers inherent in such self-indulgent lethargy and in the potential loneliness, and he emphatically replies, "No, no, no!" He warns his loved one of the monotony and of the "worm" which lives in "the lonely wood" and "pierces the liver and blackens the blood," making it "a sorrow to be."

This need to fight idleness, to maintain the supremacy of the will, and to keep control set Tennyson on a lifelong path devoted to duty and work. His devotion to work was such that during those interludes, particularly those spent at the water cures when work was denied him, he despaired. Work was an antidote to chaos. But when Tennyson was at work writing, control did not come automatically. Always he consciously and conscientiously strove to reaffirm the supremacy of his will. He worked hard to give clues to his readers, so that they would know of his control over his words, his mad subject matter, and, by extension, himself. By no means did he ever want to be thought of as a "Wild Poet." Sections in *In Memoriam*, for instance, reveal his distinct discomfort with the image of a writer who works without either "a conscience or an aim," or with the image of the "delirious man" whose "fancy fuses old and new, / And flashes false and true, / And mingles all without a plan" (lyric 16).

Tennyson also did not want to be subjected to the kind of criticism written about him during his Cambridge years. He would not have wanted to read Charles Wordsworth's comments on his award-winning "Timbuctoo." After reading it, Wordsworth complained: "If such an exercise had been sent up at Oxford, the author would have had a better chance of being rusticated, with the view of passing a few months at a Lunatic Asylum."[5] Imagine how the anxious Tennyson would have reacted to that and to Leigh Hunt's criticism of the 1830 poem "The 'How' and the 'Why.'" Facetiously Hunt wrote: "We only hope it is not sick writing, and that the author, in the mystifications of himself, only feels the pleasure of a healthy wonderment." The poem was never republished in Ten-

nyson's lifetime.[6] To make matters more difficult, Tennyson's sensitivity
to Hunt's criticism was compounded by the Victorian critics' tendency
to diagnose a literary work in terms of its mental health or its wholeness,
to trace, for instance, the idiosyncracies of Horace Walpole's prose and
Arthur Hugh Clough's verse either to "an unhealthy and disorganized
mind" or to an "almost morbid craving." Walter Bagehot is typical. He
firmly believed that the critic must surrender his mind to the "delicate
task of detecting the healthiness or unhealthiness of familiar states of
feeling" within the literary text.[7]

As might be expected, to avoid being identified with his mad subjects
and to avoid being called "sick," Tennyson developed a style that in his
poems on madness, especially, produces merely an illusion of irrationality and constantly reminds his readers that he, the poet, is very much in
control. The irrationality in these poems is continuously tugged and
challenged by an orderly and controlling current. Martin Dodsworth has
commented on this tendency. He notes that "Tennyson's poetry *is* morbid, at least in the sense that it grows from morbid feelings in the poet
himself. And yet it is surely not great *because* it is morbid, but because at
its best it allows us to feel at once the poet's intense involvement with
his subject-matter and at the same time his control over it."[8]

In *Maud*, for example, to chart the speaker's shifting and increasingly
wild moods, Tennyson adopts a style that only gives an illusion of the
speaker's instability. Throughout the poem a tension exists between the
irrational and the rational. The stronger pull is always that of a rational
voice, which even in the most irrational moments is audible.

A cursory glance at the printed poem quickly reveals its seemingly
irregular and erratic form. The lengths of the sections in part one are as
varied and as vacillating as the hero's emotions. When he begins to lose
hold of himself, the sections become erratic. After section five, for example, few sections are written in regular stanzas. The number of lines
varies in the sections from two to twenty-two. By the time the hero is
ranting in his asylum, his fragmented mind and disordered equilibrium
permit little visual organization. The visual irregularity is not the only
means by which Tennyson mirrors the irrational. Frequently the rhythm
and the rhyme emphasize the hero's distress. At the beginning of the
asylum section, for instance, the rhythm is manic. Long pauses, marked
by a dash at the end of the line, slow down the pace and introduce lines
of gathering speed that eventually slow down again. The rhyme in that
section is also nearly as unwieldy as the lover's delirious mind. In the 49-
line section, there are few repeated rhymes.

All this disorder in the number and length of lines, in the poem's beat
and rhyme is, however, in the end, merely illusory, for Tennyson never

gives in to the irrationality and never allows himself to become like the hero in the poem, who feels himself to be a puppet moved by forces beyond his control and therefore to be without a will. Tennyson is devoted to the forces of order; he is pledged to displaying a control that fights the seemingly fragmented stanzas and the poem's erratic posture. To begin with Tennyson selects an acceptable form in which to record the lover's "successive phases of passion." In the past critics have regarded Tennyson's monodrama as "experimental" and "hazardous." But recently A. Dwight Culler has suggested that the form was by no means experimental, but a widely accepted one that by the 1840s "was commonly used."[9] Tennyson has not only the security of that accepted frame but also the reassurance of using two other established forms: the sonnet and the ballad, both of which are to be expected in a poem about love, death, and madness.

Within the security of these conventional forms, Tennyson clings to many other controlling literary devices. Even though the rhyme seems erratic, even unobtrusive, throughout the poem, it never disappears. Even in its most irregular moments, patterns are still discoverable and repetitions audible. Occasionally the rhyme threatens to slip away. For example, in one of the lover's worst moments, he imagines that he is buried alive, that pedestrians' feet and the wheels of the street vehicles pass over his head. For five lines there is no end rhyme. But Tennyson cannot let that symbol of control disappear. He quickly pulls the poem back into shape and establishes control by repeating the sounds of the last two lines and by adding an even, sobering, metrically regular couplet that echoes a ballad's refrain: "But up and down and to and fro, / Ever about me the dead men go."

Not only end rhymes, but internal rhymes and alliteration bind the poem's wild thoughts tightly together. Even when he shifts the rhyming pattern, the change is not always a radical one. Often he shifts to sounds that are related, to almost half-rhymes. Perhaps the consonants change, but the vowel sounds remain, or vice versa. Repeated sounds, then, are important in his maintaining order and remind the reader with what defiance Tennyson had used rhyme to combat adversity in an early poem, "What Thor Said to the Bard before Dinner": "Wherever evil customs thicken / Break through with the hammer of iron rhyme."

Another means by which he counteracts his seemingly irrational poem is by constantly boxing it in, framing it, not only through repeated sounds, but through refrains or neat couplets which open and close sections or punctuate them. For example, in part one he opens section nineteen (one of the most threatening moments) with the couplet "Her brother is coming back to-night, / Breaking up my dream of delight." Tennyson concludes this section with a most irregular stanza, but one that ends neatly by repeating with variation the opening couplet "But that her brother come, like a blight / On my fresh hope, to the Hall to-night." This framing or binding technique exists not only in the rhyme or in the traditional refrains, but also in the repetition of thought. It is not unusual to find Tennyson closing a section by referring to the ideas or images introduced in that section's opening lines. Section five, part two concludes by returning to the notion of being buried alive—a notion that opened the section but disappeared during the central part when the mad lover was raving and seemingly freely associating ideas. As before, in the first example of the five unrhymed lines, Tennyson cannot let disorder gain too much strength. He must show his hand. Orderly syntax also creates neat boxes. Notice how the repetitive syntax in section fourteen, part one creates a visual and audible square.

> Maud has a garden of roses
> And lilies fair on a lawn;
> There she walks in her state
> And tends upon bed and bower,
> And thither I climbed at dawn
> And stood by her garden gate.
>                    [ll. 489–94]

As David Shaw notes in his recent book on Tennyson's style, the poet controls his work through "a shuttering effect by blocking off the action." [10] Shaw must also agree with Dodsworth, who senses that "Tennyson's fondness for the frame may reflect his anxiety" that his poems should not be read as the product of a person suffering from "inherited craziness." [11]

Certainly one of the most brilliant results of Tennyson's compulsion to show his controlling hand is the way he commands the poem's intricate and complex imagery. Throughout *Maud* Tennyson cleverly intertwines images of war, peace, Mammon, flowers, woods, birds, jewels, curtains, and sultans, bringing unity to the poem, linking one section and one thought to another. These intricate image patterns are by no means the work of a "wild poet" writing without an aim, mingling all without a plan. Often, though, this compulsive need to fight the image of the wild poet causes conflict. Sometimes Tennyson in his efforts to sound rational tends to conclude his poems more neatly than the thought deserves. The result is that the ending sounds more definitive than Tennyson intends. The last section of *Maud*, with its regularity and authority, its conclusive tone, creates problems. As we noted earlier, many critics mistakenly believe that the lover is fully recovered; others worry over and question Tennyson's values. It needs to be pointed out, however, that this conclusiveness is more illusory than real. Tennyson's need to be tight contradicts the ending's ambiguous dilemma. The closing of *Maud*, as a result, is a good example of what Dodsworth recognizes as "the rhetorically conclusive nature of these inconclusive endings."[12]

Ultimately, Tennyson's belief in the necessity of the will went beyond his poetic posture and affected the way in which he approached the metaphysical problems facing him and many of his contemporaries. Tennyson was faced with a dilemma. His fear of losing the will's power and his compulsion to be in control of himself made it difficult for him to surrender himself to visions and systems of thought which might possibly involve him in distortions and cause him to lose himself among shadows and harmful delusions. Worse, this surrender might cause the suspension of his will. As a result, Tennyson felt driven to qualify his experiences with the spiritual and visionary worlds. He was never completely comfortable at seances or with his dreams; yet, he felt the necessity of coming to terms with these experiences, for like others in his family and in accord with the interests of the period, Tennyson was slightly in awe of the spiritual and otherworldly dimensions of existence and was convinced, in varying degrees, of that world's validity. Although not so completely captivated as some of his brothers and sisters, Tennyson was intrigued with what he called "the great Realm of the unknown," and he was fascinated with the thought of life being continued "independently of our present bodies." Wishing he could remove the veil shielding his view of the unknown and wanting to capture glimpses of that realm, he sometimes threw himelf into a trance, experimented with mesmerism, attended seances, and collected accounts and photographs of ghosts. For Tennyson ghosts were not necessarily fictitious creations.[13] Consequently when he heard stories of phantoms, ghosts, and specters, he listened to them with his "hair on end." He also attempted to communicate with ghosts. For instance, Tennyson slept in his dead father's bed, hoping to see Dr. Tennyson's ghost, and after Arthur Henry Hallam died, Tennyson wished his friend's ghost would "descend, and touch, and enter" and "that in this blindness of the frame / My ghost may feel that thine is near" (*In Memoriam*, 93:13–16). Later in his life, still attempting to communicate with the deceased, Tennyson consulted mediums. Mrs. Warre Cornish remembers several of these occasions: "Mary Brotherton's door at Freshwater Gate never failed to admit the poet on his return from London or Aldworth, whatever the changes in his life and the ups and downs of his spirits. . . . And on more than one occasion Alfred hovered rather wistfully, waiting for results which never came. Once it was the sudden death of Matthew Arnold. . . . The natural man craved

for a message from the dead . . . where it would be safe from report-
ers."[14] Mrs. Cornish does not record the most poignant of these seances,
when Tennyson tried to reach his dead son, Lionel, and failed.[15]

As he grew older Tennyson's endeavors to understand and reach this
"great Realm" increased. Despite his wife's pious skepticism and her dis-
approval of table rapping, spiritualists frequently came to visit Tennyson. According to Emily, at times the "middle room" rang with "raps
on the table" and "A's study table" heaved "like the sea."[16] Because of
his interest in spiritualism Tennyson read a considerable amount of psychic
literature; in 1881 he joined the Society of Psychical Research, and for
years he carried on a lengthy correspondence with his brother Frederick
about psychic phenomena. One of Tennyson's letters to him reveals just
how fascinated Tennyson was, and yet how unwilling he was to give in
completely to spiritualism: "I grant you that spiritualism must not be
judged by its quacks: but I am convinced that God and the ghosts of men
would choose something other than mere table-legs through which to
speak to the heart of man. You tell me it is my duty to give up everything
in order to propagate spiritualism. I cannot see what grounds of proof
(as yet) you have to go on (July 1887)."[17] Tennyson never could allow
himself to enter the spiritual world as freely as Frederick had. As Mrs.
Cornish noted, he preferred to hover wistfully at its door.

Dreams also belonged to that sense of "otherness" Tennyson and his
family shared. From the time he was ten and composing poems in his
sleep, until his death, Tennyson shared his dreams with his family and
friends, particularly in the last decade of his life. Then, as Sir Charles
Tennyson suggests, Tennyson must have "passed many hours during that
winter [1888–1889] in a visionary state. . . . Asleep he had magnificent
visions of fir-woods, cliffs, and temples. . . . One night the face of the
clock seemed to expand and to fill up the whole end of the room in
which he was sleeping. The clock pointed to a quarter past six—'Superstitious people would say that I should die then,' he remarked to his son
next morning."[18]

Because dreams were intricately involved in Tennyson's quest to affirm
the "unknown," or at least capture a glimpse of it, they frequently became the subject of his poetry. Writing about these dreams was not an
easy task, however, for it was not a matter of merely recording the dreams.
Because of Tennyson's lifelong interest in psychology and because of his
compulsion to be "accurate" when speaking of human nature, he was
forced to come to terms with the scientific community's theories about
the dreaming experience. He had to balance these theories not only against
his own inclination to side with those believing dreams are communications from a mystical realm but also with the scientists' insistence that

such communications are false and involve the individual in the surrender of the will. Consequently, in writing about dreams Tennyson always felt it necessary to qualify their validity or explain their origins. Tennyson discovered that just as he could not surrender to table legs as proof of the spiritual world, neither could he totally trust his dreams. They too might be creations of a sickly mind.

That Tennyson had to deal with these theories is not surprising, for they were attracting many people's close attention. These theories were part of the new emphasis on a materialistic definition of experience; hence, they stressed the material origin of dreams and, in doing so, challenged people's traditional beliefs in any sort of spiritual experience and made it difficult for them to regard dreams as having any spiritual dimension. Titles of scientific studies vividly reveal the materialistic bias. For instance, in 1842 Samuel Hibbert wrote *Sketches of the Philosophy of Apparitions; or, An Attempt to Trace Such Illusions to Their Physical Causes*. His attitude was like that of other physicians who cut no corners in proclaiming their skepticism. They believed that prophetic dreams are nothing but chance; dreams of dead or absent friends are optical illusions or images of diseased brains, or products of excited memories, magnetic charges running through the brain, or nervous temperaments. The supernatural was dismissed as "humbug."[19] Some of the scientists supporting the material bases of dreams were among those Tennyson most admired. Among them, for instance, was his own Dr. Benjamin Brodie, who thought of dreams as being either the imaginative replay of the day's impressions or the products of physiological changes occurring while a person sleeps. He was one of many to believe that indigestion, gout, fever, and "intoxicating agents" shape dreams. He was also part of a school that believed that sounds "occurring when we are asleep" prompt dreams, and that a person's fears, griefs, and expectations also create dreams. A dream was nothing more than a mirror of the physical and emotional forces influencing the dreamer.[20]

When the scientists argued their case, they often took their evidence from their historical predecessors as well as from their own clinical data. They frequently relied on texts familiar to the educated public. They read Lucretius's *De Rerum Natura*, Lavater's *De Spectris*, and Burton's *Anatomy of Melancholy*, all of which insist that dreams are nothing more than either the reflections of the waking state or the products of diseased minds and organs. These physicians also respected the work of Sir Thomas Browne (1605–1682). In his books (which perhaps because of their relevant subject matter were reprinted in 1835), they found support for the physical basis of dreams and for their growing conviction that dreams are reflections of the inner life. They were also indebted to Erasmus Dar-

win, who in *Zoonomia* had devoted considerable space to the study of
sleep and dreams and had spoken of dreams as "repeating waking sensations."

Because of Tennyson's clinical bias, many of his dream poems incorporate these theories. For instance, in "Sea Dreams" the husband and
wife account for their dreams by singling out the sounds and events that
invade their sleep and predispose them to create their dreams. They are
aware that the sounds of the sea outside their window and the breaking
glass, their fears, and the experience of listening to the preacher's fiery
sermon come together to mold their dreams. Waking experiences shape
many other dreams: in "Enoch Arden" and "The Dreamer" passages
read from the Bible shape the night's visions, and in "Lucretius" images
from the reading of the master's three hundred scrolls mingle with the
love potion to create terrifying nightmares. In other poems hopes and
anxieties steer the course of Akbar's prophetic dream ("Akbar's Dream"),
form the delusive and wish-fulfilling dreams of Maud's lover, create the
prince's feverish dreams (*The Princess*), and shape the tenant's anxious
dreams about his squire ("Owd Roä"). Other poems demonstrate Tennyson's sensitivity to the role memory plays as a stimulus for dreams.
For instance, in "The Death of Oenone" Oenone's return to the valley
where Paris deserted her stimulates feelings belonging to a confusing,
unhappy past she had almost forgotten. The resurgence of those feelings
causes her to dream of her dead Paris and to bring the past into the present.

Tennyson's respect for the scientific community's theories was helpful
in allowing him to depict the dreaming state in a way which complemented his need to be "accurate." Yet, this respect also brought anxiety
and difficulty. One of the greatest challenges to Tennyson's peace of mind
was the physicians' persistent assumption that linked the madman to the
dreamer, a connection hundreds of years old but one that received much
credence in Tennyson's lifetime. Like the psychiatrist George Man Burrows, many reiterated the ancient sense that madness is the dream of him
who is awake, that the ideas of an insane person are as delusive as the
images of sleeping visions. To this prejudice they added their understanding that in the dreaming state the dreamer is passive and therefore
at the mercy of his senses, which can easily exaggerate and chaotically
combine ideas. The dreamer consequently participates in an experience
in which the will exercises no power. Because of this lack of regulation,
some suggested that it would be "better in the mind to lie in restless
ecstasy, than thus to have naked fancy stretched upon the rack. . . . What
more lurid picture of hell can be formed than that it is one long bad
dream!"[21] These physicians were not alone in promoting their theories.
In *Letters on Demonology and Witchcraft* (1830) Sir Walter Scott wasted

little time deflating the supernatural causes of dreams and apparitions and was quick to identify them as mental delusions—a conviction that must have caused the admiring Tennyson some grief.[22]

Such a menacing and often lurid link between madness and dreams often characterizes Tennyson's dream poetry. For example, in *The Princess* the prince's feverish dreams are a mark of his madness. Tennyson compares his return to sanity to waking from sleep. The lover in *Maud* also speaks of his return to a more stable state in terms of his awakening from a dream. Lucretius and Oenone, however, do not wake from their mad dreams. The increasing horror of their dreams measures their increasing instability. Lucretius's dreams are especially lurid, for they represent the loss of the will's power to guide his thoughts and control his senses. Oenone also experiences such a loss. Her judgment gone, she gets lost in her dream; she grows wild and like Lucretius commits suicide.

The reason Tennyson was willing to address the connection between dreams, madness, and the law of the will is that he recognized the dangers of such a connection. Fearing he had inherited a predisposition to madness, Tennyson could not avoid worrying about the likelihood that his dreaming experience was close to the undisciplined, untrustworthy thoughts crowding a madman's mind. As E.D.H. Johnson suggests, Tennyson could not be sure whether the dream "was a legitimate vision carrying supernatural authority, or whether it was not merely a self-imposed and superstitious delusion?"[23] Johnson's concern is to the point, for how could Tennyson know whether his dreams were either a consequence of the gout, a perverted will, or a true glimpse of that "nameless world" he speaks of in "The Ancient Sage"? To make matters worse for Tennyson, later in his life when he was becoming more anxious to affirm the existence of a nonmaterial world, an increasing number of articles and books appeared in which scientists and philosophers insisted that people's belief in a spiritual world is nothing but a grand deception. Typical of those pressing this point of view is William B. Carpenter, who in his *Principles of Mental Physiology* demonstrates how dreams, seances, visions, and ghostly apparitions are nothing more than delusions of a credulous imagination and experiences grounded in a physiological phenomenon like "unconscious cerebration"—thinking automatically without the direction of the will. Like the others he ridiculed the thought that there could be anything like a "mystic gleam" or a "flash" of spiritual insight.[24]

Carpenter and his active colleagues were not, of course, without their severe critics. The reaction came swiftly. Among these critics are the Swedenborgians, who argued for the intercourse between the body and soul, and those who wrote articles defending nonmaterial experiences in magazines like *Human Nature, The Zoist,* and *Mind.*[25] The debate was lively and for someone like Tennyson, disturbing. Like so many others he found himself stuck in the middle. On the one hand, his respect for scientific opinion and his personal fears allowed him to take Carpenter seriously, but, on the other hand, his personal otherworldly experiences, his sense of a Platonic Universal realm, and his need to affirm an "otherness" attracted him to the works of Emmanuel Swedenborg and James Hinton, whose books insisted on the reality of the spiritual world.[26]

Most certainly Tennyson's part in the founding of the Metaphysical Society originated in his need to understand the dilemma facing him. It is only natural that he would gravitate toward this group of philosophers, scientists, and clergymen who desired to discuss "with absolute freedom" such subjects as "the immortality and personal identity of the soul; the logic of the sciences; the material hypothesis."[27] One of the earliest members of the society was Carpenter, who delivered a paper in which he summarized the members' dilemma. His summary shows that he was a sympathetic person who, although adamant in his renunciation of a spiritual world, was still not wholly unsympathetic to those who, like Tennyson, felt the reality of a spiritual realm, and hence were challenged by his views. In writing "On the Fallacies of Testimony in Relation to the Supernatural" (reprinted in *The Contemporary Review,* 1876) he stated:

> Every one . . . who watches the course of educated thought at the present time, must see that it is tending towards the exercise of that trained and organized Common Sense which we call "scientific method," on subjects to which it is legitimately applicable within the sphere of Religious inquiry. Science has been progressively, and in various ways, undermining the old "bases of belief;" and men in almost every religious denomination, animated by no spirit but that of reverent loyalty to truth, are now seriously asking themselves, whether the whole fabric of what is commonly regarded as authoritative Revelation must not be carefully re-examined under the searching light of modern criticism, in order that what is sound may be preserved and strengthened, and that insecurity of some parts may not destroy the stability of the whole.[28]

Carpenter's sympathy and his willingness to admit that human beings are not entirely mechanistic—that human will does exercise some influence—drew him not only into the discussions of the Metaphysical Society but also made him more attractive to religious thinkers. For example the Dean of Lincoln, Joseph William Blakesley, one of Tennyson's college friends and a member of the Apostles, reviewed *Principles of Mental*

*Physiology* most favorably. In his review Blakesley speaks of the shadowy borderland in which many in the Metaphysical Society were living.

> There is no question that automatism, including in that term both mental and bodily activities, plays a very large part in the life of every one. What the limits of that part are is the real question at issue, and this it is the object of Dr. Carpenter's work to point out. The book is, in fact, a survey of the borderland between the region of Physical Causation and Moral Causation, taking its departure from the ground of the physiologist.[29]

Early meetings of the society included such advocates of materialism as Carpenter, Frederic Harrison, T. H. Huxley, and Richard Hutton, a bonesetter who, enamored with Herbert Spencer, argued that "what metaphysicians call an intuition or an a priori idea is probably nothing but a special susceptibility in our nerves produced by a vast number of homogeneous ancestral experiences gradually agglutinated into a single intellectual tendency."[30] And the meetings included those like Henry Sidgwick, Walter Bagehot, F. D. Maurice, James Hinton, and Bishop C. J. Ellicott who were not willing to accept materialism. These men were more ready to believe in intuitive knowledge and to recognize a world beyond that of man's immediate senses. For example, rather than champion Spencer, Ellicott reacted against Spencer's definition of death as "the final equilibration which precedes dissolution," or as "the bringing to a close all those integrated motions in any body which arose during its evolution."[31] Ellicott refused to see death in such materialistic terms. He preferred to argue for the immortality of the soul.

In addition to Carpenter's paper, Tennyson heard nine others at the meetings of the society. Two of these must have touched him deeply, for their contents seem to come close to mirroring the dilemma facing him. Questions addressed in these papers were Tennyson's: How is a person to trust the dream's or trance's occasional revelation of a spiritual world? How is a person to trust any sort of intuitive sense of a world beyond this? How is a person to maintain any religious faith? Moments in Sidgwick's paper, "The Verification of Beliefs," (later published in *Contemporary Review*, July 1871) center on these disturbing questions: if the erroneousness of some beliefs is ascertained, then he wonders whether it "suggests the possible erroneousness of all."[32] Bagehot's paper "On the Emotion of Conviction" (also later published in *Contemporary Review*, April 1871) questions the trustworthiness and nature of belief. Sobered by the reasonableness of the scientists' challenge, he warns his audience to "be very careful how we let ourselves believe that which may turn out to be error. . . . Always keep an account in our minds of the degree of evidence on which we hold our convictions, and be most careful that we do not permanently permit ourselves to feel a stronger conviction than the evidence justifies."[33] Tennyson probably felt most sympathetic with Sidgwick's and Bagehot's questions not only because they were similar to his, but also because these speakers cling to the value of intuitive or emotional belief as well as that based on scientific evidence or the intellect. Sidgwick affirms "the force of the direct original intuition which declared them [beliefs] true," and Bagehot acknowledges those convictions coming like "a hot flash" burning across the brain: "Once acutely felt, I believe it is indelible; at least, it does something to the mind which is hard for anything else to undo."[34] The experiences of Bagehot and Sidgwick with intuitive revelation must have given Tennyson much support, for he wished to believe in flashes of spiritual insight or the "heat of inward evidence" ("The Two Voices").

Bagehot's double-bind must have also touched Tennyson. In "On the Emotions of Conviction" Bagehot reveals that he too has trouble believing in flashes of insight and dreams, for they are untrustworthy and, worse, are comparable to "certain forms of insanity, where fixed delusions seize upon the mind and generate a firmer belief than any sane person is capable of."[35] His answer to this double-bind is to temper intuitive enthusiasm or flashes with scientific fact. With this answer in mind, Bagehot is able to conclude his paper in a neat and straightforward manner. Sidgwick has answers too. The conclusion to his paper gives no sense of an uneasy ambiguity: "One may say generally that as the intuitive verification cannot be made entirely trustworthy, it requires to be supplemented by a discursive verification—which consists generally in ascertaining the harmony between the proposition regarded as intuitively certain and other propositions belonging to the same department of fact, and of which Baconian verification is the most important, but by no means the only species."[36]

But Tennyson is not like Bagehot and Sidgwick. Tennyson never seems to be able to believe their neat, conclusive, and confident statements. In fact, Tennyson's only written contribution to the society, "The Higher Pantheism," is structured around ambiguous yet balanced questions and phrases beginning with "if." Typically, the poem ends with a question rather than an answer or a declarative statement. In the poem Tennyson admits he cannot accept that "all dreams" are "true." Yet he cannot deny their validity. The poem shows that Tennyson is a person who is able to identify rather than solve a dilemma.

Later, still searching for answers and seeking confirmation of a world beyond the limits of his immediate senses, Tennyson was among the founders of the Society of Psychical Research, which recorded and examined people's dreams, visions, and communications from the dead. His role in the founding of this society shows his bias. As much as he respected scientific fact and felt it necessary to incorporate it into his poetry, and as much as Huxley could call him "the modern Lucretius," Tennyson could not help but lean toward those who were more spiritual than factual. His earlier admiration for Hinton's work is indicative of his prejudice. He felt drawn toward Hinton's insistence on the reality and necessity of the spiritual world and to this doctor's lengthy, at times strangely repetitive, statements concerning the "nature" of the material world as a shadow or "fictitious image" of the spiritual. He studied and admired Hinton's sense that people can fall into as much error and "obstruct the road to truth" by limiting their thoughts to sense impressions. Tennyson probably envied the doctor's seemingly strong belief in a spiritual presence after death. He would have liked to have been able to write what Hinton wrote in a letter (1851): "I think a correct application of material and physiological science to the facts of man's nature proves that there *is* some 'substance' or agent connected with him which is not appreciable by our senses after his death. I call that the spirit, but it really makes no difference what it is called."[37] Tennyson's desire to confirm a spiritual reality was not, however, strong enough to allow him to write Hinton's words, to keep him at Mary Brotherton's table, or to allow him to ignore medical men like Carpenter. Rather, Tennyson was compelled to acknowledge them all, especially the scientists. As Sidgwick once remarked, Tennyson's "general acceptance" of the world as known to us through physical science "is real and sincere, even when he utters the intensest feeling of its inadequacy to satisfy our deepest needs."[38] Consequently, dreams must constantly be qualified. Only infrequently is there unqualified belief that dreams and visions lead to truth, and then that belief always seems to bring with it a slight trepidation and a compulsion to list the accompanying physiological phenomena. On those few occasions when Tennyson believes he touches that spiritual realm, there is often a sigh of relief, a relaxation on his part, as if momentarily he has won a battle toward survival—survival because for him a world without dreams is unthinkable and deadly.

One result of being caught in the middle was that rarely could Tennyson allow himself to enjoy those moments that seemed to touch the "great Realm." In "The Ancient Sage" he describes one of those rare moments when he does pass "into the Nameless . . . without a shade of doubt." More typically, Tennyson has to envy others and allow them to have these experiences. For example, there is the grandmother who never doubts that the ghosts of her dead children and husband accompany her ("The Grandmother"). More often Tennyson feels compelled to draw

back and qualify the visionary experience either by grounding it in scientific materialism or by sharing his lack of trust in it. An example comes,
significantly, in "The Dreamer," the last poem he completed. In this poem
the doubts are stronger than the vision. He must wonder: "Was it only
the wind of the Night shrilling out / Desolation and wrong / Through a
dream of the dark?"

In one poem, however, Tennyson makes a valiant attempt to reconcile
the debate. *In Memoriam* is a poem in which Tennyson tries to combine
the material and nonmaterial worlds so that he will not be crushed by
materialism. The poem is a fight for survival, a fight to revive his faith
in a world that is not defined by physiologists and geologists. He is
searching for a world in which he can acknowledge scientists' truths
without risking the loss of the spiritual dimensions of life and, of course,
without surrendering the power of the will. At the beginning of the
poem the speaker can only feel the immediate pain of his loss, the death
of Hallam. This pain originates in what Tennyson calls an "absence of
spiritual light." Cut off from the nonmaterial world, the speaker dreams
only those materialistic dreams prompted by his waking thoughts. These
dreams of the ship carrying Hallam's dead body back to England do not
free the speaker from his grief and do not put him in touch with a living
Hallam; rather, they root the speaker deeper in himself. Those dreams
offer him neither release nor the chance to touch the mystic "deep" where
he might meet Hallam's soul. Not only does the grief bind the speaker,
but so do the speaker's doubts. He fears that his dreams are delusive, the
consequences of his fancy, the canker of his brain. The speaker begins to
break away from this difficulty only when he reads Hallam's letters, which
remind him of Hallam's vigorous faith in the nonmaterial, spiritual world.
Hallam's words momentarily release the speaker from his dreamless,
faithless world; consequently, for the first time, he falls into a dreamlike
trance and senses "at last / The living soul was flashed on mine." Even
though that moment is quickly canceled by doubt, the path is open and
the possibility exists. With renewed trust, the speaker's dreaming powers
gradually return. Moreover, with that return comes a sense of a universal
wholeness which permits the speaker to think of the material and the
nonmaterial experiences as being united in that wholeness. The result is
that in lyric 123 he can combine images from Charles Lyell's *Principles of
Geology* with the more shadowy images belonging to a spiritual experience, and he can write: "The hills are shadows, and they flow / From
form to form, and nothing stands; / They melt like mist, the solid lands, /
Like clouds they shape themselves and go." With this sense of wholeness,
the speaker can allow himself to trust his dreams. No longer need he be
distracted by "iron truths" of materialism. Toward the end of *In Memo-*

*riam* he feels comfortable enough to exclaim, "But in my spirit will I dwell / And dream my dream, and hold it true" (lyric 123). The speaker will survive.

The conclusion, however, is more hopeful than Tennyson felt was true. Speaking of *In Memoriam* Tennyson confessed to his friend John Knowles, "It's too hopeful, this poem, more than I am myself. . . . I think of adding another to it, a speculative one, bringing out the thoughts of *The Higher Pantheism*, and showing that all arguments are about as good on one side as the other, and thus throw man back more on the primitive impulses and feelings." [39] Perhaps, in the end, what counted for Tennyson were the primitive impulses and feelings that allowed him occasional glimpses of the spiritual realm. Tennyson knew that he would have to take the risk that his dreams might be erroneous, for if he denied himself those experiences, he would not be a complete person. His view would be limited and cramped and, therefore, even more erroneous. Dreams and visions could help him break through the limits of the material world. They could revive the past and sometimes reach into the future. They could occasionally join the body with the whirring music of the spheres. Consequently, as much as Tennyson respected those physicians and philosophers like Carpenter, he could not remain with them. For sanity's sake he needed to keep looking beyond. He did not wish to become like the knights in King Arthur's court who lost sight of the dream and the ideal and, thereby, lost their sense of self and went mad. That risk was far worse than any other, for in losing the ideal and the self he would be losing the powers allowing him to exercise the sublime repression.

# Notes

## Notes to the Introduction

1. Ralph Wilson Rader, *Tennyson's "Maud": The Biographical Genesis*, Perspectives in Criticism, no. 15 (Berkeley and Los Angeles: University of California Press, 1963).

2. *The Poems of Tennyson*, ed. Christopher Ricks, Longmans Annotated English Poets, ed. F. W. Bateson (London: Longmans, 1969), pp. 846–48.

3. James Anthony Froude, *Thomas Carlyle: A History of His Life in London*, 2 vols. (London: Longmans, Green, 1884), 2: 81.

4. Charles Richard Sanders, "Carlyle and Tennyson," *PMLA* 76 (1961): 82–97.

5. William Knight, "A Reminiscence of Tennyson," *Blackwood's Edinburgh Magazine* 162 (1897): 264–70.

6. Hallam Tennyson, *Alfred Lord Tennyson: A Memoir*, 2 vols. (London: Macmillan, 1897), 1: xi.

7. As quoted in Thomas R. Lounsbury, *The Life and Times of Tennyson from 1809 to 1850* (New Haven: Yale University Press, 1915), p. 14.

8. Charles Tennyson, "The Somersby Tennysons," Christmas Supplement to *Victorian Studies* 7 (1963): 7–55.

9. Knight, "A Reminiscence of Tennyson," p. 266. In *Tennyson and Tradition* (Cambridge: Harvard University Press, 1979), Robert Pattison emphasizes Tennyson's "sensitiveness" about his "originality." Pattison wrote that "Tennyson, one of the most tradition-bound of English poets, was deeply incensed by the charge that he was not original, more incensed than by any other criticism brought against him during all his years of following the critics" (pp. 7, 8).

10. Robert Bernard Martin, *Tennyson: The Unquiet Heart* (Oxford: Clarendon Press, 1980), p. 1.

11. Until Robert Martin's *The Unquiet Heart* (1980) surprisingly few critics have written of Tennyson's experiences with madness and the effect of those experiences on his poetry. Most critics have been and are still content to make a statement about Tennyson's morbidity and then drop the subject. Several critics follow Sir Charles Tennyson's lead by noting biographical allusions to madness in a few of the poems (especially "Locksley Hall" and *Maud*). Only a handful of critics, however, attempt to explore how Tennyson's experiences with madness

influence his poetry. Martin Dodsworth is one. In his essay "Patterns of Morbidity: Repetition in Tennyson's Poetry," Dodsworth sees Tennyson's repetitive style as a product of the poet's instability. See Isobel Armstrong, ed., *The Major Victorian Poets: Reconsiderations* (London: Routledge and Kegan Paul, 1969), pp. 7–34. E. D. H. Johnson is another. His discussion in *The Alien Vision of Victorian Poetry* (Princeton: Princeton University Press, 1952) is the most concentrated and, perhaps, extensive one on madness and Tennyson's poetry. Johnson speaks of madness as a tool for Tennyson, as a way of talking about subjects and attitudes that were alien to Victorian society.

12. It was not long after the Tennyson family left Somersby in 1837 and bought a house in High Beech, Essex, that Tennyson became friendly with Dr. Allen. For a more detailed explanation of Tennyson's visits to Dr. Allen's asylum see Martin, *The Unquiet Heart*, pp. 253–54.

13. Clare remained in the asylum until 1841, when he escaped and walked eighty miles home. Soon after he was placed in the Northampton General Lunatic Asylum, where he stayed until his death in 1864. For details of John Clare's life see J. W. Tibble and Anne Tibble, *John Clare: His Life and Poetry* (London: William Heinemann, 1956). Sir Charles Tennyson suggests that even though there is no evidence that the two met, "it may well be that Allen's kindness to Clare was one cause of Tennyson's attraction to" the doctor (*Alfred Tennyson* [New York: Macmillan, 1949], p. 186).

14. The allusion to the "dark passages" is to the phrase used by John Keats in his letter to John H. Reynolds, 3 May 1818, in *The Letters of John Keats*, ed. Hyder Edward Rollins, 2 vols. (Cambridge: Harvard University Press, 1958), 1: 281. The allusion is a liberal one in that Keats was writing of the mind weighed down by the "burden of mystery," a mystery in which "we see not the balance of good and evil." The phrase, however, is appropriate, for the burden is not only the ensuing "mystery" but also the misery, heartbreak, pain, sickness, and oppression that occasion it.

15. See *The Letters of John Keats*, 2: 88–90. Of course, Keats is by no means the only example of a Romantic poet who explored his dreams. Samuel Taylor Coleridge, for instance, wrote about dreams. At times he could become quite analytical. For example, see his analysis of Martin Luther's dream in essay two of "The Landing-Place" in *The Friend* (London: G. Bell and Sons, 1906).

16. *The Letters of John Keats*, 1: 184–85.

17. "Sanity of True Genius" in *Essays of Elia I: Last Essays of Elia*, ed. Geoffrey Tillotson (London: J. M. Dent and Sons, 1962), p. 219. See also Clare's poems addressed to Charles Lamb: "To Charles Lamb on His Essays" and "To Charles Lamb" in *The Poems of John Clare*, ed. J. W. Tibble (London: J. M. Dent and Sons, 1935).

18. *The Letters of John Keats*, 1: 254–55.

19. Matthew Allen, *Essay on the Classification of the Insane* (London: John Taylor, [1837]), p. 148.

20. *The Letters of John Keats*, 1: 280–81.

21. Ibid., 1: 277.

# Notes to Chapter One

1. For more examples see John R. Reed, "Madness in Literature," in *Victorian Conventions* (Athens: Ohio University Press, 1975), pp. 198–215. See also Sandra M. Gilbert and Susan Gubar, *The Madwoman in the Attic: The Woman Writer and the Nineteenth-Century Literary Imagination* (New Haven: Yale University Press, 1979), pp. 77–83. The emphasis in this study of women writers is that madness offers the writers and their female characters "moments of escape" from "male houses and male texts" and allows them through "the phenomenon of the mad double" to express "hunger, rebellion, and rage" as well as to explore the costs of such anger.

2. Too frequently the interest attached to these mad figures is "literary." That is, the critic's energy tends to be directed toward tracing the literary conventions associated with the madness. For example, although John R. Reed is aware that "madness was a real part of every man's consciousness" (*Victorian Conventions*, p. 214), he does little to put his understanding to work. The thrust of his discussion is toward the influence of the literary conventions over the various portraits of madness.

3. See *Macaulay's Essay on Lord Clive*, ed. J. W. Pearce (New York: Macmillan, 1907). It originally appeared in the January 1840 *Edinburgh Review*. See also John Henry Newman, *The Idea of a University: Defined and Illustrated*, ed. I. T. Ker (Oxford: Clarendon Press, 1976), pp. 126–29.

4. For a fuller discussion of King George III's illness, see "George III," in Richard Hunter and Ida Macalpine, ed., *Three Hundred Years of Psychiatry, 1535–1860* (London: Oxford University Press, 1963), pp. 509–14. This book is an invaluable anthology for anyone interested in the history of psychology. The anthology offers selections from numerous treatises, essays, and books on insanity. Other materials that survey attitudes toward insanity in the nineteenth century are: John R. Reed, "Insanity: An Overview," in *Victorian Conventions*, pp. 193–98, and Vieda Skultans, ed., *Madness and Morals: Ideas on Insanity in the Nineteenth Century* (London: Routledge and Kegan Paul, 1975). See also Vieda Skultans, *English Madness: Ideas on Insanity, 1580–1890* (London: Routledge and Kegan Paul, 1979); Andrew Scull, ed., *Madhouses, Mad-Doctors and Madmen: The Social History of Psychiatry in the Victorian Era* (London: Athlone Press, 1981), and Klaus Doerner, *Madmen and the Bourgeoisie: A Social History of Insanity and Psychiatry* (Oxford: Basil Blackwell, 1981).

5. Philippe Pinel, "Insanity without Chains," in *Three Hundred Years of Psychiatry*, p. 606.

6. Introduction to "John Conolly," in *Three Hundred Years of Psychiatry*, p. 806.

7. Sir Benjamin Brodie, *Lectures Illustrative of Certain Local Nervous Affections* (London: Longman, Rees, Orme, Brown, Green, and Longman, 1837), p. 3.

8. For an example see the 1848 volume of the *Athenaeum: Journal of Literature, Science, and the Fine Arts* and see the 17 January 1852 issue of *Household Words*. Charles Dickens, who edited *Household Words*, was a friend of Dr. John Conolly and of John Foster, an officer of the Lunacy Commission. Dickens's interest in

insanity prompted him not only to feature articles on it in his journal, but also to visit mental asylums during his tour to America. In England on Boxing Day 1851 Dickens visited St. Luke's Hospital. An account of that visit is in the 17 January 1852 issue of *Household Words*. On a later visit to St. Luke's, Dickens wrote the following in the visitor's book (January 1858): "Much delighted with the great improvements in the Hospital, under many difficulties—with the excellent demeanour of the attendants—and with the benignant and wise spirit of the whole administration."

9. For examples see: J. Scoffern, "Insanity," *St. James' Magazine* 13 (May–July 1865): 373–81; "Clouded Intellects," *St. James' Magazine* 27 (October 1870–March 1871): 383–94; Sir James Clark, "Mad Folk," *Belgravia*, n.s. 9 (July 1869): 109–13; and W. H. Lewis, "Tame Lunatics," *Belgravia*, n.s. 10 (February 1870): 467–78.

10. [Andrew Wynter], "The First Beginnings," *Cornhill Magazine* 5 (1862): 481–94.

11. George Cheyne's book *The English Malady; or, A Treatise on Nervous Diseases of All Kinds* (London: Strahan and Leake, 1733) seems to have set a trend for the English to think of insanity as their disease. It should be remembered, however, that Cheyne was picking up a commonplace that, for example, is visible at the end of the seventeenth century when Sir William Temple wrote that "our country must be conferred to be what a great foreign physician called it, the region of spleen; which may arise a good deal from the great uncertainty and many sudden changes of our weather in all seasons of the year" ("Of Poetry" in *The Works of Sir William Temple, Bart. Complete in Four Volumes To Which Is Prefixed, The Life and Character of the Author, Considerably Enlarged*, new ed., 4 vols. [New York: Greenwood Press, 1968], 3: 440). Later Thomas Arnold's *Observations on the Nature, Kinds, Causes, and Prevention of Insanity, Lunacy, or Madness* (1782–86; reprint ed., London: Richard Phillips, 1806) keeps the question of the nation's sanity very much alive by devoting a whole section to it. See also *Madness and Morals*, p. 10, and two studies of madness in eighteenth-century England: Michael DePorte, *Nightmares and Hobbyhorses: Swift, Sterne, and Augustan Ideas of Madness* (San Marino: Huntington Library, 1974), and Max Byrd, *Visits to Bedlam: Madness and Literature in the Eighteenth Century* (Columbia: University of South Carolina Press, 1974).

12. Parliamentary committees investigating the welfare and treatment of lunatics were convened frequently. In the first half of the century alone, special committees were formed eleven times. Perhaps the most important result of these committees was the 1827 Lunacy Bill, which stipulated that asylums should be inspected four times a year, that records should be kept of each patient, and that there should be one medical officer for at least every hundred patients. Another important act was that of 1828, which empowered commissioners to visit private asylums in the metropolitan area four times a year. These commissioners had the right to grant or revoke licenses.

13. *Report from the Committee Appointed to Examine the Physicians Who Have*

*Attended His Majesty, during His Illness; Touching the State of His Health,* in *Three Hundred Years of Psychiatry,* p. 674.

14. Benjamin Rush invented a number of new terms. "Among these were 'Tristimania' for a 'form of madness when erroneous opinions respecting a man's person, affairs, or condition, are the subjects of his distress' replacing 'hypochondriasis' . . . 'Amenomania' for 'a higher grade of hypochondriasis' going over into frank madness; 'Manicula' for 'Mania' in a 'reduced' or 'chronic' state; 'Manalgia' for a 'general madness' characterised by . . . a total neglect of dress" ("Benjamin Rush," in *Three Hundred Years of Psychiatry,* p. 664).

15. As early as 1809 a reviewer wrote, "the distinction of the different kinds of insanity is a matter of no less delicacy than the definition of insanity itself: for these varieties pass into each other still more frequently and more imperceptibly than insanity passes into health" ("Haslam, Arnold, etc. on Insanity," *Quarterly Review* 2, no. 3 (1809): 155–80). In the 1830s Dr. John Abercrombie, a physician interested in the mental aspects of medicine, wrote, "When the mental impression is of a depressing character, the modification of the disease is produced which is called melancholia. It seems to differ from mania merely in the subject of hallucination, and accordingly we find the two at one time, in a state of melancholic depression, and at another of maniacal excitement" ("John Abercrombie," in *Three Hundred Years of Psychiatry,* p. 803). Later Dr. Matthew Allen, Tennyson's friend, repeated the belief when he stated that the "excitement of the depressing and exhilirating passions alternately, is the most striking characteristic of the insane." See Matthew Allen, *Essay on the Classification of the Insane* (London: John Taylor, [1837]), p. 17.

16. "Jean Étienne Dominique Esquirol," in *Three Hundred Years of Psychiatry,* p. 735. Following the lead of Esquirol, in the 1830s James Cowles Prichard, commissioner of lunacy, pointed out that the melancholia had "become improper in modern times" ("James Cowles Prichard," in *Three Hundred Years of Psychiatry,* p. 837).

17. Michel Foucault, *Madness and Civilization: A History of Insanity in the Age of Reason,* trans. Richard Howard (New York: Random House, 1973), p. 68.

18. Brodie, *Lectures Illustrative of Certain Local Nervous Affections,* p. 46.

19. Ibid. p. 2.

20. In the 1830s Dr. James Cowles Prichard defined moral insanity as a "form of mental derangement" in which there is "a morbid perversion of the feelings, affections, and active powers, without any illusion or erroneous conviction impressed upon the understanding. . . . The most frequent forms . . . of the disease are those which are characterised either by the kind of excitement already described [bad temper], or by the opposite state of melancholy dejection. . . . A state of gloom and melancholy depression occasionally gives way after an uncertain period to an opposite condition of preternatural excitement. . . . In this form of moral derangement the disordered condition of the mind displays itself in a want of self-government, in continual excitement, an unusual expression of strong feelings, in thoughtless and extravagant conduct" ("James Cowles Prichard," in

*Three Hundred Years of Psychiatry*, p. 839). For more examples of discussions on moral insanity see Alexander Morison, "Moral Causes of Insanity, 1824," and George Man Burrows, "Moral Causes of Insanity as They Affect Different Social Classes, 1828" and "Moral Insanity," in *Madness and Morals*, pp. 32–33; 36–38; 186–200.

21. For a discussion of madness in the eighteenth century see DePorte, *Nightmares and Hobbyhorses*, pp. 3–53. In 1815 Thomas Bakewell, owner of Spring Vale Asylum in Staffordshire, summarized this continued equation between madness and false reason when he wrote, "The whole may be reduced to this, that Insanity consists in the power of erroneous conceptions of thought." ("Thomas Bakewell," in *Three Hundred Years of Psychiatry*, p. 709).

22. For an account of Daniel McNaughton's trial see "The McNaughton Rules," in *Three Hundred Years of Psychiatry*, pp. 919–22.

23. It is John Barlow who wrote, "The madman has the false report from his own senses" (*Madness and Morals*, p. 164).

24. In "Haslam, Arnold, etc. on Insanity," the reviewer states that "among the physical causes of madness, Mr. Haslam enumerates, in his fifth chapter," are "intoxication, blows, fever, the use of mercury, suppressed eruptions and discharges, hereditary disposition, and paralytic affections" (p. 170). Haslam's belief lived on. By the 1840s, like many of his colleagues, Thomas Octavius Prichard stressed that "insanity always originates in a corporeal cause" ("Thomas Octavius Prichard," in *Three Hundred Years of Psychiatry*, p. 898).

25. "Thomas Trotter," in *Three Hundred Years of Psychiatry*, pp. 588–91.

26. Benjamin Rush believed, for example, that children born prior to the attack of madness in their parents are less likely to be insane than those born after the attack ("Benjamin Rush," in *Three Hundred Years of Psychiatry*, p. 667). In 1854 Alfred Beaumont Maddock claimed that the mental state or attitude of the parents at the moment of conception affects the children (*Madness and Morals*, p. 206).

27. In 1873 the belief in the hereditary transmission of a predisposition toward madness was strong enough for Henry Maudsley, professor of medical jurisprudence at University College, London, to exclaim, "No one can escape the tyranny of his organization; no one can escape the destiny that is innate in him" (*Madness and Morals*, p. 23). In the same year Sir James Paget delivered a lecture in which he said: "The family relationship between nervous mimicries and mental insanity is specially worth considering. . . . I believe that a large majority of the worser [*sic*] cases of nervous mimicry occur in members of families in which mental insanity has been frequent." He opened his lecture on the premise that "facts relating to inheritance deserve great weight in the diagnosis of any doubtful case of nervous mimicry" ("Clinical Lectures on the Nervous Mimicry of Organic Diseases, Delivered at St. Bartholomew's Hospital," *Lancet*, no. 2616 (18 October 1873), p. 547).

28. For discussion of blood circulation and mental health see Ilza Veith, *Hysteria: The History of a Disease* (Chicago: University of Chicago Press, 1965), pp. 98, 124, 131–32, 156, 227.

29. Paul Slade Knight, *Observations on the Causes, Symptoms, and Treatments of*

*Derangement of the Mind, Founded on Extensive Moral and Medical Practice in the Treatment of Lunatics*, (1827), in *Three Hundred Years of Psychiatry*, p. 774.

30. It was the French doctor Antoine Laurent Jesse Bayle who gave an impetus to English doctors like George Man Burrows. Dr. Bayle confidently connected "specific symptoms of mental disorder with specific morbid conditions of the encephalon, with which there is a uniform correspondence,—but also to shew, that in a great proportion of cases, the commencement of the mental disturbance is to be imputed to a chronic disease of the membranes" (*Three Hundred Years of Psychiatry*, p. 781).

31. For example, William Willis Moseley in his book *Eleven Chapters on Nervous and Mental Complaints* (London: Simpkin, Marshall, 1838) wrote: "Strong passions are dangerous adjuncts to all, but especially to youth." So concerned was he that in italics he wrote, "*Let moderation, therefore, govern thee, O, Reader!* " (*Madness and Morals*, pp. 42, 45).

32. Many French physicians were intrigued with the excesses of the French Revolution. Philippe Pinel was one who wrote, "The storms of the revolution, stirred up corresponding tempests in the passions of men, and overwhelmed not a few in total ruin of their distinguished birthright as rational beings" (*Three Hundred Years of Psychiatry*, p. 607). Dugald Stewart, professor of moral philosophy at Edinburgh University, was also interested in the phenomenon of "sympathetic imitation." He used the phrase to explain the "contagious nature of convulsions, hysteric disorders, panics, and various enthusiasms" ("Dugald Stewart," in ibid., pp. 641–43). This fascination with and fear of the excesses of the French Revolution and with the phenomenon of mass hysteria also finds expression in Thomas Carlyle's *The French Revolution: A History* (1837) and in Charles Dickens's *Tale of Two Cities* (1859). This fascination and fear are prominent in Dickens's *Barnaby Rudge: A Tale of the Riots of 'Eighty* (1840–41), in which Dickens's attitude toward the lawlessness of the mob and the burning of Newgate Prison echo the fall of the Bastille. Dickens's conception of Barnaby is also rooted in the madness associated with such mob violence, for the character of Barnaby is partially based on that of Lord George Gordon who led the riots and who was reputed to suffer from a mad streak.

33. "Haslam, Arnold, etc. on Insanity," p. 172. Samuel Foart Simmons, the physician to St. Luke's Hospital, offered another example of the interest in statistical data. He was able to produce "the first actual figures from a large institution for the insane to substantiate what before had only been an impression gained from isolated cases, namely that old age in general and 'fatuity' or dementia in particular adversely affected the chance of recovery" ("Samuel Foart Simmons," in *Three Hundred Years of Psychiatry*, p. 672).

34. For discussions concerning the indiscriminate uses of physical cures such as bleeding and blistering see Robert Gardiner Hill, "Total Abolition of Personal Restraint in the Treatment of the Insane" (1830), in *Three Hundred Years of Psychiatry*, pp. 886–92. See also the works of Benjamin Rush, who was an advocate of large bleedings. In 1795 Rush believed that mania is "in nearly all cases accompanied by inflammation of the brain," and so he began his notorious copious bleedings—up to forty ounces at a time. He wrote a defense of his bloodletting

in his *Medical Inquiries and Observations, upon the Diseases of the Mind.* See *Three Hundred Years of Psychiatry,* pp. 662–64.

35. For illustrations of the swinging machine see figs. 118 and 131 in *Three Hundred Years of Psychiatry,* pp. 601, 605.

36. For an illustration of the Tranquillizer see fig. 134 in *Three Hundred Years of Psychiatry,* p. 671.

37. Introduction to "Thomas Bakewell," in *Three Hundred Years of Psychiatry,* p. 705. Bakewell felt comfortable enough with his convictions to admit that when "a maniac confined in a room over my own . . . bellowed like a wild beast, and shook his chain, almost constantly for several days and nights . . . I . . . got up, took a hand whip, and gave him a few smart stripes on the shoulder . . . he disturbed me no more."

38. Foucault, *Madness and Civilization,* p. 72.

39. See, for example, Fitzjames Stephen, "Commissions of Lunacy," *Cornhill Magazine* 5 (1862): 220–32; John Charles Bucknill, "Abolition of Proprietary Madhouses," *Nineteenth Century* 17 (1885): 263–79; J. R. Gasquet, "Lunacy Law Reform," *Nineteenth Century* 17 (1885): 857–68.

40. See fig. 199 in *Three Hundred Years of Psychiatry,* p. 887.

41. "Robert Gardiner Hill," in *Three Hundred Years of Psychiatry,* p. 887.

42. Ibid., p. 891.

43. Ibid., p. 892.

44. Allen, *Essay on the Classification of the Insane,* pp. 29–32.

45. John Abercrombie, "Moral Discipline," in *Madness and Morals,* pp. 157–59. Many other physicians were also to emphasize the will's power. John Charles Bucknill was an advocate of "The Supremacy of the Will" (in ibid., p. 174); Daniel Hack Tuke also believed in the importance of developing a patient's will. In 1872 he wrote, "The power of the Will in resisting disease, apart from the influence of the Imagination or the concentration of the Attention, is unquestionable" ("The Importance of Arousing the Patient's Will," in ibid., p. 175). Earlier Daniel Noble's "Elements of Psychological Medicine" (1853) had concluded by emphasizing "the importance of energetically exercising the will. . . . If this were well-understood and acted-upon, there is no doubt that many cases of melancholia and notional delusion would be prevented" (in ibid., p. 171).

46. Paget, "Clinical Lectures on the Nervous Mimicry of Organic Diseases," pp. 511–13.

47. See, for example, Alexander Comfort, *The Anxiety Makers: Some Curious Preoccupations of the Medical Profession,* National History and Society Series (London: Thomas Nelson and Sons, 1967), pp. 69–113, and figs. 5, 6a, 6b, facing pp. 104–5.

48. For a strong argument for clitoridectomies see I. Baker Brown, *On the Curability of Certain Forms of Insanity, Epilepsy, Catalepsy, and Hysteria in Females* (London, 1866). See also A. Eyer, "Clitoridectomy for the Cure of Certain Cases of Masturbation in Young Girls," *International Medical Magazine* 3 (1894–95): 259–62. Although John S. Haller, Jr., and Robin M. Haller in their book *The Physician and Sexuality in Victorian America* (Urbana: University of Illinois Press, 1974) do not discuss clitoridectomies, they do address the connection between attitudes

toward sexual behavior, the sexual organs, and the emotional well-being of an individual. Haller and Haller write specifically about the electric shock treatments that were used to treat numerous sexual complaints including masturbation.

49. In 1843 John Barlow, for example, wrote in "Man's Power over Himself to Prevent or Control Insanity" that "to educate a man, in the full and proper sense of the word, is to supply him with the power of controlling his feelings, and his thoughts, and his actions." (in *Madness and Morals*, p. 166).

50. See, for example, Emily Davies, "Women and University Degrees," *Thoughts on Some Questions Relating to Women, 1860–1900* (1901; reprint ed., New York: Doubleday, 1971).

51. Elizabeth Jenkins, *Tennyson and Dr. Gully*, Tennyson Society Occasional Papers, no. 13 (Lincoln: Tennyson Research Centre, 1974), p. 5.

52. For examples see Reed, *Victorian Conventions*, pp. 198–201. For a review of attitudes toward madness in the middle ages see Penelope B. R. Doob, *Nebuchadnezzar's Children: Conventions of Madness in Middle English Literature* (New Haven: Yale University Press, 1974), pp. 1–53.

53. It is not unusual to find nineteenth-century physicians quoting Robert Burton as an authority on insanity. For example, Benjamin Rush wrote: "Dr. Burton, in his *Anatomy of Melancholy*, remarks that children born of parents who are in the decline of life, are more predisposed to one of the forms of partial insanity than children born under contrary circumstances" (*Three Hundred Years of Psychiatry*, p. 667). John Ferriar, physician to Manchester Lunatic Hospital, borrowed many ideas from Burton's *Anatomy* ("John Ferriar," in ibid., p. 543).

54. Robert Burton, *Anatomy of Melancholy*, 3 vols. (New York: Armstrong and Son, 1889), 1: 64.

55. D. Hack Tuke, "Modern Life and Insanity," *Macmillan's Magazine* 37, no. 218 (1877): 130–40.

56. In his biography of Tennyson, Sir Charles Tennyson writes about Tennyson's literary preferences: "He had all his life been an assiduous student of the Elizabethan and Ancient Greek theatre and of the romantic drama of Goethe and Schiller." *Alfred Tennyson* (New York: Macmillan, 1949), p. 410.

57. Byrd, *Visits to Bedlam*, p. 5. Byrd, of course, is not the only critic to consider madness as a metaphor of tragedy. For example, T. B. Tomlinson, in *A Study of Elizabethan and Jacobean Tragedy* (Cambridge: Cambridge University Press, 1964), speaks of madness as a metaphor of chaos and instability (p. 3); and Theodore Lidz, in *Hamlet's Enemy: Madness and Myth in Hamlet* (New York: Basic Books, 1975), points out how Shakespeare uses madness "to convey the disillusion and despair that pervade the characters . . . to express the dissolution of the world" (p. 33).

58. M. C. Bradbrook, *Themes and Conventions of Elizabethan Tragedy* (Cambridge: Cambridge University Press, 1960), p. 222.

59. For a discussion of how closely John Ford studied Burton's *Anatomy* see S. Blaine Ewing, *Burtonian Melancholy in the Plays of John Ford*, Princeton Studies in English, no. 19, ed. G. H. Gerould (Princeton: Princeton University Press, 1940). See also Lawrence Babb, *The Elizabethan Malady: A Study of Melancholia*

*in English Literature from 1580–1612* (East Lansing, Mich.: State College Press, 1951).

60. Hallam Tennyson, *Alfred Lord Tennyson: A Memoir*, 2 vols. (London: Macmillan, 1898), 2: 503.

61. For a full discussion of *The Dunciad* and madness see Byrd, *Visits to Bedlam*, pp. 13–59.

62. In *Nightmares and Hobbyhorses*, pp. 55–105, DePorte talks at length about madness as "a staple of satire" and discusses Jonathan Swift's use of madness as a satirical tool.

63. *Poems of Jonathan Swift*, ed. Harold Williams, 3 vols. (Oxford: Clarendon Press, 1937), 3: 831, ll. 47–62.

64. In *Victorian Conventions*, Reed talks briefly about madness as a metaphor of moral disorder: "Clearly Dickens was mainly concerned with madness as a metaphor for aspects of the human condition. He made no more attempt at precise delineation than did Scott or Charlotte Brontë. But more suggestively than either, he implied through the convention of madness some monstrous consequences of conduct that violated a natural moral order" (p. 203).

65. Fredson Bowers, *Elizabethan Revenge Tragedy* (Princeton: Princeton University Press, 1940), p. 115. In *Visits to Bedlam* Byrd also alludes to the convention. In speaking of *King Lear* he says: "The idea that Lear has taken over the role of the Fool means that he has also taken over both the exile and the license of the fool: an outcast, he is now free to talk in ways normally forbidden; has the license to criticize with impunity. Such license has always been the prerogative of the fool, but it has been the prerogative of madness as well. Indeed, one of the fascinating things about the madman to ordinary men is the leave he has to speak his mind" (p. 4). In his own way Tennyson also recognized this convention. Hallam Tennyson recalls that "the parts of Irving's *Hamlet* which my father thought best were the dreamy and poetical sides, and when he showed 'a method in his madness as well as the madness in his method'" (*Memoir*, 2: 151).

66. Reed, *Victorian Conventions*, pp. 209, 211.

67. Byrd, *Visits to Bedlam*, p. 96.

68. One example is the blunt soldier in John Fletcher's *Mad Lover* who can only kneel before his object of affection and ludicrously exclaim, "O Venus." Other examples are the lover in John Ford's *The Lover's Melancholy* who "runs a headlong course to desparate madness," Penthea in Ford's *The Broken Heart*, and Ophelia in Shakespeare's *Hamlet*, who can no longer bear the anguish of frustrated love and dies singing mad songs. Added to these crazed lovers are Tamora in Shakespeare's *Titus Andronicus*, whose insane ambition destroys and makes mad all who stand in her way, and the characters in Ben Jonson's *Sejanus, His Fall* who ruin themselves with a maddening single ambition. Then there are many more like Hieronimo in Thomas Kyd's *The Spanish Tragedy* whose excessive grief and obsession rip them apart.

69. Ann Radcliffe, *The Mysteries of Udolpho: A Romance*, ed. Bonamy Dobrée (London: Oxford University Press, 1966), pp. 278, 296.

70. For a fuller discussion of madness in these novels see Reed, *Victorian Conventions*, pp. 203–8.

71. For examples of these stock figures see Thomas Percy's *Ballads*, book one of William Cowper's *The Task*, and chapter 32 of Sir Walter Scott's *Ivanhoe*. It is interesting to note that Tennyson's father composed a Tom O'Bedlam ballad. Tennyson wrote out a copy for himself.

72. Thomas Middleton and William Rowley, *The Changeling*, ed. Matthew W. Black, Mathew Carey Library of English and American Literature (Philadelphia: University of Pennsylvania Press, 1966), act 3, sc. 3, lines 196–98.

73. Penelope B. R. Doob, *Nebuchadnezzar's Children*, pp. 54–55.

74. M. C. Bradbrook, *The Growth and Structure of Elizabethan Comedy* (London: Chatto and Windus, 1961), pp. 181–85.

75. For a lengthy treatment of this willingness to engage the extraordinary see Mario Praz, *The Romantic Agony*, trans. Angus Davidson (Cleveland: World, 1951).

76. Shelley uses these words to describe the "gloomy passion" belonging to the Protestant religion. See "Preface to the Cenci" in *The Cenci: A Tragedy in Five Acts*, Shelley Society Publications, 4th series, miscellaneous, no. 3 (New York: AMS Press, 1975), p. 5.

77. *"So late into the Night": Byron's Letters and Journals*, ed. Leslie A. Marchand, 6 vols. (Cambridge: Harvard University Press, 1976), 5: 165.

78. [Arthur] Rimbaud, *Oeuvres Complètes*, ed. Antoine Adam (Paris: Gallimard, 1972), p. 251.

79. In the spirit of the beautiful suicide, Gustave Flaubert recalls dreaming of suicide. He speaks of his friends who "lived in a strange world . . . we swung between madness and suicide; some of them killed themselves . . . another strangled himself with his tie, several died of debauchery in order to escape boredom; it was *beautiful*" (as quoted in A. Alvarez, *The Savage God: A Study of Suicide* [New York: Random House, 1970], p. 211).

80. Charles Tennyson, *Alfred Tennyson*, p. 604.

## Notes to Chapter Two

1. Charles Tennyson and Hope Dyson, *The Tennysons: Background to Genius* (London: Macmillan, 1974), pp. 32–42.

2. From a letter written by Dr. Tennyson to his brother Charles in February 1824, as quoted in Charles Tennyson, *Alfred Tennyson* (London: Macmillan, 1968), p. 31.

3. Robert B. Martin in *Tennyson: The Unquiet Heart* (Oxford: Clarendon Press, 1980), pp. 10–11 emphasizes Dr. Tennyson's epilepsy and tends to treat it as a purely physical disease.

4. In February 1824 Dr. Tennyson wrote to his brother Charles, "I fear my powers are sensibly declining and the attacks to which I am subject must necessarily injure the intellect. I have had two in the last five days" (Charles Tennyson, *Alfred Tennyson*, p. 46). At the same time, Dr. Tennyson's son Charles was writing to his grandfather, "My father at this moment excessively ill from spasms of

the chest, desires me to say that he feels utterly unable to meet you. . . . Last night he suffered very much from the same cause. Tonight it has returned with greater violence. My father is lying for ease on the floor and it is now midnight" (Tennyson and Dyson, *The Tennysons*, p. 70). In his biography of Tennyson, Robert Martin discusses at length Dr. Tennyson's epilepsy and the family's fear that the epilepsy was hereditary. See Martin, *Tennyson: The Unquiet Heart*, pp. 32–51.

5. In 1822 Dr. Tennyson went to Cheltenham for a "cure" (Tennyson and Dyson, *The Tennysons*, p. 59). Later Dr. Bousfield strongly suggested that Dr. Tennyson go on a continental tour to help restore his equilibrium. Consequently, in 1827 Dr. Tennyson went to Paris (Charles Tennyson, *Alfred Tennyson*, p. 53). Two years later he returned to the continent for yet another tour, but with little long-lasting benefits. Soon after his return to England in 1830, he began to drink excessively, and he also began to take increasing amounts of laudanum (Charles Tennyson, *Alfred Tennyson*, pp. 79–81). For more details of Dr. Tennyson's life see Tennyson and Dyson, *The Tennysons*, pp. 55–69.

6. Charles Tennyson and Hope Dyson write about the night when Dr. Tennyson "was found with a large knife and a loaded gun in his room. He was with difficulty restrained from firing the gun through the kitchen window and threatened to kill Frederick and others with the knife" (*The Tennysons*, p. 72). This behavior was not unusual for Dr. Tennyson in the 1820s. He often collapsed into rage after drinking. A nephew describes Dr. Tennyson's behavior: "He is sometimes perfectly sensible—at others, talks wildly and is evidently deranged for the time being" (as quoted in Christopher Ricks, *Tennyson*, Masters of World Literature Series, ed. Louis Kronenberger [New York: Macmillan, 1972], p. 27). Dr. Tennyson's instability caused an old family friend, Rev. William Chaplin, great concern. On 10 October 1827, Rev. Chaplin wrote to Dr. Tennyson's brother telling him that Dr. Tennyson "is now dangerously disposed to his wife and children: I dread the fatal effects towards some of them, which would consign him to perpetual confinement for his life— . . . this excessive habit of drinking brings on such fits, that he is deranged as madness can be described. . . . The children are alarmed at him" (in Tennyson and Dyson, *The Tennysons*, p. 66). Dr. Tennyson's instability, in fact, was alarming enough to make it desirable that Alfred and Charles leave home and join their brother Frederick at Cambridge (ibid., p. 68).

7. Tennyson and Dyson, *The Tennysons*, p. 73. Elizabeth wrote to her father-in-law expressing her fear for her safety and her desire to take rooms elsewhere. See also Martin, *Tennyson: The Unquiet Heart*, pp. 48–50.

8. Charles Tennyson, *Alfred Tennyson*, p. 47.

9. For an account of Tennyson's fears of blindness see Charles Tennyson, *Alfred Tennyson*, p. 112 and Ricks, *Tennyson*, pp. 65–66. See also Martin, *Tennyson: The Unquiet Heart*, p. 25. For an account of his throwing himself on the grave see Hallam Tennyson, *Alfred, Lord Tennyson: A Memoir*, 2 vols. (London: Macmillan, 1898), 1: 15. Charles Tennyson repeats the story in *Alfred Tennyson*, p. 48.

10. "Song [A spirit haunts the year's last hours]," in *The Poems of Tennyson*, ed. Christopher Ricks, Longmans Annotated English Poets, ed. F. W. Bateson

(London: Longmans, 1969), pp. 215–16, ll. 1–6. Subsequent references to poems from this book are given in text.

11. "The Hall" is an allusion to Bayons Manor, the Tennyson family home, which would have belonged to Dr. Tennyson if his father had not disinherited him in favor of the second son, Charles.

12. For a study of Tennyson's sensitivity to literary tradition see Robert Pattison, *Tennyson and Tradition* (Cambridge: Harvard University Press, 1979). In his study of Tennyson's early poetry, W. D. Paden writes that Tennyson's "own emotional state" is responsible for his being drawn to Byron's melancholic verse. See *Tennyson in Egypt: A Study of the Images in His Earlier Work* (Lawrence: University of Kansas Press, 1942), p. 60.

13. Tennyson and Dyson, *The Tennysons*, p. 78.

14. Note for example the following lines from "The Voyage of Maeldune":

And we stayed three days, and we gorged and we maddened, till every
    one drew
His sword on his fellow to slay him, and ever they struck and they slew;
And myself, I had eaten but sparely, and fought till I sundered the fray,
Then I bad them remember my father's death, and we sailed away.

[ll. 67–70]

15. For another summary of the emotional difficulties of Tennyson's brothers and sisters see Martin, *Tennyson: The Unquiet Heart*, pp. 136–38.

16. Ricks, *Tennyson*, p. 62.

17. Ibid., p. 63. Edward remained in an asylum until his death in 1890.

18. In Tennyson and Dyson, *The Tennysons*, pp. 80–81.

19. Charles Tennyson, *Alfred Tennyson*, p. 60.

20. "There is a tradition in the family that she [Matilda] had at the age of six months been dropped on a coal scuttle which injured her head and caused some mental derangement in after years" (Tennyson and Dyson, *The Tennysons*, p. 146).

21. Ibid., p. 195.

22. From a letter written by George Clayton Tennyson to his son Charles, 21 March 1823, as quoted in ibid., p. 62. The opening of the letter reads: "I understand your brother is in his usual state of health and spirits. You may write to him [Dr. Tennyson] if you think proper, he will not consent to see us! but we have and always will do our Duty to him and all our children as well as we can yet we cannot but feel his condition of mind and more on his account than on our own. I believe he is in a very bad state of health, and you too our dutiful Charles are a great invalid and sufferer. Eliza and Mary also. You may be sure we cannot be happy. God be thank'd your dear Mother is in as good health as she commonly is."

23. As quoted in ibid., p. 31.

24. Ibid., pp. 9–38. When Arthur's nervousness and alcoholism sent him to the Crichton Institute in 1842, the family must have thought the sins of the father had passed on to the son. The convictions of the public and the institute's superintendent, Dr. Browne, would have encouraged their fears, for in the 1840s Dr.

Browne was reflecting public opinion when he declared, "whatever tends to exalt or depress, or disturb the function of the nervous system (such as alcohol) in the parent tends to create a predisposition to mental imperfection, or irregularity, or vitiation in the child."

25. For a list of medical books in Dr. Tennyson's library see George Moore, "A Critical and Bibliographical Study of the Somersby Library of Doctor George Clayton Tennyson," (Ph.D. diss., University of Nottingham, 1966), p. 49.

26. Tennyson and Dyson, *The Tennysons*, p. 63.

27. Hallam Tennyson, *Memoir*, 1: 101–2.

28. Ricks, *Tennyson*, p. 235.

29. *The Letters of Emily Lady Tennyson*, ed. James O. Hoge (University Park: Pennsylvania State University Press, 1974), pp. 210, 217.

30. Charles Tennyson, "The Somersby Tennysons," Christmas Supplement to *Victorian Studies* 7 (December 1963): 7–55. Picture faces p. 9. Sir Charles suggests that the two "Brothers in Misery" are Alfred and Charles.

31. These letters were collected by Sir Charles Tennyson for the biography of his grandfather. They are housed in the Tennyson Research Centre, Lincoln.

32. The story is a popular one, therefore, it is often repeated. See Charles Tennyson, *Alfred Tennyson*, p. 199 and Ricks, *Tennyson*, p. 63.

33. *William Allingham's Diary*, ed. Geoffrey Grigson (Fontwell, Sussex: Centaur Press, 1967), p. 132. Entry is dated Wednesday, 13 June [1866]. Allingham always referred to Alfred Tennyson as "T."

34. Typical of this reaction is that of Aubrey deVere and Agnes Grace Weld. DeVere wrote to Miss Fenwick on 24 September 1854 exclaiming, "A. Tennyson has been very greatly blessed in his marriage. . . . He is much happier and proportionally less morbid than he used to be." See Wilfrid Ward, *Aubrey deVere: A Memoir* (London: Longmans, 1904), p. 227. Agnes Grace Weld recalls, "After his marriage my uncle found it much easier to shake off these fits of depression than he had done in the days when my mother knew him as one sorely tried by the long deferment of that marriage with her sister which at last brought the 'peace of God' into his life." See Agnes Grace Weld, *Glimpses of Tennyson and of Some of His Relations and Friends* (London: Williams and Norgate, 1903), p. 50. For more recent responses see Joanna Richardson, *The Pre-Eminent Victorian* (London: Jonathan Cape, 1962), p. 63; *The Letters of Emily Lady Tennyson*, p. 7, and *Lady Tennyson's Journal*, ed. James O. Hoge (Charlottesville: University of Virginia Press, 1981), p. 7: "Emily adored Tennyson, and, though without question he was periodically restless and troubled even after he married her, she tempered the periods of discontent and enabled him to survive them."

35. The letter is housed in the Tennyson Research Centre, Lincoln, Eng.

36. *The Letters of Emily Lady Tennyson*, p. 317.

37. Ibid., p. 317.

38. Emily Lady Tennyson, "Recollections of My Early Life," in *Tennyson and His Friends*, ed. Hallam, Lord Tennyson (London: Macmillan, 1911), p. 7.

39. In 1852, shortly after their marriage, Alfred and Emily visited Malvern, where Dr. Marsden, one of Dr. Gully's partners, saw Emily. During that visit

the doctor encouraged Tennyson to learn the art of mesmerism. See Charles Tennyson, *Alfred Tennyson*, p. 268 and Elizabeth Jenkins, *Tennyson and Dr. Gully*, Tennyson Society Occasional Papers, no. 3 (Lincoln, Eng.: 1974), pp. 10–11. Two years later Tennyson used his skill to alleviate Emily's troubles. In March 1854 Tennyson wrote to a friend: "My wife's kind regards to you: she has been in a great state of suffering and sleeplessness for nine days, but at last I set her right by mesmerizing,—the effect was really wonderful" (Hallam Tennyson, *Memoir*, 1: 374). For another reference to this experience with mesmerism see *Lady Tennyson's Journal*, p. 222.

40. *The Letters of Emily Lady Tennyson*, p. 115. Letter to Edward Lear, 17 November 1857. In the introduction to his edition of the letters, Hoge states that he does not believe Emily's troubles were psychological. He writes: "Certainly it was fashionable for Victorian ladies to be delicate, and refinement seems often to have entailed sickliness or its accepted and expected corollary. From all indications, however, Emily's weakness was physical, not psychic, or more anatomical than affected, though her specific ailments are rarely particularized, and her womanish infirmities may well have been expected by a husband predisposed to regard the highest type of woman as a rather unphysical being" (p. 8).

41. Ibid., p. 114; 177; 80; 225, letter to Alfred Tennyson, 19 November 1868.

42. When Emily Tennyson wrote, she was writing innumerable letters of an official nature as well as of a friendly nature—to her husband's friends. It seems she frequently wrote letters for Alfred. She also wrote many letters to Hallam and Lionel when they were away at school. She also read the incoming correspondence before Alfred received it and at times protected him from harsh criticism by not showing him letters from those who strongly objected to his poems. Tennyson wrote to J. Knowles about Emily's letter writing: "'She has overwrought herself,' he wrote to me, 'with the multifarious correspondence of many years, and is now suffering for it. I trust that with perfect quiet she will recover; but it will never again do for her to insist upon answering every idle fellow who writes me. I always prayed her not to do so, but she did not like the unanswered (she used to say) to feel wroth and unsatisfied with me.'" See "Aspects of Tennyson—II," *Nineteenth Century* 33 (1893): 188. In his biography of Tennyson Robert Martin speaks of Emily Tennyson's problems at this time as a "breakdown." See *Tennyson: The Unquiet Heart*, pp. 504–5.

43. Sir James Paget, "Clinical Lectures on the Nervous Mimicry of Organic Diseases," *Lancet*, no. 2615 (11 October 1873): pp. 511–13.

44. Ralph Wilson Rader, *Tennyson's "Maud": The Biographical Genesis*, Perspectives in Criticism, no. 15 (Berkeley and Los Angeles: University of California Press, 1963), p. 25.

45. Letter to Aunt Elizabeth Russell, 10 March 1833, Tennyson Research Centre, Lincoln, Eng.

46. *Remains in Verse and Prose of Arthur Henry Hallam*, ed. Henry Hallam (London: John Murray, 1863), p. xxxi. For discussions and examples of Arthur Henry Hallam's depression see *An Eton Boy: Being the Letters of James Milner Gaskell from Eton and Oxford: 1820–1830*, ed. Charles Milner Gaskell (London: Constable, 1939);

*Richard Chenevix Trench, Archbishop: Letters and Memorials*, ed. M. Trench, 2 vols. (London: Kegan Paul, Trench, 1888); Arthur M. Brookfield, "Some Letters from Arthur Hallam," *Fortnightly Review* 74 (1903): 173; T. Wemyss Reid, *The Life, Letters and Friendships of Richard Monckton Milnes, First Lord Houghton*, 2 vols. (London: Cassell, 1890); James Pope-Henessey, *Monckton Milnes: The Years of Promise, 1809–1851* (London: Constable, 1949); and Ricks, *Tennyson*, pp. 37–38. For another discussion of Hallam and Tennyson's friendship see Martin, *Tennyson: The Unquiet Heart*, pp. 67–79. Martin is also sensitive to the fact that "like Tennyson . . . Hallam was despondent about his own health" (p. 76).

47. Brookfield, "Some Letters from Arthur Hallam," pp. 177, 179. The second of the two letters was probably written in August 1832.

48. As quoted in Jack Kolb, "Arthur Hallam and Emily Tennyson," *Review of English Studies* 28 (1977): 32–48. See also *The Letters of Arthur Henry Hallam*, ed. Jack Kolb (Columbus: Ohio State University Press, 1981), p. 697.

49. *The Writings of Arthur Hallam*, ed. T. H. Vail Motter, Modern Language Association of America General Series, no. 15 (New York, 1943), p. 102. The letter is postmarked 12 July 1831.

50. "Essay on Philosophical Writings of Cicero," in *The Writings of Arthur Hallam*, p. 176. The essay won the Trinity College Prize in 1831.

51. Hugh L'Anson Fausset, *Tennyson: A Modern Portrait* (London: Selwyn and Blount, 1923), p. 23. See also Tennyson's poem "To—[Thou mayst remember what I said]" (1830). The poem speaks of R. J. Tennant's despondency. See also Tennyson's "To—[Clear-headed friend]" (1830), a poem addressed to J. W. Blakesley.

52. Walter E. Houghton, "Anxiety," in *The Victorian Frame of Mind: 1830–1870* (New Haven: Yale University Press, 1957), pp. 54–89.

53. See for example letters in *Richard Chenevix Trench, Archbishop*. See also Alfred McKinley Terhune, *The Life of Edward FitzGerald, Translator of "The Rubaiyat of Omar Khayyam"* (London: Oxford University Press, 1947), pp. 55–57. Terhune attributes FitzGerald's and his contemporaries' despondency and ill health to their lack of faith. To support this point, he prints a letter from FitzGerald to John Allen, 24 February 1883: "I was unhappy and in low spirits on account of the same turmoil in my head that I once had at Seaford. The other night when I lay in bed feeling my head get warmer and warmer, I felt that if I should pray to some protector for relief, I should be relieved" (pp. 56–57).

54. See Hallam Tennyson, *Memoir*, 1: 177n.

55. As quoted in Ricks, *Tennyson*, p. 107. Originally published in *Edinburgh Review* 10 (1843): 373–91.

56. Reid, *The Life, Letters and Friendships of Richard Monckton Milnes*, pp. 92–93. The letter was written 13 March 1830.

57. Another reason Tennyson became so involved with Dr. Allen was their shared enthusiasm for a wood-carving scheme. For a fuller account of Allen's wood-carving scheme see Charles Tennyson, *Alfred Tennyson*, pp. 185–86 and Tennyson and Dyson, *The Tennysons*, pp. 150–59.

58. Tennyson went to Prestbury for a water cure in February 1844 and perhaps again in November 1844. In the spring of 1847 he went to Umberslade Hall

near Birmingham. Later in 1847 he became a patient at Dr. James B. Gully's establishment in Malvern. Tennyson was there also in the autumn of 1848.

59. Evidence of how nervous his mother was is found in a letter Tennyson wrote to Emily Sellwood when they were engaged: "My Mother is afraid if I go to town even for a night" ([Hallam Tennyson], Ms. *Materials*, Notebook, no. 1 [Lincoln, Eng.: Tennyson Research Centre], pp. 209–17).

60. Letter to Frederick Tennyson, 17 April 1830, as quoted in *Letters and Literary Remains of Edward FitzGerald*, ed. William Aldis Wright, 3 vols. (London: Macmillan, 1889), 1: 202–3.

61. James Anthony Froude, *Thomas Carlyle: A History of His Life in London: 1836–1881*, 2 vols. (London: Longman, Green, 1884), 2: 80.

62. *Letters and Literary Remains of Edward FitzGerald*, 1: 203. The letter was written in December 1851. Froude also remarks on how little good the water cure did Carlyle. See Froude, *Thomas Carlyle*, 2: 81.

63. *William Allingham's Diary*, p. 136.

64. Several contemporaries noted Tennyson's attraction to James Hinton's works. See Hallam Tennyson, *Memoir*, 2: 206. *The Letters of Emily Lady Tennyson*, p. 219, includes a letter from Emily to Thomas Woolner, 24 March 1868: "How pleased Ally, who is studying Hinton, would be by this last part of my sentence." See also Charles Tennyson, *Alfred Tennyson*, p. 368.

65. Letter to Mr. Berry, a medical man and friend, dated September 1864 in *Life and Letters of James Hinton*, ed. Ellice Hopkins (London: C. Kegan Paul, 1878), p. 183.

66. Mrs. Havelock Ellis, *James Hinton: A Sketch* (London: Stanley Paul, 1918), p. 10.

67. In a biography of Alfred Tennyson published in 1884 and sanctioned by the Tennyson family, there is the following account of Arthur Henry Hallam's death: "A sudden determination of blood to the head—his old disorder—caused by a weak action of the heart, had over-charged the cerebral vessels, and death must have been instantaneous" in Henry J. Jennings, *Lord Tennyson, 1809–1892: A Biographical Sketch*, rev. ed. (London: Chatto and Windus, 1892), p. 41.

68. *The Letters of Emily Lady Tennyson*, p. 48.

69. Ibid., p. 236. The proposal comes in a letter from Emily to Alfred, Farringford, 16 June 1869.

70. Ibid., pp. 259–60.

71. Charles Tennyson, *Alfred Tennyson*, p. 347.

72. See Edgar F. Shannon, Jr., "The Critical Reception of Tennyson's *Maud*," *PMLA* 68 (1953): 397–414.

73. Some letters exchanged between Tennyson and Dr. Robert J. Mann are at the Tennyson Research Centre, Lincoln, England. Recently A. Dwight Culler published some of these letters. See A. Dwight Culler, *The Poetry of Tennyson* (New Haven: Yale University Press, 1977), pp. 200–202.

74. For a record of the visit see Artem Lozynsky and John R. Reed, *A Whitman Disciple Visits Tennyson: An Interview Describing Dr. Richard Maurice Bucke's Visit of August 9th, 1891 at Aldworth*, Tennyson Society Monographs, no. 8 (Lincoln, Eng.: Tennyson Research Centre, 1977).

## Notes to Chapter Three

1. Robert B. Martin, *Tennyson: The Unquiet Heart* (Oxford: Clarendon Press, 1980), p. 140.

2. [Hallam Tennyson], Ms. *Materials*, Notebook, no. 3 (Lincoln, Eng.: Tennyson Research Centre), p. 3. Dr. Ker was Charles Tennyson's homeopathic doctor.

3. Christopher Ricks, *Tennyson*, Masters of World Literature Series, ed. Louis Kronenberger (New York: Macmillan, 1972), pp. 65–67. Ricks quotes Tennyson: "In my youth I knew much greater unhappiness than I have known in later life. When I was about twenty, I used to feel moods of misery unutterable! I remember once in London the realization coming over me, of the *whole* of its inhabitants lying horizontal a hundred years hence. The smallness and emptiness of life sometimes overwhelmed me—" (p. 65).

4. Charles Tennyson, *Alfred Tennyson* (New York: Macmillan, 1949), p. 99.

5. *Letters to Frederick Tennyson*, ed. Hugh J. Schonfield (London: Hogarth Press, 1930), p. 23. Portions of the letter are also quoted in Ricks, *Tennyson*, p. 66.

6. Charles Tennyson, *Alfred Tennyson*, p. 145.

7. For a lengthy treatment of Tennyson's friendship with Rosa Baring see Ralph Wilson Rader, *Tennyson's "Maud": The Biographical Genesis*, Perspectives in Criticism, no. 15 (Berkeley and Los Angeles: University of California Press, 1963), pp. 11–20. For more recent reflections on Tennyson's friendship with Rosa Baring see Martin, *Tennyson: The Unquiet Heart*, pp. 214–21. Martin tends to consider the friendship as being less intense than Rader sees it.

8. As quoted in Rader, *Tennyson's "Maud,"* p. 70. It should be pointed out that Emily had her doubts too. She also feared the responsibilities accompanying marriage. In her journal she looks back at those years of indecision and writes "I had lost courage and I don't know if I should ever have ventured to become his wife knowing the greatness of the responsibility had not [Charles] Kingsley not merely encouraged but urged me—Thank God." See *Lady Tennyson's Journal*, ed. James O. Hoge (Charlottesville: University of Virginia Press, 1981), p. 16.

9. See for example George H. Savage, "Marriage in Neurotic Subjects," *Journal of Mental Science*, n.s. 29 (April 1883): 49–54. Robert Martin in *Tennyson: The Unquiet Heart*, p. 237 speculates that Tennyson's reluctance to marry was influenced by his fear of passing on Dr. Tennyson's epilepsy to any children he might have.

10. Matthew Allen, *Essay on the Classification of the Insane* (London: John Taylor, [1837]), pp. 24, 194.

11. For a more detailed explanation of Dr. Allen's wood-carving scheme see Martin, *Tennyson: The Unquiet Heart*, pp. 254–56.

12. Ms. *Materials*, "1835–1847," p. 128.

13. As quoted in Charles Tennyson, *Alfred Tennyson*, p. 201.

14. Wilfrid Ward, *Aubrey de Vere: A Memoir* (London: Longmans, 1904), p. 87.

15. "My father told me, 'When I wrote "The Two Voices" I was so utterly

miserable, a burden to myself and to my family, that I said, "Is life worth anything?"'" as quoted in Hallam Tennyson, *Alfred, Lord Tennyson: A Memoir*, 2 vols. (London: Macmillan, 1898), 1: 193n.

16. Charles Tennyson, *Alfred Tennyson*, p. 77. See also September 1829 letter to James Milner Gaskell in *An Eton Boy: Being the Letters of James Milner Gaskell*, ed. Charles Milner Gaskell (London: Constable, 1939), p. 206: "I am changed now: changed, I willingly allow for the worse."

17. From "Lines Addressed to Alfred Tennyson," in *The Writings of Arthur Hallam*, ed. T. H. Vail Motter, Modern Language Association of America General Series, no. 15 (New York, 1943), p. 66.

18. "Gully, James Manby, M.D.," in *Dictionary of National Biography*, eds. Leslie Stephen and Sidney Lee (London: Smith, Elder, 1890), 23: 325.

19. As quoted in Charles Tennyson, *Alfred Tennyson*, p. 201. The discussion of Tennyson's experiences at Prestbury has already appeared. See Ann Colley, "Alfred Tennyson's 'Four Crisises': Another View of the Water Cure," *Tennyson Research Bulletin* 3, no. 2 (November 1979): 64–68.

20. As quoted in Ricks, *Tennyson*, pp. 180–81. The letter is dated 23 February 1844. The original is at the Tennyson Research Centre, Lincoln, England.

21. Richard Beamish, *The Cold Water Cure as Practised by Vincent Priessnitz at Gräfenberg, in Silesia with an Account of Cases Successfully Treated at Prestbury, near Cheltenham* (London: Samuel Highley, 1843).

22. Beamish, *The Cold Water Cure*, pp. 54–55. The errors in German spelling are in original text.

23. Elizabeth Jenkins, *Tennyson and Dr. Gully*, Tennyson Society Occasional Papers, no. 3 (Lincoln, Eng.: 1974), p. 5.

24. "Life at the Water Cure," *Fraser's Magazine* 14, no. 320 (August 1856): 197–207.

25. Beamish, *The Cold Water Cure*, p. 90.

26. Ibid., pp. 86–87.

27. In a February 1844 letter quoted in Charles Tennyson, *Alfred Tennyson*, p. 201. The letter reads: "it is very kind of you to think of such a poor body as myself—The perpetual panic and horror of the last two years had steeped my nerves in poison: now I am left a beggar, but I am or shall be shortly somewhat better off in nerves. . . . They were so bad six weeks ago that I could not have written this, and to have to write a letter on that accursed business threw me into a kind of convulsion. I went through Hell. Thank you for inquiring after me. I am such a poor devil now I am afraid I shall very rarely see you. No more trips to London and living in London, hard penury and battle will be my lot."

28. As quoted in Hallam Tennyson, *Memoir*, 1: 221. To Edmund Lushington 29 July 1844.

29. A review of Herbert Mayo's *The Cold Water Cure, Its Use and Misuse Examined*, in *Athenaeum*, no. 970 (May 1846), p. 552. In 1843 people in England were more than usually involved in the pros and cons of the water cure. Books and articles defending or "objectively" describing the methods and miraculous cures flooded the market.

30. Like many water cure doctors Dr. James M. Gully was himself interested in mesmerism, phrenology, and homeopathy. See Jenkins, *Tennyson and Dr. Gully*, p. 9.

31. James Wilson and James M. Gully, *The Dangers of the Water Cure* (London: Cunningham and Mortimer, 1843), pp. 99–100.

32. Ibid., p. 93.

33. As quoted in Charles Tennyson, *Alfred Tennyson*, p. 232.

34. Joanna Richardson, *The Pre-Eminent Victorian* (London: Jonathan Cape, 1962), p. 179.

35. Robert Martin in *Tennyson: The Unquiet Heart* is less willing to subscribe to the notion that with marriage came emotional security. He does write, however, that "What is certain is that she [Emily] brought a new order into his life without which he could hardly have continued his existence" (p. 335).

36. F. T. Palgrave, "Tours with Alfred Tennyson 1853–1867," Ms. Notebook, p. 8, in Tennyson Research Centre, Lincoln, Eng.

37. Ibid., pp. 8, 25–27.

38. Ibid., "1860 Tour in Cornwall."

39. From Richardson, *The Pre-Eminent Victorian*, p. 179.

40. *The Letters of Emily Lady Tennyson*, p. 322.

41. Richardson, *The Pre-Eminent Victorian*, p. 186.

42. On 15 October 1892, Emily wrote to her sister Anne Weld: "My own belief is that my Ally's illness has something to do with influenza. The doctors talked of nervous exhaustion and this might well have been the case" (*The Letters of Emily Lady Tennyson*, p. 359).

43. Ms. *Materials* "1860 Etc.," Notebook no. 5, p. 61. The entry is dated 29 June 1863.

44. *The Letters of Emily Lady Tennyson*, pp. 161–62.

45. For an account of the voyage to Venice see Charles Tennyson, *Alfred Tennyson*, pp. 449–53.

46. Benjamin Brodie, *Lectures Illustrative of Certain Local Nervous Affections* (London: Longman, Orme, Brown, Green, and Longman, 1837), p. 70.

47. Wilson and Gully, *The Dangers of the Water Cure*, p. 146.

48. For an account of an attack of palpitations see Charles Tennyson, *Alfred Tennyson*, p. 330. See also Richardson, *The Pre-Eminent Victorian*, p. 187: "In March [1871] Tennyson had 'so much palpitation of the heart and fluttering of the nerves' that he had to spend a few days at Aldworth."

49. According to the story, in 1889 Tennyson claimed that "his youthful 'fits of melancholy' had been really 'just gout.'" See H. D. Rawnsley, *Memories of the Tennysons* (Glasgow: James MacLehose, 1900), pp. 129–30.

50. T. Herbert Warren, *The Centenary of Tennyson, 1809–1909* (London: Oxford University Press, 1909), p. 18.

51. Rader, *Tennyson's "Maud,"* p. 76.

52. For more examples of the oar image, see "The Lotos-Eaters" (l. 40), and see discussion of sources in *The Poems of Tennyson*, ed. Christopher Ricks, Longmans Annotated English Poets, ed. F. W. Bateson (London: Longmans, 1969), p. 560.

53. For an investigation into Tennyson's activity following Arthur Henry Hallam's death see Joyce Green, "Tennyson's Development during the 'Ten Years' Silence' (1832–1842)," *PMLA* 66 (1951): 662–97.

54. Ms. *Materials,* "1835–1847," p. 166.

55. Amy Woolner, *Thomas Woolner, R.A.: His Life in Letters* (London: Chapman and Hall, 1917), p. 213.

56. Humphrey House, "Tennyson and the Spirit of the Age," in *All in Due Time: The Collected Essays and Broadcast Talks of Humphrey House* (London: Rupert Hart-Davis, 1955), p. 129.

57. A new biography of Tennyson, although it underplays the subject's experiences with madness, gives an excellent sense of Tennyson's resilience—his joy in survival. See Philip Henderson, *Tennyson: Poet and Prophet* (London: Routledge and Kegan Paul, 1978).

## Notes to Chapter Four

1. "Memory (Memory! dear enchanter)" is, in fact, an excellent example of what W. D. Paden implied when he spoke of Tennyson's indebtedness to Byron as being "indicative" of Tennyson's "own emotional state." W. D. Paden, *Tennyson in Egypt: A Study of the Imagery in His Earlier Work* (Lawrence: University of Kansas Press, 1942), p. 60.

2. Robert Martin, *Tennyson: The Unquiet Heart* (Oxford: Clarendon Press, 1980), p. 107.

3. A recurrent, but dying, theme in criticism of Tennyson's work is that Tennyson is reluctant or unable to face his problems or the outside world. As a result, critics often speak of Tennyson's "retreat from life." See, for example, Jerome Hamilton Buckley, *Tennyson: The Growth of a Poet* (Cambridge: Harvard University Press, 1961), p. 19, and Clyde de L. Ryals, *Theme and Symbol in Tennyson's Poems to 1850* (Philadelphia: University of Pennsylvania Press, 1964), p. 40. It was probably Arthur J. Carr who helped readers to see Tennyson as a poet who is not evasive. See Carr, "Tennyson as a Modern Poet," *University of Toronto Quarterly* 9 (1950): 361–82. Sir Charles Tennyson often speaks of Tennyson as a "straight-forward" poet. John D. Rosenberg also thinks of Tennyson as a straight-forward poet: "He is not an escapist, as his critics of the past generations have foolishly charged, but a hyper-realist." See Rosenberg, "Tennyson and the Landscape of Consciousness," *Victorian Poetry* 12 (1974): 303.

4. Recently Paul Turner remarked that when Tennyson was composing "Marion," he was making "an attempt, almost clinical in tone, to define the peculiar charm of a very ordinary person." See Paul Turner, *Tennyson,* ed. B. C. Southam, Routledge Author Guides (London: Routledge and Kegan Paul, 1976), p. 44. Turner is not the only critic to sense Tennyson's interest in analyzing the characters in these poems. For instance, Robert Pattison writes of Tennyson's interest in the emotional states of these characters (*Tennyson and Tradition,* [Cambridge: Harvard University Press, 1979], p. 13). A. Dwight Culler also regards these

poems as character studies. He, however, concludes that "the poems are efforts to explore different aspects of formal beauty through the metaphor of the feminine soul and form" (*The Poetry of Tennyson* [New Haven: Yale University Press, 1977], pp. 39–40).

5. Case studies were the necessary adjuncts of most nineteenth-century psychological treatises. Drs. Brodie, Allen, Gully, and Paget, like all physicians of their time, devoted much of their professional energy to writing up their cases. Gully, for example, published an account of cases treated at his hydropathic establishment, and Allen described selected cases of patients treated in his asylum.

For examples of case studies see Matthew Allen, *Cases of Insanity with Medical, Moral, and Philosophic Observations and Essays upon Them* (London: George Swire, 1831), vol. 1 [other volumes never completed], and Matthew Allen, *Essay on the Classification of the Insane* (London: John Taylor [1837]). In a footnote Christopher Ricks comments on Tennyson's sensitivity to the practice of publishing case histories. Ricks reads the lines "And Yonder a vile physician, blabbing / The case of his patient" (*Maud*, 2: 274–75), and suggests that Tennyson is "possibly recalling" Allen's *Essay on the Classification of the Insane* (*The Poems of Tennyson*, ed. Christopher Ricks, Longmans Annotated English Poets, ed. F. W. Bateson (London: Longmans, 1969), p. 1088n). Tennyson's distrust, however, probably had more to do with his attitude toward Allen than the practice of publishing case studies.

6. As quoted in Hallam Tennyson, *Alfred, Lord Tennyson: A Memoir*, 2 vols. (London: Macmillan, 1897), 1: 500.

7. 15 January 1834 letter to Uncle Charles, as quoted in Charles Tennyson, *Alfred Tennyson* (London: Macmillan, 1968), p. 150.

8. Later in life Tennyson explained to his son Hallam, "I used, from having early read in my father's library a great number of medical books, to fancy at times that I had all the diseases in the world, like a medical student" (Hallam Tennyson, *Memoir*, 1: 269).

9. Shortly after the poet's death, John Tyndall wrote to Hallam praising Tennyson's "profound" interest in science (ibid., 2: 469); later Oliver Lodge stated that regarding Tennyson as a "Poet of Science . . . is now a commonplace of letters, and requires no emphasizing," in "The Attitudes of Tennyson towards Science," in *Tennyson and His Friends*, ed. Hallam, Lord Tennyson (London: Macmillan, 1912), p. 280. Recently many have discussed Tennyson's interest in science. The studies, however, tend to dwell on Tennyson's knowledge of astronomy, biology, chemistry, electricity, geology, and physiology. These critics overlook his interest in psychology or "the secrets of the brain."

*Lady Tennyson's Journal*, ed. James O. Hoge (Charlottesville: University of Virginia Press, 1981) offers the reader a vivid sense of Tennyson's interest in science, for in it are titles of articles and books Tennyson read to her. Among these are: "Physiognomy of the Human Form," *London Quarterly Review* 98 (October 1856): 247–68; Samuel Brown, *Lectures on the Atomic Theory; and Essays Scientific and Literary* (Edinburgh: T. Constable, 1858): 99–120; and John Tyndall, *Heat: A Mode of Motion* (London: Longmans, Green, 1868).

10. Charles Tennyson, *Alfred Tennyson*, p. 303. In her journal, Emily Tenny-

son records that on 17 February 1857 "A reads to me the reign of John in Sharon Turner, some of Burton's *Anatomy of Melancholy* in the evenings." See *Lady Tennyson's Journal*, p. 85.

11. For examples of poems using this physiological vocabulary see: "I dare not write an Ode for fear Pimplaea," "The Outcast," and "The Bridal."

12. John Killham points out that in *The Princess* Tennyson alludes to Friedrich Tiedemann's theory concerning the brain's foetal development. John Killham, "'The Princess' and Evolution," in *Tennyson and the Princess: Reflections of an Age* (London: Athlone Press, University of London, 1958), p. 237. Christopher Ricks notes another allusion to Tiedemann's theory in the 1832 version of "The Palace of Art." Ricks, *The Poems of Tennyson*, p. 409n.

13. Sir Charles Tennyson has written of his grandfather's interest in the process of dreams. He notes, for instance, that in "The Lover's Tale" Tennyson seems to be trying to grapple with a dream phenomenon based on personal experiences, but too elusive for clear verbal description. Sir Charles Tennyson, "The Dream in Tennyson's Poetry," *Virginia Quarterly Review* 40, no. 2 (1964): 228–42.

14. Psychiatrists interested in dream theory were indebted to Erasmus Darwin, who in *Zoonomia* (1794–1796) devoted considerable space to a study of sleep and dreams. Darwin spoke of dreams as "repeating waking sensations"; he distinguished between various kinds of dreams and examined sensations peculiar to the dreaming state such as the ceaseless flow of ideas, variety of scenery, the novelty of combination, distinctness of imagery, rapidity of transaction, and their loss of self, time, or place. Erasmus Darwin, *Zoonomia or the Laws of Organic Life* 2 vols. (London: Printed for J. Johnson, 1801), 2: 334.

15. James Sully, "Genius and Insanity," *Nineteenth Century* 17 (1885): 948–69.

16. "A man and his wife the other day flung themselves into a river with the intention of committing suicide. The man was rescued, the woman drowned. I have substituted the sea for the river and hypothesized the feelings of a would-be-suicide in this latter half of the nineteenth century." As quoted in Ricks, *The Poems of Tennyson*, p. 1299.

17. Among the critics to praise Tennyson for his "accuracy" is Roy P. Basler, who, in his study of *Maud*, explores the nature of Tennyson's accuracy. He, however, is not as interested in pursuing Tennyson's knowledge of nineteenth-century psychology as he is interested in demonstrating how Tennyson antedates by half a century the writings of Sigmund Freud. For his comments on Tennyson's "accuracy" see Basler, "Tennyson's Maud," in *Sex, Symbolism, and Psychology in Literature* (New York: Octagon Books, 1970), p. 75. For examples of others who have thought Tennyson "accurate," see Jerome Buckley, *Tennyson: The Growth of a Poet* (Cambridge: Harvard University Press, 1961), p. 55; Basil Willey, "Tennyson," in *More Nineteenth-Century Studies: A Group of Honest Doubters* (London: Chatto and Windus, 1956); Christopher Ricks, *Tennyson*, Masters of World Literature Series, ed. Louis Kronenberger (New York: Macmillan, 1972), p. 310; Paul Turner, *Tennyson*, Routledge Author Guides, ed. B. C. Southam (London: Routledge and Kegan Paul, 1976), p. 146; and E. D. H. Johnson, *The Alien Vision of Victorian Poetry*, Princeton Studies in English, no. 34 (Princeton: Princeton

University Press, 1952), p. 29. Johnson writes that Tennyson's poetry "shows an acquaintance with symptoms of insanity which is as uncommon in its period as the somewhat similar interest in dream psychology." More recently Henry Kozicki has noted Tennyson's love of accuracy in the early poems. Kozicki writes that Tennyson "takes pride in an exact knowledge of his subject matter and, further, looks without squeamishness or illusions upon the ordained ways of the world" (*Tennyson and Clio: History in the Major Poems* [Baltimore: Johns Hopkins University Press, 1979], p. 11).

18. Arthur Henry Hallam pointed out "five distinct excellencies" of Tennyson's poetry. The second of these was Tennyson's "power of embodying himself in ideal characters, or rather moods of character, with such extreme accuracy of adjustment, that the circumstances of narration seem to have a natural correspondence with the predominant feeling, and, as it were, to be evolved from it." In "On Some Characteristics of Modern Poetry, and on the Lyrical Poems of Alfred Tennyson," *Englishman's Magazine* 1 (August 1831): 616–28.

19. J. C. B. [John Charles Bucknill], "Review of *Maud and Other Poems*," *Asylum Journal of Mental Science*, no. 15 (October 1855): 94–104; and R. J. Mann, *Tennyson's "Maud" Vindicated: An Explanatory Essay* (London: Jarrold, 1856), p. 64. Dr. Mann and Tennyson were friends. They spent time together looking through microscopes and telescopes.

20. Joshua Adler, "Tennyson's 'Mother of Sorrows': 'Rizpah,'" *Victorian Poetry* 12 (1974): 363–69.

21. Mrs. Warre Cornish, "Memories of the Tennysons—I," *London Mercury* 5, no. 26 (December 1921): 155.

22. François Xavier Swedjuar, ed., *The Philosophical Dictionary; or, The Opinions of Modern Philosophers on Metaphysical, Moral, and Political Subjects*, 4 vols. (London: G. G. J. and J. Robinson, 1786), 2: 135, 159; Gerard Van Swieten, *Commentaries upon the Aphorisms of Dr. Herman Boerhaave: Concerning the Knowledge and Cure of the Several Diseases Incident to Human Bodies* (London: R. Horsfield and T. Longman, 1765), 2: 2; Mann, *Tennyson's "Maud" Vindicated*, p. 10.

Several critics have noted parallels between Tennyson's and Allen's views. Charles Tennyson, *Alfred Tennyson*, p. 286; Johnson, *The Alien Vision of Victorian Poetry*, p. 29; Turner, *Tennyson*, pp. 146–48; Culler, *The Poetry of Tennyson*, pp. 190, 193, 207; and Ricks, *Tennyson*, p. 249.

23. "Haslam, Arnold, etc. on Insanity," *Quarterly Review* 2, no. 3 (1809): 155–80. It is probably helpful to be reminded also of Tennyson's letter to Wilfrid Ward. In the letter Tennyson said that the hero of *Maud* "is dismayed by the first appearance of difficulty and pain in the world, as he had been satisfied for a time with the immediate pleasures within his reach. He is unable to steady the nerve of his brain (so to speak), and trace the riddle of pain and trouble in the universe to its ultimate solution. In thought, as in conduct, he is filled and swayed by the immediate inclination and first impression, without self-restraint and without the habit of concentrated reflection which go hand in hand with self-restraint. Failing, in spiritual life within, he is impressed, probably by experience, with this one truth, that uncontrolled self-indulgence leads to regret and pain; and he is consequently pessimistic in his ultimate view of things." As quoted in Ralph

Wilson Rader, *Tennyson's "Maud": The Biographical Genesis*, Perspectives in Criticism, no. 15 (Berkeley and Los Angeles: University of California Press, 1963), pp. 100–101.

24. For example, Robert Martin in *Tennyson: The Unquiet Heart* writes that the lover is "at last cured of his madness by a purified love of the dead Maud that leads to a more generalized love of mankind" (p. 384).

25. Swieten, *Commentaries upon the Aphorisims of Dr. Herman Boerhaave*, 11: 2. In *Essay on the Classification of the Insane*, Dr. Allen states a similar theory: "What is called mania and melancholia are for the most part effects of the same power being overactive, but overactive in different directions. If the distressing passions are overactive, we have melancholics—if the animal propensities, we have furious maniacs" (p. 16).

26. As quoted in Vieda Skultans, ed., *Madness and Morals: Ideas on Insanity in the Nineteenth Century* (London: Routledge and Kegan Paul, 1975), p. 82. The selection is dated 1832.

27. "But for this purpose, travelling excels [*sic*] all other methods; because thus a perpetual variety of new objects is offered to the mind, upon which they operate with strength enough to change the inherent thoughts. For like reasons, physicians so often advise the mineral waters . . . especially such as lie considerable distant from the patient." In Swieten, *Commentaries upon the Aphorisms of Dr. Herman Boerhaave*, 11: 43.

28. Bucknill's review of *Maud* acknowledges memory's disastrous role in precipitating a person's decline: "This mixed state of reason and delusion, and of wild emotion, partly the natural sequence of the latter, partly arising from agonizing memories, is depicted with terrible reality" (Bucknill, "Review of *Maud and Other Poems*," p. 102).

29. Mann, *Tennyson's "Maud" Vindicated*, p. 65.

30. As quoted in "John Johnstone," in Richard Hunter and Ida Macalpine, eds., *Three Hundred Years of Psychiatry, 1535–1860* (London: Oxford University Press, 1963), p. 577.

31. As quoted in "Haslam, Arnold, etc., on Insanity," p. 170.

32. William Willis Moseley, *Eleven Chapters on Nervous and Mental Complaints* (London: Simpkin, Marshall, 1838), pp. 123–40.

33. As quoted in William B. Neville, *On Insanity: Its Nature, Causes, and Cure* (London: Longman, Rees, Orme, Brown, Green, and Longman, 1836), p. 75.

34. Introduction to "Amariah Brigham," in *Three Hundred Years of Psychiatry*, p. 821.

35. Robert Burton, *Anatomy of Melancholy*, 3 vols. (New York: Armstrong, 1889), 3: 190.

36. Ibid., 3: 308.

37. Janice C. Sinson alludes to the popularity of Burton's *Anatomy*. See *John Keats and the Anatomy of Melancholy* (London: Keats-Shelley Memorial Association, 1971), p. 10. Arthur Henry Hallam's father, for example, read *The Anatomy*, even though he was said not to think much of it. New editions with translations of the Latin passages were published, allowing *The Anatomy* to reach a larger audience. Tennyson's interest might also have been stimulated by those

Romantic poets whom he admired and who were indebted to Burton. Tennyson read Lamb's essays and evidently admired him, for on one occasion he took Emily by the window of Charles Lamb's room at India House. (Charles Tennyson, *Alfred Tennyson*, p. 425.)

38. For a discussion of how closely John Ford studied Burton's *Anatomy* see S. Blaine Ewing, *Burtonian Melancholy in the Plays of John Ford*, Princeton Studies in English, no. 19, ed. G. H. Gerould (Princeton: Princeton University Press, 1940).

39. For a survey of literary attitudes toward madness see chapter one of this book.

40. Herbert G. Wright, *The Decameron in England from Chaucer to Tennyson* (London: University of London Press, 1957), p. 438. For a discussion of the genesis of "The Golden Supper," see Culler, *The Poetry of Tennyson*, pp. 257–58 (n. 4). In her journal, Emily Tennyson wrote that Tennyson thought of publishing "The Golden Supper" with a preface (29 November 1869). See *Lady Tennyson's Journal*, p. 299.

41. It is impossible to speak of *Maud* without discussing its ending or the hero's decision to commit himself to war. When the poem was first published in 1855, it was the hero's commitment to war and his belief that war is a noble act which caused people to attack Tennyson and call him a warmonger. See, for example, Edgar F. Shannon, Jr., "The Critical Reception of Tennyson's *Maud*," *PMLA* 68 (1953): 397–414.

42. Many critics tend to believe that the hero has regained his sanity at the end of the poem. For example, John D. Jump speaks of the hero's "recovery of reason" in *Alfred Tennyson: "In Memoriam," "Maud," and Other Poems* (London: J. M. Dent, 1974), p. xv. Culler also holds on to the idea that the hero "frees himself from his disease" (*The Poetry of Tennyson*, pp. 206–13); so does John R. Reed in *Perception and Design in Tennyson's "Idylls of the King"* (Athens: Ohio University Press, 1969), pp. 44–45; and so does John Killham in "Tennyson's *Maud*—The Function of the Imagery," in *Critical Essays on the Poetry of Tennyson*, ed. John Killham (New York: Barnes and Noble, 1960), p. 235. Martin in *Tennyson: The Unquiet Heart* states that he believes the hero to be cured (p. 387), and Kozicki in *Tennyson and Clio* writes that at the end of *Maud* the hero "is reconstructed, and he sails off to join the knighthood setting up a new social order, perhaps a Camelot" (p. 111).

43. One instance occurred when Tennyson received an anonymous letter that read: "sir, I used to worship you, but now I hate you. I loathe and detest you. You beast! so you've taken to imitating Longfellow." As quoted in Hallam Tennyson, *Memoir*, 1: 400.

44. Turner, *Tennyson*, pp. 142–46.

45. Allen, *Essay on the Classification of the Insane*, p. 17.

46. See, for example, "How Atmospheric Influence Is Modified among the Insane, and the Application of This Knowledge," "On Lunar Influence," "On the Influence of the Seasons," and "On Planetary Influence" in Allen, *Cases of Insanity*, 1: 13–111. (Allen never completed any of the other volumes.)

## Notes to Chapter Five

1. Alfred Beaumont Maddock, *Practical Observations on Mental and Nervous Disorders* (London: Simpkin, Marshall, 1854), p. 13.

2. Matthew Allen, *Essay on the Classification of the Insane* (London: John Taylor, [1837]), p. 18.

3. John D. Rosenberg, *The Fall of Camelot: A Study of Tennyson's "Idylls of the King"* (Cambridge: Harvard University Press, 1973), p. 24. See also Rosenberg, "Tennyson and the Landscape of Consciousness," *Victorian Poetry* 12 (1974): 303–10. Other critics following Rosenberg's lead speak of the *Idylls'* emphasis on psychological experience. Donald S. Hair in *Domestic and Heroic in Tennyson's Poetry* (Toronto: University of Toronto Press, 1981) writes, for example, of the "emphasis on inner psychological experience in the second idyll" (p. 166), and Robert Pattison in *Tennyson and Tradition* (Cambridge: Harvard University Press, 1979) thinks of the *Idylls* as "a series of portraits of the Arthurian characters, not in the process of action, but in the throes of internal debate" (p. 137).

4. See for example Penelope B. R. Doob, *Nebuchadnezzar's Children: Conventions of Madness in Middle English Literature* (New Haven: Yale University Press, 1974), p. 154. Doob argues that Merlin's madness is not merely the result of "excessive grief and melancholia," but it is also a consequence of his "disgust at human sinfulness masquerading as virtue." She points out that this larger concern for human sinfulness also influences Lancelot's and Tristram's madness, a concern that not only colors the Arthurian legends, but also other medieval pieces. Doob concludes that in medieval literature madness is a symbol of the deformity of the soul and tangible proof of sin. This understanding of madness had its equivalent in Tennyson's *Idylls*. Here too madness becomes an emblem of the continuing assault of the passions on Arthur and his kingdom, the "Ideal Soul." Furthermore, madness erupts from those like Guinevere and Lancelot who are caught in a "masquerade." They appear to be virtuous, but in reality they are symbols of "human sinfulness."

This medieval understanding of madness as a symbol of excessive grief and sin was still popular when Burton was compiling his *Anatomy*. Fully aware of the continuing tradition, Doob opens her discussion with a selection from the *Anatomy* which demonstrates that there was a precedent for using madness as a central image in the *Idylls*.

5. Robert Martin, *Tennyson: The Unquiet Heart* (Oxford: Clarendon Press, 1980), pp. 215–21.

6. For discussions of literary madness in the nineteenth century see, for example, Sandra M. Gilbert and Susan Gubar, *The Madwoman in the Attic: The Woman Writer and the Nineteenth-Century Literary Imagination* (New Haven: Yale University Press, 1979).

7. Walter E. Houghton, *The Victorian Frame of Mind, 1830–1870* (New Haven: Yale University Press, 1975), p. 368. In *Alfred Tennyson* (New York: Macmillan, 1949) Charles Tennyson writes that Tennyson "had a deep-seated loathing for recent tendencies in French politics and art. 'The frightful corruption of their

literature makes me fear that they are going straight to Hell,' he said" (p. 390). Tennyson also thought it upsetting that Swinburne wrote a sonnet in praise of Mademoiselle de Maupin.

8. Paul Turner, *Tennyson*, Routledge Author Guides, ed. B. C. Southam (London: Routledge and Kegan Paul, 1976), p. 176. In discussing Tennyson's political poems of the early fifties, Henry Kozicki states that they "were occasioned by his concern that the nation was falling into anarchy on the plane of ordinary providence as a result of its failure to engage the historically formative power of active providence. More specifically, man microcosmically . . . was failing to make base passions (selfishness, sensuality, covetousness) subservient to the nobler conditions of selfishness, struggle, and sacrifice" (*Tennyson and Clio: History in the Major Poems* [Baltimore: Johns Hopkins University Press, 1979], pp. 98–99).

9. One example of the popular interest in epidemics of madness is the publication of Charles Mackay's *Memoirs of Extraordinary Popular Delusions*, 3 vols. (London: R. Bentley, 1841). Another example is B. G. Babington's translation of J. F. C. Hecker's *The Epidemics of the Middle Ages* (London: Sydenham Society, 1846). For a lengthier treatment of the interest in political or social revolution as a cause of insanity see Richard Hunter and Ida Macalpine, *Three Hundred Years of Psychiatry, 1535–1860* (London: Oxford University Press, 1963), pp. 821–22. See also Richard Robert Madden, "Epidemic Insanity," ibid., pp. 1040–42.

10. As quoted in introduction to "Amariah Brigham," in *Three Hundred Years of Psychiatry*, p. 821.

11. George Man Burrows, *Commentaries on Insanity* (London: Underwood, 1828), p. 20.

12. E. D. H. Johnson recognizes the fact that madness is an important motif in the *Idylls of the King*. See *The Alien Vision of Victorian Poetry*, Princeton Studies in English, no. 34 (Princeton: Princeton University Press, 1952), p. 42.

13. For a discussion of the *Idylls of the King* and its serial evolution see J. M. Gray, *Thro' the Vision of the Night* (Edinburgh: Edinburgh University Press, 1980), pp. 3–9, and for a discussion of the *Idylls* in chronological sequence see J. Philip Eggers, *King Arthur's Laureate: A Study of Tennyson's "Idylls of the King"* (New York: New York University Press, 1971), pp. 139–84.

14. There are numerous explanations of Arthur's multiple birth. Paul Turner, for example, links the multiple birth to the theme of "truth" and "falsehood" which runs throughout the *Idylls of the King* (*Tennyson*, p. 167). A. Dwight Culler sees the multiple birth as a means of questioning and establishing Arthur as a "spiritual absolute" (*The Poetry of Tennyson* [New Haven: Yale University Press, 1977], pp. 214–15). James R. Kincaid relates the multiple birth to the question, "how do we know, what is the nature of knowledge, what sort of knowledge is authentic? The question is Arthur himself: who is he, where does he come from, how does he operate?" See *Tennyson's Major Poems: The Comic and Ironic Patterns* (New Haven: Yale University Press, 1975), p. 158.

15. In *Domestic and Heroic in Tennyson's Poetry*, Donald S. Hair emphasizes the importance of marriage in the *Idylls*. He writes "the central action is his [Arthur's] marriage, and on that marriage the fate of civilization depends. The link

between an individual and the state is thus much more than just an analogy" (p. 217).

16. Hallam Tennyson, 2 vols. *Alfred, Lord Tennyson: A Memoir* (London: Macmillan, 1897), 2: 131.

17. Ibid.

18. Alexander Morison, *Outlines of Moral Diseases* (Edinburgh: MacLachlan and Stewart, 1824), pp. 70–71.

19. George Man Burrows, *Commentaries on Insanity*, p. 33.

20. The number of articles on mesmerism seems endless and indicates just how mesmerized the nineteenth-century public was. For a good account of the popular interest in mesmerism see Fred Kaplan, "The Mesmeric Mania," in *Dickens and Mesmerism: The Hidden Springs of Fiction* (Princeton: Princeton University Press, 1975), pp. 3–33.

21. Tennyson's sensitivity to those whose expectations deceive them and lead them into false beliefs must have been encouraged not only by those who were doing studies in popular delusions, but also by those like Samuel Hibbert (1824) who "concluded that whatever their exciting cause apparitions, that is illusions and hallucinations, resulted from the recall of forgotten memories which being emotionally charged attained a vividness exceeding that of external sensory impressions." As quoted in "Samuel Hibbert," in *Three Hundred Years of Psychiatry*, pp. 760–63. Tennyson must also have been influenced by W. B. Carpenter's doctrine of unconscious cerebration or muscular action—a doctrine receiving much attention while Tennyson was at work on "The Holy Grail." It is helpful to recall what Tennyson said about the visions of the Holy Grail—that "the differences between the five visions of the Grail" are dependent on the nun's and the knights' "peculiar natures and circumstances, their selflessness, and the perfection or imperfection of their Christianity" (Hallam Tennyson, *Memoir*, 2: 63 [originally an 1869 entry in Emily Tennyson's journal]).

22. A. Dwight Culler has stated, "Tennyson treats the quest for the Holy Grail as an example of mass hysteria. The whole thing originated, he makes perfectly clear, in the frustrated sexual desires of a young woman who had been disappointed in love and gone into a nunnery" (*The Poetry of Tennyson*, p. 228). Donald S. Hair writes that when the nun "does have a vision of the Grail, it is hard to distinguish the Grail from the phallus and her ecstasy from sexual orgasm" (*Domestic and Heroic in Tennyson's Poetry*, pp. 191–92).

23. Critics tend to think that Galahad's vision is the exception to that of the others. For instance Donald S. Hair in his discussion of the *Idylls* writes that "Nonetheless, Galahad is genuine. He alone of all the knights is suited for the Grail quest, and he alone is successful" (*Domestic and Heroic in Tennyson's Poetry*, p. 192).

24. The idea of the last idyll being a reversal of Arthur's order can be found in Donald S. Hair's study. He writes, "When we look back over these four idylls [the last four], we can see that parody is one of Tennyson's main techniques. Men and women are still attracted to each other; the Order of the Round Table still exists; and quests are undertaken. But the character of all these has dwindled from the original, or become uneven. If James R. Kincaid is right in arguing that

*Gareth and Lynette* provides 'the standard against which all else is measured' . . .
then we can say these four idylls are parodies of this one" (*Domestic and Heroic in
Tennyson's Poetry*, p. 210).

25. A typical response to Arthur's lecture to Guinevere is in Ward Hellstrom,
*On the Poems of Tennyson* (Gainesville: University of Florida Press, 1972): "Arthur, in a rather self-righteous tone of moral superiority which is at once priggish
and quite human, makes Guinevere's culpability paramount" (p. 132). Another
version of that response can be seen in James R. Kincaid's *Tennyson's Major Poems*:
"'Guinevere' apparently had quite a spectacular effect on many Victorians. It
seems astonishing, for instance, that the idyll 'made George Eliot weep when
Tennyson read it.' These days the idyll is more likely to seem an unaccountable
lapse on Tennyson's part. Less open about our emotions and also less struck by
the novelty of domestic realism, we are prone to blame the whole episode on
sexual prudery. In any case, it seems thematically narrow, generically and tonally
inappropriate" (pp. 206–7). I agree with J. M. Gray, who in *Thro' the Vision of
the Night* writes, "One class of criticism condemns the cold, passionless Arthur. . . . The proper critical question to ask is whether Arthur's conduct at this
point is consistent with his character and with the spirit of Tennyson's Arthurian
world. There is not a single passage to suggest that Arthur's condemnation of
Guinevere is out of character" (pp. 133–34).

26. Hallam Tennyson, *Memoir*, 1: 317.

27. Most readers have trouble with the phrase because they feel separated from
Victorian values. I agree with Ward Hellstrom when he writes, "The tendency
of modern audiences is, I think, to concur with [John] Sterling's criticism of the
*Idylls*, that 'the miraculous legend of "Excalibur" does not come very near to
us'" (*On the Poems of Tennyson*, p. 133).

## Notes to Chapter Six

1. See chapter one for a discussion of moral insanity.

2. John Barlow, *Man's Power Over Himself to Prevent or Control Insanity* (London: William Pickering, 1843), p. 59.

3. John Charles Bucknill, "The Supremacy of the Will," in *Unsoundness of Mind
in Relation to Criminal Insanity* (London: Longman, Brown, Green, and Longmans, 1854) as quoted in Vieda Skultans, *Madness and Morals: Ideas on Insanity in
the Nineteenth Century* (London: Routledge and Kegan Paul, 1975), p. 174.

4. William B. Carpenter, *Principles of Mental Physiology* (London: H. S. King,
1874), p. 366.

5. Hallam Tennyson, 2 vols. *Alfred, Lord Tennyson: A Memoir* (London: Macmillan, 1897), 1: 46.

6. It is also intriguing to wonder how Tennyson might have reacted to John
Ruskin's sense of him as a poet who is "morbid" enough to fall prey to the
pathetic fallacy; whose perception is "diseased." John Ruskin, "Of the Pathetic
Fallacy," in *Modern Painters*, 5 vols. (New York: J. Wiley, 1865), 3: 156–72. Be-

cause Tennyson was sensitive to such criticism he never reprinted and sometimes never published his irregular sonnets. See, for example, "Sonnet [Guess well, and that is well]" first published by Sir Charles Tennyson in 1931. Dougald B. MacEachen, in his "Tennyson and the Sonnet," *Victorian Newsletter*, no. 14 (1958): 1–8, suggests that two later sonnets were not published because their rhyme scheme was irregular. See also the irregular "Dualisms" (1830), which was not reprinted. According to Hallam Tennyson his father felt uneasy about his experiments with unhyphenated compound words. See *Memoir*, 1: 50. Tennyson's uneasiness also can be heard in a letter to Arthur Henry Hallam. He wrote that Hallam's "Timbuctoo" was much better "than that wild and unmethodized performance of my own." As quoted in Tennyson's *Works*, ed. Hallam, Lord Tennyson (London: Macmillan, 1907–1908), 3: 258–59.

7. As quoted in Bruce Haley, *The Healthy Body and Victorian Culture* (Cambridge: Harvard University Press, 1978), p. 46. Haley points out the emphasis Victorian critics placed on a "thoroughly healthy mind."

8. Martin Dodsworth, "Patterns of Morbidity: Repetition in Tennyson's Poetry," in Isobel Armstrong, ed., *The Major Victorian Poets: Reconsiderations* (London: Routledge and Kegan Paul, 1969), p. 22.

9. A. Dwight Culler, *The Poetry of Tennyson* (New Haven: Yale University Press, 1977), p. 195.

10. W. David Shaw, *Tennyson's Style* (Ithaca: Cornell University Press, 1976), pp. 170–71.

11. Dodsworth, "Patterns of Morbidity," p. 21.

12. Ibid.

13. Philip Eliot, "Tennyson and Spiritualism," *Tennyson Research Bulletin* 3, no. 3 (1979): 89–100.

14. Mrs. Warre Cornish, "Memories of Tennyson—II," *London Mercury* 5, no. 27 (January 1922): 266–75. See also Hallam Tennyson, *Memoir*, 2: 59. On occasion Tennyson corresponded with friends about mediums. The following excerpt from an 1857 letter from Frederick is an example: "Mrs. Browning is anxious to know if Alfred takes any interest in the 'spiritual manifestations,' she herself I believe is totally absorbed in this subject and believes that 'good will come out of it.' Browning like most literary men either denies the evidence in favour of the facts, or the faculty of observation in others, appearing to me, like all skeptics of this slapdash school, to wind through the most labyrinthine intricacies of credulity in order to justify their incredulity" (Ms. *Materials*, Notebook no. 2 [Lincoln, Eng.: Tennyson Research Centre], p. 293).

15. Robert Martin in *Tennyson: The Unquiet Heart* (Oxford: Clarendon Press, 1980), p. 558 records the event. According to William Allingham's diary Laura Gurney took Tennyson to a seance where he painfully asked, "Are you my boy Lionel?" Laura Troubridge, *Memories and Reflections* (London: William Heineman, 1925), pp. 28–29.

16. Emily Tennyson wrote to Hallam and Lionel in October 1869: "Dr. and Mrs. Acworth and her maid are coming tomorrow, not to my delight. I am not prepared for strangers— . . . and she is a spiritualist and I dread her." In her journal, Emily wrote: "A and Tilly much amazed by *raps on the table* in the middle

room. In A's study a table heaves like the sea. Mrs. Acworth is a great medium. A delicate little creature with very bright eyes. Something there must be in it. What I cannot say but it seems to me a power more liable to abuse than others— more like sorcery when abused than anything else." There is also an entry (19 October 1869) in her journal about Dr. and Mrs. Acworth's visit. See *Lady Tennyson's Journal*, ed. James O. Hoge (Charlottesville: University of Virginia Press, 1981), p. 297.

17. Hallam Tennyson, *Memoir*, 2: 342–43.

18. Sir Charles Tennyson, "The Dream in Tennyson's Poetry," *Virginia Quarterly Review* 40, no. 2 (1964): 228–48.

19. Carpenter, *Principles of Mental Physiology*, p. 612. When introducing his section on mesmerism and spiritualism, Carpenter mentioned those who think them "all humbug." Carpenter was not alone. For example, Walter Cooper Dendy in *On the Phenomena of Dreams, and Other Transient Illusions* (London: Whittaker, Treacher, 1832) wrote that "in reasoning on the cause or nature of dreams, we must discard the sophisms of the pseudo psychologists, who consider the dream as the uninfluenced and independent flight of the soul;— And, as a convincing proof of an immaterial mind during life, and of the existence of soul itself." For other examples of those who dismissed the supernatural see Henry Maudsley, "Hallucinations of the Senses," *Fortnightly Review* 30 (1878): 370–86; [Thomas Richards], "The Philosophy of Apparitions," *Fraser's Town and Country Magazine* 2 (1830–31): 33–41; Andrew Lang, "Ghosts and Right Reason," *Cornhill Magazine*, n.s. 21 (1897): 629–41; F. H. Bradley, "The Evidences of Spiritualism," *Fortnightly Magazine* 44 (1885): 811–26.

20. *The Works of Sir Benjamin Collins Brodie*, ed. Charles Hawkins (London: Longman, Green, Longman, Roberts, and Green, 1865), p. 64. These studies arguing for the material bases of dreams and other psychic phenomena naturally set off a flurry of reviews and debates. The *Quarterly Review*, *Westminster Review*, *Fortnightly Review*, *Contemporary Review*, *Blackwood's Magazine*, and *Fraser's Magazine* were all brimming with commentary. Such was the strength of the arguments against psychic experiences that David Brewster in "The Philosophy of Apparitions," *Quarterly Review* 48 (1832): 287–320 commented on the "eagerness with which almost all educated persons disclaim a belief in the supernatural, and denounce, as a vulgar absurdity, the very notion of apparitions." The debates also prompted many more physicians to investigate and write books on the nature of sleep and to examine, most clinically, the truths involved in superstition.

21. George Man Burrows, "The Character of Insanity," in *Commentaries on Insanity* (London: Underwood, 1828), pp. 260–62.

22. Sir Walter Scott, "Unreal Ghosts" and "True Ghosts," in *Letters on Demonology and Witchcraft* (London: J. Murray, 1830), pp. 41–56, 57–71.

23. E. D. H. Johnson, *The Alien Vision of Victorian Poetry*, Princeton Studies in English, no. 34 (Princeton: Princeton University Press, 1952), p. 23. For a study of a nineteenth-century French writer confronted by a similar dilemma see Irving Massey, "The Contribution of Neurology to the Scepticism of Alfred de Vigny." *Journal of the History of Medicine* (1954).

24. Carpenter's most extensive treatment of "Unconscious Cerebration" is in

his book *Principles of Human Physiology* (London: Churchill, 1852 and 1855). The book went through several editions. Later Carpenter expanded his work and published *Principles of Mental Physiology*. The book was reviewed widely. See, for example, Joseph Williams Blakesley, "Dr. Carpenter's *Mental Physiology*," *Quarterly Review* 143 (1877): 83–104.

25. In a pamphlet published in 1844 and found in Tennyson's library, Emmanuel Swedenborg strongly argues for the intercourse between the soul and the body and, in the process, turns the tables on those psychologists who claim that such insights are products of diseased minds. He claims, instead, that it is insane not to believe in such intercourse. Mary Brotherton or possibly Frederick gave Tennyson the pamphlet, and underlined the following passage: "It is believed by many that the soul, lives from his own life, thus of himself, consequently, not by the influx of life from God. But such persons cannot avoid twisting of fallacies a sort of Gordian knot in which they entangle all the judgments of their mind, till nothing but *insanity in regard to spiritual things is the result.*" Obviously the Swedenborgians were not the only ones to react strongly to the medical psychologists. An 1845 article in *Blackwood's Magazine* probably speaks for a large group who continued to believe in dreams as one "*natural* link by which the material and immaterial within and without ourselves may be connected" (John Eagles, "A Few Passages Concerning Omens, Dreams, Appearances, etc. in a Letter to Eusebius (No. II)," 58 [1845]: 737–51).

26. Emily Tennyson records in her journal that Tennyson read a review of Swedenborg in the February 1857 issue of *Fraser's Magazine* and that Tennyson read to her from Hinton's *Man and His Dwelling Place* (*Lady Tennyson's Journal*, pp. 83, 129).

27. Alan Willard Brown, *The Metaphysical Society: Victorian Minds in Crisis, 1869–1880* (New York: Columbia University Press, 1937), p. 26.

28. William B. Carpenter, "On the Fallacies of Testimony in Relation to the Supernatural," *Contemporary Review* 27 (1876): 279–95.

29. Blakesley, "Dr. Carpenter's *Mental Physiology*," p. 89.

30. Richard Hutton, "On Mr. Herbert Spencer's Theory of the Gradual Transformation of Utilitarian into Intuitive Morality by Hereditary Descent," as quoted in Brown, *The Metaphysical Society*, p. 60. The paper was read at the society's first meeting. Richard Hutton was the uncle of R. H. Hutton. Tennyson was not present at that meeting, but John Knowles recited Tennyson's "Higher Pantheism," which he had written for the occasion.

31. Bishop C. J. Ellicott, "What Is Death?" *Contemporary Review* 8 (1871): 56–66. Tennyson heard this paper.

32. Henry Sidgwick, "The Verification of Beliefs," *Contemporary Review* 17 (1871): 582–90. Tennyson heard this paper. It is perhaps helpful to be reminded of an observation about intuition and its role in Tennyson's education at Cambridge. In *Tennyson and Clio: History in the Major Poems* (Baltimore: Johns Hopkins University Press, 1979), Henry Kozicki writes that "intuitionism, combined, unparadoxically, with rigorous learning, was characteristic for the period. . . . Charles Tennyson writes that Jowett 'grasped truth intuitively, apprehending one aspect of it after another, but making little effort to trace their logical con-

nexion—"I put down my thoughts like sparks," he once wrote, "and let them run into one another"'" (p. 17).

33. Walter Bagehot, "On the Emotion of Conviction," *Contemporary Review* 17 (1871): 32–40. Tennyson heard this paper.

34. Sidgwick, "The Verification of Beliefs," p. 583, and Bagehot, "On the Emotion of Conviction," p. 34.

35. Bagehot, "On the Emotion of Conviction," p. 34.

36. Sidgwick, "The Verification of Beliefs," p. 590.

37. *Life and Letters of James Hinton*, ed. Ellice Hopkins (London: C. Kegan Paul, 1878), p. 79. James Hinton, on Tennyson's suggestion, was one of the earliest members of the Metaphysical Society. He presented only one paper, "On the Relation of the Organic and Inorganic Worlds" (18 November 1873). He attended the meetings regularly "until his premature death in 1875" (Brown, *The Metaphysical Society*, pp. 122–23).

38. Hallam Tennyson, *Memoir*, 1: 303.

39. John Knowles, "Aspects of Tennyson—II," *Nineteenth Century* 33 (1893): 182.

# Index